PARAGRAPH PRACTICE

PARAGRAPH

Kathleen E. Sullivan
Merritt College

PRACTICE

Writing the Paragraph
and the Short Composition

SIXTH EDITION

MACMILLAN PUBLISHING COMPANY
New York
COLLIER MACMILLAN PUBLISHERS
London

Copyright © 1989 by Macmillan Publishing Company,
a division of Macmillan, Inc.

Printed in the United States of America

Earlier edition copyright © 1967, 1971, 1976, 1980, 1984
by Kathleen E. Sullivan.

Macmillan Publishing Company
866 Third Avenue, New York, New York 10022

Collier Macmillan Canada, Inc.

Library of Congress Cataloging-in-Publication Data

Sullivan, Kathleen E.
    Paragraph practice : writing the paragraph and the short
composition / Kathleen E. Sullivan.—6th ed.
        p.   cm.
    ISBN 0-02-418390-3
    1. English language—Rhetoric.   2. English language—Paragraphs.
I. Title.
PE1408.S779   1989
    808'.042—dc19   88-3933
                                                                      CIP

Printing: 2 3 4 5 6 7   Year: 9 0 1 2 3 4 5

Preface

The sixth edition of *Paragraph Practice: Writing the Paragraph and the Short Composition* has been revised to include a new opening chapter, "Getting Started," designed to prompt students to plunge into the writing process before they later begin to analyze the basic elements of composition. The chapter opens with a recognition of the blank paralysis beginners often feel when asked to take up the unfamiliar activity of writing, proceeds to validate their ordinary daily experiences as valuable source material and themselves as authentic and dynamic voices, and then moves on to methods by which they may trigger their best written responses. The major portion of the chapter consists of prewriting exercises using Gabriele Rico's technique of clustering, each followed by exercises, with examples in writing practice paragraphs. The chapter concludes with a list of additional topics for clustering and paragraphing and with some simple relaxation exercises to help ease tension before writing. In addition, the sixth edition includes improvements in the text and exercises in Parts I and II as well as new model exercises in the paragraph and short composition. It is the aim of this edition to be clearer and more comprehensive than its predecessors.

With the expansion of Part I in the fifth edition, which introduced the chapter "Coherence and Continuity," and the enlargement of Part II in the fourth edition, which added new chapters in organizing, developing, introducing, and concluding the short composition, *Paragraph Practice* combines virtually two little books into one. The first half of the book concentrates on the topic sentence and the paragraph, and the second half focuses on the thesis statement and the short composition. This expansion should make it possible for *Paragraph Practice* to serve the needs of a broader range of college students than it did in its original edition, as well as to increase the extent of its usefulness to the students for whom it was originally designed. This new edition also contains Appendix B, "Correction Symbols," which was expanded in the third edition into a mini-handbook of grammar and usage.

Like its predecessors, the sixth edition is a workbook designed not so much to *talk about* the paragraph as to provide models and exercises in *writing* the paragraph. It is intended to give the same experience with the topic sentence, the thesis sentence, and the short composition. The main theme of this workbook, as Professor Strunk might have put it, is *practice, practice, practice!*

Why practice the paragraph? The paragraph is ideally suited to meet the needs of college students who, for one reason or another, need extra practice in writing. The paragraph is comparatively short and contains many of the basic elements to be considered in studying any form of writing. Because of its brevity, the paragraph permits frequent writing practice without overburdening either the student or the instructor. In addition, the brevity of the paragraph makes it ideal as a medium for controlled composition in which specific mechanics or techniques of writing can be studied.

Organization is the primary concern of this workbook. Organization does not come naturally to most students in college composition courses. Because it is unfamiliar and strikes many students as unnecessary pain, they often resist it. As a result, instructors frequently neglect it. Nonetheless, organization is vital to good composition. It is the aim of this workbook to make it as painless to learn and as enjoyable to teach as possible. Consequently, the book begins with relatively simple problems and proceeds, by degrees, to problems of greater complexity.

The order of the text and exercises in Part I that precede the actual practice of the paragraph may be modified. For example, the section in Chapter 4 called "Find the Right Word" may be deferred as a refinement that digresses from more essential requirements of the topic sentence. It can easily be taken up later when, for instance, problems of variety and imagination are introduced in Chapter 8.

Paragraph Practice may be used in combination with other books, or it may serve by itself as a reader and as a workbook in composition. The subject matter of the model sentences, paragraphs, and compositions can serve as topics for class discussions and for written exercises based on the discussions that will be of genuine interest to both instructor and students.

The advice and suggestions of many people have contributed greatly to improving this edition of *Paragraph Practice.* I would especially like to thank Anne Anderson, Marjorie Smith, Marion Trentman, Richard Vietti, and my editor, D. Anthony English, for their understanding and help.

K. E. S.

Contents

1

Getting Started

2

Introduction to the Paragraph

PART 1

Practicing the Paragraph

6

Elementary Problems of Form and Organization   73

7

Advanced Problems of Form and Organization   87

Problems of Variety
and Imagination   112

PART II

Writing the Short Composition

The Short Composition   133

10

The Thesis Statement 139

11

Practicing the Thesis Statement 144

12

Organizing the Discussion 154

Developing the Discussion   160

Introducing and Concluding the
Short Composition   169

Practicing the Short Composition   174

Appendixes

1

Getting Started

1. DO YOU RECOGNIZE THIS EXPERIENCE?

As a student you are probably familiar with the following experience: You are sitting in a classroom, paper in front of you, pencils sharp, pens poised for action. Your assignment is to write a five-hundred-word composition within the hour. You understand the directions and are ready to begin. But the clock on the wall begins to jerk away the minutes as you stare at the blank page, defying you to write on it. What can you write about? What is there to say? You feel as blank as the page itself and sit there, paralyzed, waiting for inspiration. No ideas come. You begin to twist and turn in your hard chair, desperately looking around the room for some kind of miracle. Why can't you get started?

2. YOU HAVE PLENTY TO WRITE ABOUT

Deep down you know you have a lot to say. Just think about your last telephone call. Can you hear how you jabbered away to one of your best friends? You had plenty of ideas then. Think about the last time you griped to someone about your life. You were loaded with complaints, weren't you? Or consider all the effort you have made to find a decent job and the humiliation and frustration you have experienced. You have had no trouble sharing your feelings with people close to you, some of them in the same boat. How about the directions you recently gave a younger sister or brother who was trying to learn to do something you already knew all about? That effort took clear explanation as well as patience, didn't it? Think of all the skill you have developed in discussing controversial issues with your parents and others older if not wiser than you. You have proved to be quite a survivor, haven't you? Remember the intricate beginnings when you met that very important person in your life. Conversation may not have been easy at first, but you ultimately learned to speak volumes to each other. Take stock of the fact that you are an authority about your life and your experiences, and that you have a lot to say and plenty to write about.

3. BE YOURSELF

You have within you a gold mine of source material to draw on for writing. Moreover, you are unique. No one else has lived your life. No one else knows quite what you know or sees through your particular eyes. Therefore, what you have to say is special and should be alive and interesting. If you can reveal what you know, value, think about, worry about, fear, or look forward to, you are bound to find an attentive audience. But you must write from yourself and with your own authentic voice. Do not be a phony. Do not try to sound like someone else, some stranger, and do not distance yourself from what you write, trying vaguely to deliver what you imagine is expected from those writing (or not writing) with you in the classroom. Do not nonperson yourself or become bland, colorless, and dull. Be yourself when you pick up that pen to write. Be genuine. Be willing to risk showing your reader who you are.

Revealing who you are, of course, also includes letting your imperfections as a writer show. For example, you may not always be as clear or as well organized as you would like to be. Your vocabulary may not be as exact and as fully developed as you might wish. You may be shaky about mechanics such as spelling, grammar, and punctuation. However, you cannot afford to worry about these problems when you are first getting started. If you do, you may risk blocking yourself, being unable to write at all, becoming self-conscious, intimidated, confused, stiff, and wooden instead of your spontaneous, dynamic self! Since no one expects you to be perfect in the beginning, anyway, you may as well relax and be yourself, all the best and worst of you. Perfection can come later. First you must worry about getting your thoughts on paper, no matter how they may come out, before they slip away!

4. THINK ABOUT *WHAT* MORE THAN *HOW*

In the beginning, think about *what* you want to say more than *how* you want to say it. In most writing situations, you will be able to write more than one version or "draft" of what you want to say. In the first or "rough draft" of your composition, you should dwell on *content*—that is, on subject matter, the thoughts or ideas you want to express—more than on *form* or the various means by which you express those ideas. Your rough draft may be quite sketchy, in fact, and consist of little more than notes to yourself in a kind of shorthand that only you can read and understand. Form is not important at this point. What is important is to pin down those thoughts that come to you just as they appear, direct and honest, maybe even crude or half-conceived, semithoughts, ghosts of thoughts, but possibly very vital fragments that you can later develop more clearly. If time permits, and your energy and motivation are strong enough, you may write several drafts, gradually developing and refining your composition. In your final drafts, your attention can rightly turn to form, structure, and mechanics, but not in the beginning, when you need to focus on content.

5. CONTENT MAY NEED TO BE TRIGGERED

Content will not always leap to your call. Although you have within you an abundant source of subject matter to draw on for writing, what you need at any given moment may not always be immediately accessible. You may not always know what you know or be able to bring it to mind with ease so that you can write about it. Suppose you "can't think of anything"? What can be done to trigger your thoughts or to tap into them?

6. THE OUTSIDE WORLD CAN BE HELPFUL

The thoughts or ideas that exist somewhere in the hidden reaches of your mind may be teased into your consciousness with the help of the outside world or may depend on your own ability to trigger them. Forces in the outer world can be very helpful. For instance, writing assignments are frequently preceded by classroom discussion that can stimulate your thoughts. Your instructor may put penetrating questions to the class that make you think, that remind you of something in your past experiences, that encourage you to put together new combinations or fresh applications of ideas. Besides your classroom activities, your personal world is probably full of people who can assist you. It may prove enjoyable as well as enormously helpful for you to go to family members or other people who know you well and ask them, "Can you remind me of what I know about this subject? Have I had experience with this topic? Help me remember." The result can be not only entertaining but can bring you still closer together.

To illustrate, suppose you are asked to write a composition in which you have to discuss your earliest experience with right and wrong behavior, particularly in relation to violation of law. You think back through your career as a less-than-perfect child, and you realize you are hazy on the subject, but fortunately a parent is available. You sit down together and begin to reflect on your childhood, one of you remembering one thing, the other another. The discussion calls to mind a poignant memory of your stealing a small item from a neighborhood store, and you remember how bothered you were as weeks went by and your guilt about the theft mounted until you finally revealed your secret to your parent. Sharing this memory, you both smile as you recall the lesson you learned that day when the two of you returned to that small store, your parent watching as you made your apology and paid the proprietor.

Bringing what you know to consciousness is not always so much a matter of *remembering* as it is of *realizing* something about which you may be only vaguely aware or which you may not have thought about at all. For instance, imagine a classroom discussion of a complex word such as *ambivalence,* which means feeling conflicting emotions about a person or thing, such as love and hate, at the same time. Suppose you are asked to write about the word and you wonder what to say. You have lunch with a friend after class, and you begin to toss the word around, trying it out. At some point your friend says, "Isn't that how you used to feel about your Ex? Didn't you sometimes love and hate him at the same time?" Of course, you "know that" or sometimes almost let yourself feel that, but it may take your friend to bring your dim awareness to full recognition. When you realize you have had real experience with the word—that is, with the feelings the word represents—you have much to write about. Thus can the outside world help you to tap into your inner resources.

7. YOU MAY NEED TO HELP YOURSELF

Although your writing can benefit from the outside world in this and other ways, some of your most vivid writing may depend on your ability to tap into your memory or to trigger your realization on your own. To do this requires a special state of mind and may also be facilitated by some special prewriting exercises.

8. CONSIDER A SPECIAL STATE OF MIND

All writing classes might well begin with relaxation exercises, for one of the greatest blocks to good writing is tension—feeling "uptight," threatened, insecure, defensive. Notice how you hold your pen or pencil as you write in class. Do you squeeze it so tightly that it feels like a weapon stabbing the page and your dented hand in armed combat? While a rush of adrenaline or excitement may help you to write well, feeling tense and defensive will likely make it difficult for you to write. Hopefully, you will have a chance, before you write, to stretch, breathe deeply, and loosen up, just as you would before engaging in an athletic event requiring intense concentration and skill. (For some simple exercises designed to help you relax before writing, see the end of this chapter.) Further, early in your class, you may also have an opportunity to get acquainted with your classmates, at least those sitting in your vicinity, to discover that they are human, too, and quite possibly as unsure of themselves as you may be. Sharing your mutual anxiety can do much toward making it tolerable or even diminishing it to the point that it ceases to matter. These activities should help you feel more relaxed, confident, and ready to write.

Feeling stimulated but not tense and defensive, you are ready to experience the special state of mind called for in the beginning or "rough draft" stage of writing. (Remember, at this point you are concentrating on *content*, on *what* you want to express, *not* on *form* or *how* to express it, which comes later.)

First you need to "look outward" to your instructor or elsewhere for direction, for as clear a sense of the writing assignment as you can obtain. After that, however, you must become somewhat detached from the outer world and "look inward." At this stage you need to tap into your inner resources, to become creative and original. This is when you want most to be your unique self, to dwell on subject matter, attitudes, or feelings only you know about. This is also the moment when you need most to trust yourself, indeed, to allow yourself to *be*, to see who you are, to learn how you think and feel. This can be a striking moment of self-discovery, certainly a prime benefit of writing. A scary but exciting time, this is when you need to take a risk, to be open and therefore vulnerable, if only to yourself. No one should intrude on this moment, nor should you look to others for help, for this is your time to be with yourself. Look inward to your own experience, to your own reality. Listen to yourself. Get in touch with your own inner voice. Discover, explore, and develop your unique core.

9. TRY SOME SPECIAL PREWRITING EXERCISES AND PRACTICE PARAGRAPHS

If you are still hesitant about plunging into the writing of your first rough draft, you may find the special prewriting exercises that follow helpful. They should get you started, ease you into the writing process, facilitate the flow of ideas, possibly even make you eager to begin writing. As noted earlier, you have within you a wealth of subject matter to draw on for writing. However, what you need at any given moment may not be immediately accessible. The outside world or you, yourself, may help to trigger your thoughts. The exercises that follow are designed to assist you to do that, to stimulate you to action, perhaps to little bursts of activity, and ultimately to the writing of your rough draft.

To begin with, your instructor may put a word on the blackboard, enclosing it in a circle or rectangle to set it off, and then ask you and your classmates to tell what you think of or associate with that word. Take, for example, the word *chance*. Imagine yourself in class now. What comes to mind when you think of that word? What else? Does something contrary also come to mind? Try to be free and spontaneous rather than studied or analytical. To tap your inner resources, you may need to surprise yourself, to catch yourself "off guard." Therefore, do not be too careful. Do not "think it through." Instead, say whatever pops into your mind about the word. Can you imagine what others in your class might say also? Picture your instructor writing each contribution from the class (a single word or group of words) on the board, encircling it, and making these "word bubbles" or "balloons," connected by little lines or "strings," float out and about the core word, *chance*. After a short period of class participation, with many members of the class contributing a "bubble," the blackboard should be filled. A simplified version of it might look something like Figure 1–1.

The process represented in Figure 1–1 is called *clustering*, which is a special way of brainstorming designed to develop ideas, images, and feelings around a core or stimulus word (in this case, the word *chance*) that can motivate or help lead to writing.* After you sample the process two or three times as part of a group in class, you may be on your own (though you may want to share the results in class) to try the exercises that follow. Keep in mind that the words you see around the core word, *chance*, do not result from careful and deliberate planning but rather from spontaneous, free association; that is, from whatever you happen to think of when you see the word. Further, you do not need to arrange the "word bubbles" in any special way around the core word, though a pattern may emerge, but let them connect and float about as they may.

As represented in Figure 1–1 the right-hand side of the core or stimulus

---

*Based on the process originated by Gabriele Rico, California State University, San Jose.

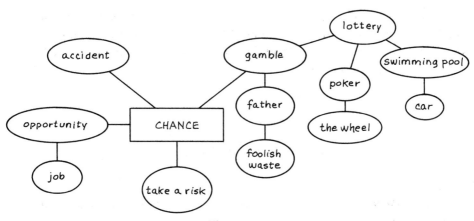

Figure 1–1

word is busier (contains more "word bubbles") than any other space around it, suggesting greater interest or responsiveness in that direction. You may also see a kind of pattern or form of thinking developing there. When such a pattern becomes clear in your own clustering, when it begins to call to you, the clustering process may give rise to the desire to write, to test the developing pattern. When you are clustering on your own, you may feel at such a point, "Aha! Maybe this is something I can write about!" When this feeling strikes you, it is time to stop clustering and to begin writing. Examine the following paragraph based on the clustering developed in Figure 1–1.

"A fool and his money are soon parted," I can imagine my father saying as I buy my state lottery ticket. "So I pay for a little fantasy life," I argue back, in my mind, as I consider how best to spend my millions, always including a swimming pool and a new car in my plans. Taking a chance on the lottery or a game of poker or, my favorite long shot at a Nevada gambling house, the big wheel, is certainly a debatable use of money. The rare times I gamble, I seem to have to clear the way for it with this little imaginary argument with my father. I think of him, too, when I throw away the ticket that had once shown such promise, or when I lose at poker, or when the big wheel flicks slowly toward my number but then dies next to it. "It's only a game, Dad," I mutter to myself, and then maybe I'll get in my old car and drive to the Y for a swim.

You need to "follow your own star," so to speak, when clustering. That is, there is no one "right way" to cluster, no formula, no correct method. What you need most is to be tuned to your own impulses, to let happen what will, to permit yourself to go off in any direction that suits you. Thus, everyone will cluster a word somewhat differently, often enormously differently, and the writing that comes from clustering will vary with each person. The preceding examples give only one way to cluster and write about the word *chance*. Keep in mind that there are numerous different ways, including others suggested but unexplored in Figure 1–1 as well as your own individual approach.

EXERCISE 1A

Directions

Cluster the words *ice cream*, or choose another "fun food" such as *pizza*, *popcorn*, *French fries*, *peanuts*, or *potato chips*.

To encourage your spontaneous rather than planned and considered responses, limit yourself in time to approximately *3 minutes*. An example for comparison follows; however, remember the example reflects the reactions of someone else whereas your own reactions are called for here.

EXAMPLE

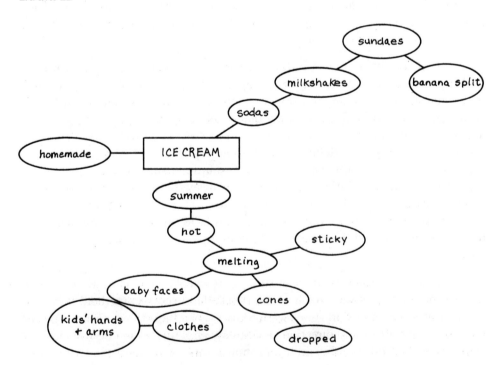

EXERCISE 1B

Directions

Write a paragraph—a group of sentences about one central topic—based on one point or aspect you developed in Exercise 1A.

In your clustering of the words ice cream (or some other word you chose), you very likely developed the core word in more than one worthwhile and interesting direction, but now you need to select just one direction on which to base a paragraph. Think about what you want to say—the content—as you write your paragraph. Do not worry about the form of the paragraph (you will study form in depth later in the book); concentrate on one topic and develop it until it "feels" finished. Follow through on one of the ideas that came to you or that you found most interesting as you clustered. Compare the following example to the cluster example in Exercise 1A. Can you see how the paragraph grew from the cluster?

EXAMPLE

Ice cream makes me think of summer. It is hot, and everyone tries to keep cool by eating ice cream. I can imagine happy baby faces messy with ice cream, globs of it stuck to their noses and chins, layers of it smeared around their mouths and cheeks. I can see little kids with ice cream cones melting in their hands, running down their arms, and dripping on their clothes. Suddenly there is a tragedy. A cone slips from a small hand and lands, plop, on a hot sidewalk. Then what agony and flood of tears! An impatient parent scolds the child and they rush home. The fallen cone soon becomes a sticky feast for flies, then a faint stain in the concrete.

EXERCISE 2A

Directions

Cluster the word throw, or choose another action word such as run, kick, jump, smash, or hold.

To foster your spontaneous or free association rather than planned and studied responses, limit yourself in time to approximately 3 minutes. Use the following example for reference or comparison, but keep in mind that your own reactions are what is called for here.

EXAMPLE

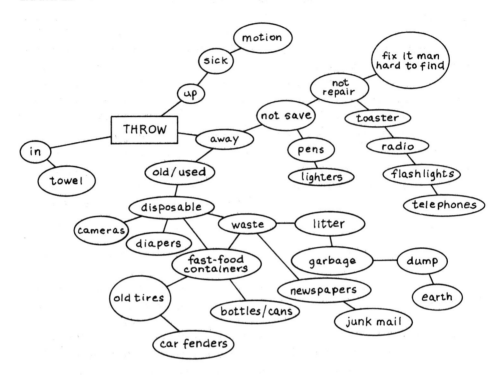

EXERCISE 2B

Directions

Write a paragraph—a group of sentences about one central topic—based on one point or aspect you developed in Exercise 2A.

Follow through on one of the ideas that came to you or that you found most interesting as you clustered in Exercise 2A. It may be helpful to compare the following example to the cluster example in Exercise 2A.

EXAMPLE

This is a throw-away culture, maybe a throw-away world. People don't save things anymore, such as pens and lighters and clocks; they toss them out. They don't repair things anymore, like radios and toasters, unless by chance they find that rare member of a dying breed, a fixit man, located in some off-beat place, dimly lighted and covered with dust. Most people just throw things away, whatever they may be: flashlights, car fenders, junk mail, fast-food containers, cameras, bottles, cans, diapers, newspapers, old tires, and telephones. Most things can be replaced; practically everything is disposable. As a result, the world is covered with litter. The great cities of the world, its rivers, lakes, and mountains, its seas and deserts, have become eyesores, slopped with garbage. That old movie line uttered by Bette Davis now applies to most parts of the earth, "What a dump!"

EXERCISE 3A

Directions

Cluster the word <u>hill</u>, or choose a word for another natural place such as <u>beach</u>, <u>meadow</u>, <u>creek</u>, <u>mountain</u> or <u>lake</u>.

To prompt a spontaneous rather than a planned reaction, limit yourself in time to approximately <u>3 minutes</u>. Use the following example for reference or comparison, but remember that your own responses, not those of someone else, are called for here.

EXAMPLE

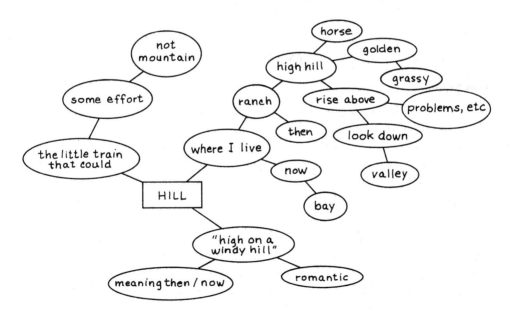

EXERCISE 3B

Directions

Write a paragraph—a group of sentences about one central topic—based on one point or aspect you developed in Exercise 3A.

Follow through on one of the ideas that came to you or that you found most interesting as you clustered in Exercise 3A. It may be helpful to compare the following example to the cluster example in Exercise 3A.

EXAMPLE

The word *hill* strikes at my core. I am a hill person. The house where I live now is on a hill. The ranch where I grew up was on a hill in back of this one. I've always lived in hilly country. I feel strange and restless on flat land, as if I'm not tall enough, as if there's no way to get perspective on reality, no high place from which to look down and see and understand. As a youngster I used to get on my horse and ride to the highest hill I could find whenever I was troubled or had a problem to work out. There, on a golden, grassy, wind-swept peak, I could literally rise above it all. The valley below me retreated in a distant haze. Even the nearest barns and houses looked tiny and insignificant. Now when I walk to the top of this hill, I can look out on a beautiful bay with its great bridges, surrounding cities, and a mountain that looks like a sleeping lady. The view is lovely and complex, but the way to the peak is paved, and houses follow me as I go.

EXERCISE 4A

Directions

Cluster the word afraid, or choose another word that suggests strong feeling such as angry, lonely, joyful, grateful, or embarrassed.

To promote spontaneity rather than a studied, planned response, limit yourself in time to approximately 3 minutes. Use the following example for reference or comparison, but bear in mind that your own reaction, not that of someone else, is called for here.

EXAMPLE

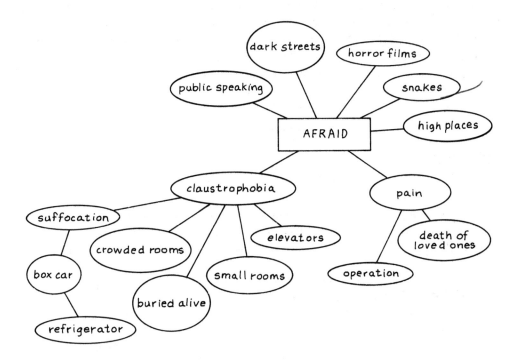

EXERCISE 4B

Directions

Write a paragraph—a group of sentences about one central topic—based on one point or aspect you developed in Exercise 4A.

Follow through on one of the ideas that came to you or that you found most interesting as you clustered in Exercise 4A. It may be helpful to compare the following example to the cluster example in Exercise 4A.

EXAMPLE

Claustrophobia gives me nightmarish thoughts. . . . I am alone in an elevator, stuck between floors. The power in the building has gone off; it is dark, and no one can hear my call for help. . . . I am in a large room filled with people wedged together, moaning and screaming; I am at the center of the mass, held in place by sweating arms and elbows, so that I cannot reach a door. I can barely breathe. . . . I am locked in a box car on a railroad siding; the blazing sun has pushed the temperature to 120 degrees inside the car where I am writhing on the floor, throwing up and tearing at my clothes. . . . I am a curious child who has wandered alone into a junkyard, and I have found an open refrigerator. I will play house, I think, as I step inside and close the door, not realizing, until too late, that I cannot get out. . . . I am lying in a narrow box, my head and feet pressing against each end. I can hear dirt being dumped on the box, but there is no way of telling anyone that I am still alive. . . . Claustrophobia—the word alone makes me afraid.

EXERCISE 5A

Directions

Cluster the word <u>singer</u>, or choose another word for a performer such as <u>pianist</u>, <u>actor</u>, <u>dancer</u>, <u>magician</u>, or <u>acrobat</u>.

To encourage spontaneity rather than a carefully planned response, limit yourself in time to approximately <u>3 minutes</u>. Use the following example for reference or comparison, but keep in mind that your own reaction, not that of someone else, is called for here.

EXAMPLE

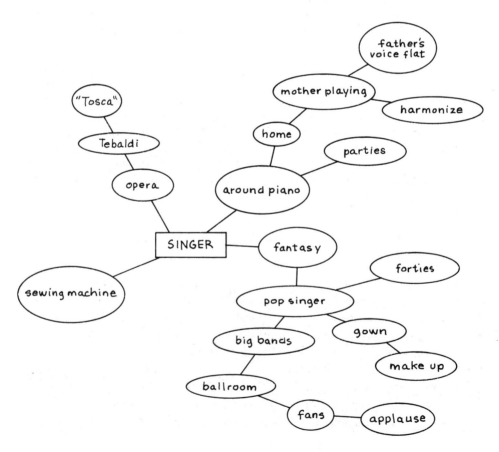

EXERCISE 5B

Directions

Write a paragraph—a group of sentences about one central topic—based on one point or aspect you developed in Exercise 5A.

Follow through on one of the ideas that came to you or that you found most interesting as you clustered in Exercise 5A. It may be helpful to compare the following example to the cluster example in Exercise 5A.

EXAMPLE

The word *singer* calls to mind one of my favorite fantasies in which I am a professional popular singer. I can put my fantasy in a time warp and zing back into the late forties with the big bands and marvelous singers such as Helen Forrest, Anita O'Day, and Margaret Whiting. I imagine myself, a new star, standing in a shimmering gown in front of one of the big orchestras in a large and elegant ballroom filled with couples dancing. The band quiets down, and I step up to the microphone, a soft spot catching the sequins of my silver dress, my Lauren Bacallish face and figure, my glowing eyes with just the right color and amount of blue eye shadow, my lips glistening with a perfect reddish-purpleish lipstick, my hair, lovely and long, slipping down my back, just so. I begin to sing in tones so sultry and intriguing that the people on the crowded floor turn my way, stop dancing, and move toward the band stand, where they stand and gently sway to the music, captivated by my charm and talent. For a time it is as if we are all caught in a kind of magic spell that holds us enchanted until my song ends. Then I modestly acknowledge the applause and step back to my chair in front of the band, where I sit, looking cool and perfect, until my next number.

10. CONSIDER THESE AFTERTHOUGHTS ON CLUSTERING AND PARAGRAPHING

A. You have probably noticed, especially after gaining experience with the process, that when you cluster, you sometimes find yourself developing "word bubbles" (your ideas and impressions) first in one direction, then another, and then another with almost equal fullness. You may end up with a luxurious problem: having too much to write about! Since a paragraph can contain only one main topic lest it explode with overload, you have to make a decision. Which direction developed in clustering will you take in paragraphing? If you do not know right away because of gut feeling or intensity of interest, then you might decide another way. Try writing your paragraph on first one topic, then another, and then another to see which one "writes best." A good paragraph sometimes has a way of almost writing itself, so when you feel that kind of ease as well as interest, your choice is clear. Such was the case in the last cluster and paragraph examples in the exercise on the word *singer*. The temptation to write a paragraph about *singer* in terms of being at home and singing around a piano was great, but the fantasy direction had a stronger pull. When that direction was tried out, the paragraph practically wrote itself.

B. One of the benefits that clustering brings to paragraphing is detail, without which writing is inclined to be not only vague but also limp and lifeless. Quite a bit of space is given elsewhere in this book to the subject of detailing, but it is helpful to think about it now and to appreciate clustering as a valuable source of detail. When you tap your inner resources by means of clustering, what comes to you tends to be something like snap shots your mind has taken in the past but forgotten about. The stimulus or core word triggers your memory, and those old pictures come back to you, often in sharp detail. Thus, you think about the word *hill*, for example, not in general terms or in some vague way but in relation to specific hills you have known, hills you have glimpsed or "snapped" in the past. You may see again such fine details as the grass on those hills, the color of the soil, the movement of the ground with a gopher underneath, the soil being pushed up, the bobbing nose, or whatever it was you saw originally. It is important to appreciate these details because they can make your writing rich, alive, and interesting. Be sure to make use of them, to note them in your "word bubbles" when clustering, and to use them in paragraphing.

C. At this early stage in your writing, you should concentrate on content, on what you want to say, more than on form or how to say it. However, you may realize by now that clustering gives you a sense of direction and some sense of form in paragraphing. The "word bubbles" you create around the core or stimulus word do not float about in total chaos. An idea (or perhaps two or three) tends to take shape somewhere in your clustering, a pattern of thought begins to grow. Examine again the cluster example of the word *afraid* on page 13. Clustering began with a miscellaneous assortment of things feared, which are given above and to the right of the core word. Then one of the worst fears, claustrophobia, came to mind. This word suggested a central topic, a whole category of fears, including various conditions or circumstances of claustrophobia. Thus, clustering led not only to the content of the paragraph but also to its form. Similarly, with the cluster example of the word *throw* on page 10, once the word *away* came to mind, a topic was recognized, a series of related ideas and examples tumbled onto the page in a cluster, and a paragraph quickly followed. It is not surprising that the cluster prepares the way so well for the paragraph. After all, clustering means a gathering or grouping together of similar things. A paragraph, being a group of sentences expressing one central idea, is little more than an expanded and modified cluster.

D. Do not stop clustering when you complete this chapter. If the process is working for you here, why not use it in later chapters that give you further exercises in paragraphing? Clustering should prove especially helpful to you in Chapter 6, "Elementary Problems of Form and Organization"; Chapter 7, "Advanced Problems of Form and Organization"; and Chapter 8, "Problems of Variety and Imagination." You may find the process useful, as well, when you begin to practice the short composition in Chapter 15. In fact, you may get in the habit of clustering and want to use it before you write much of anything. One well-known innovator in the teaching of writing thinks so highly of the clustering process that she uses it even outside the field, for problem solving in general.

11. TRY CLUSTERING; THEN PRACTICE PARAGRAPHING SOME ADDITIONAL TOPICS

Remember what clustering is as you use the words in the following list. You should *not* try to define the words according to a dictionary or to collect ideas from other sources. *Your own free, spontaneous reaction* to the words is all that is called for here. How do you feel about the word? What impressions does it call to mind? What associations with the word do you have? What do you think of when you see it? To encourage your spontaneity rather than a planned and studied response, limit yourself to approximately *3 minutes* with each clustering exercise. Refer to the cluster and paragraph examples given earlier in this chapter if necessary.

A. Use the word *rain,* or choose another word for a weather element such as *snow, sunshine, fog, wind,* or *clouds.*

B. Use the word *twenty-one,* or choose another age such as *thirty, ten, eighteen, forty,* or *seventy.*

C. Use the word *green,* or choose another color such as *blue, red, pink, tan,* or *gold.*

D. Use the word *aggressive,* or choose another descriptive word such as *assertive, elegant, wimpy, shy,* or *dignified.*

E. Use the word *car,* or choose another land vehicle such as *truck, bus, bicycle, motorcycle,* or *sled.*

F. Use the word *handsome,* or choose another descriptive term such as *beautiful, sexy, romantic, earthy,* or *sensitive.*

G. Use the word *Help!,* or choose another exclamation such as *Stop!, Fire!, Look out!, Mayday!,* or *Thief!*

H. Use the word *rose,* or choose another flower such as *carnation, plumeria, orchid, magnolia,* or *tulip.*

I. Use the word *sailboat,* or choose another means of sea or air transport such as *canoe, surfboard, hang glider, airplane,* or *space shuttle.*

J. Use the word *carpenter,* or choose another occupation such as *farmer, dentist, chef, mechanic,* or *teacher.*

12. TRY THESE SIMPLE EXERCISES TO HELP YOU RELAX BEFORE WRITING

A. Sitting or standing as erect and tall as you can, stretch both arms straight up above your head as far as they will reach. Can you reach higher still, trying to touch the ceiling with your finger tips? Relax a moment, then try again, stretching as far as you can. Higher, please. Now relax.

B. Sitting or standing as erect and tall as you can, hold your arms out to each side, level with your shoulders. Minimizing any other movement of your body, first stretch your right arm out, reaching, reaching, as far as it will go. Next, do the same with your left arm, stretching, stretching, as far as you possibly can. Drop both arms and relax.

C. Sitting or standing, your arms relaxed at your side, draw your shoulders up as high as you can and then slowly roll them back and around several times.

D. Sitting or standing up straight, slowly bring your head down until your chin touches your chest. Then roll your head slowly toward your right shoulder, next to the back, then toward the left shoulder, finally back until it touches your chest again. Reverse the direction, making a slow move first toward the left shoulder, next to the back, then to the right shoulder, returning to the front. Straighten and relax.

E. Sitting or standing, dangle your arms and gently shake your wrists, as if you were trying to dry your hands.

F. Sitting or standing, let your body slump forward, bending your back, dangling your arms, letting your head slowly fall forward, your chin resting on your chest. If standing, bend your knees slightly. Hang that way for a few seconds. Then straighten up again.

G. Take a deep breath and slowly sigh. Take another deep breath and let it out slowly, humming softly from a middle to a lower note, sounding something like a faint foghorn. Inhale and exhale several times deeply and slowly. Can you breathe more slowly still? Keep breathing.

SUMMARY

You do not need to feel blank and paralyzed when you are asked to write a composition. You are an authority about your life, your experiences, and that means you have plenty to write about. Appreciate who you are and be yourself when you write, concentrating on content more than form in the beginning, becoming concerned with structure and mechanics later, after you have written your first rough drafts. You have within you an abundant source of subject matter to draw on for writing; however, this content may need to be triggered by forces in the outside world or by your own efforts. Special prewriting exercises using a process called *clustering* should help you get started. Follow these exercises with practice paragraphs. Before you begin, prepare yourself to write with relaxation exercises.

2

Introduction to the Paragraph

1. WHAT IS A PARAGRAPH?

A *paragraph* is composed of a group of sentences expressing one central idea. A paragraph is complete in itself and is also a subdivision or part of something larger, such as a composition or a chapter in a book.

2. WHAT DOES A PARAGRAPH LOOK LIKE ON THE PAGE?

A paragraph begins with an empty space called an *indentation*. The indentation of a paragraph indicates where the paragraph begins. A composition, which contains several paragraphs, will have several indentations, making it easy for the reader to see where each new paragraph or idea in the composition begins. One paragraph, however, contains only one indentation because there is only one beginning point. Figure 2–1 shows how a paragraph should look. Indent—once only! Figure 2–2 shows a paragraph indented too many times.

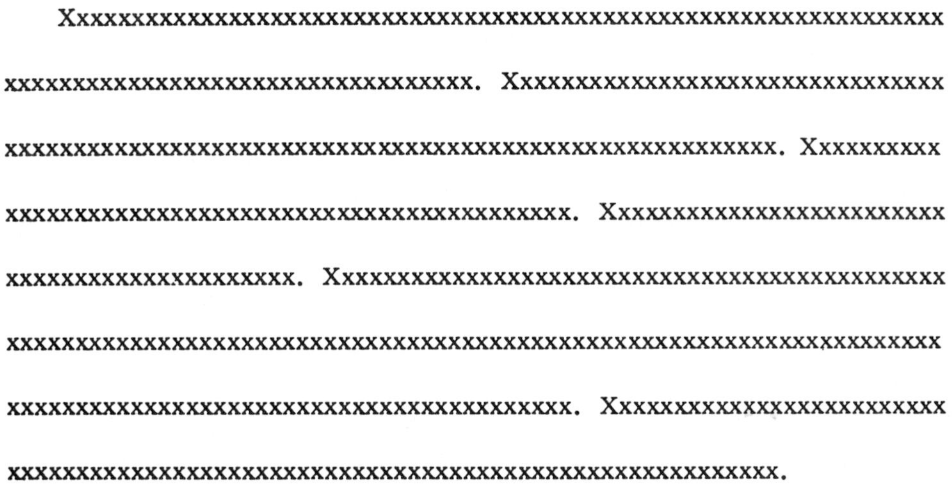

Xxxxxxxxxxxxxxxxxxxxxxxxxxxxxxxxxxxxxxxxxxxxxxxxxxxxxxxxxxxxxxxx
xxxxxxxxxxxxxxxxxxxxxxxxxxxxxxxxxxxxx. Xxxxxxxxxxxxxxxxxxxxxxxxxxxxxx
xxxxxxxxxxxxxxxxxxxxxxxxxxxxxxxxxxxxxxxxxxxxxxxxxxxxxxxxxxx. Xxxxxxxxx
xxxxxxxxxxxxxxxxxxxxxxxxxxxxxxxxxxxxxxxxxx. Xxxxxxxxxxxxxxxxxxxxxxxxx
xxxxxxxxxxxxxxxxxxxxxx. Xxxxxxxxxxxxxxxxxxxxxxxxxxxxxxxxxxxxxxxxxxxx
xxxxxxxxxxxxxxxxxxxxxxxxxxxxxxxxxxxxxxxxxxxxxxxxxxxxxxxxxxxxxxxxxxxx
xxxxxxxxxxxxxxxxxxxxxxxxxxxxxxxxxxxxxxxxxxx. Xxxxxxxxxxxxxxxxxxxxxxxx
xxxxxxxxxxxxxxxxxxxxxxxxxxxxxxxxxxxxxxxxxxxxxxxxxxxxxxxxxxx.

Figure 2–1

Xxxxxxxxxxxxxxxxxxxxxxxxxxxxxxxxxxxxxxxxxxxxxxxxxxxxxxxxxxxxxxxxxxxx
xxxxxxxxxxxxxxxxxxxxxxxxxxxxxxxxxxx.

Xxxxxxxxxxxxxxxxxxxxxxxxxxxxxxxxxxxxxxxxxxxxxxxxxxxxxxxxxxxxxxxxxx
xxxxxxxxxxxxxxxxxxxxxxxxxxxxxxxxxxxxxxxxxxxxxxxxx.

Xxxxxxxxxxxxxxxxxxxxxxxxxxxxxxxxxxxxxxxxxxxxxxxxxxxxxxxxxxxxxxx
xxxxxxxxxxxxxxxxxxxxxxxxxxxxxxxxxxxxx. Xxxxxxxxxxxxxxxxxxxxxxxxxxxxx
xxxxxxxxxxxxxxxxxxxxxxxxxxxxxxxxxxxxxxxxxxxxxxxxxxx.

Xxxxxxxxxxxxxxxxxxxxxxxxxxxxxxxxxxxxxxxxxxxxxxxxxxxxxxxxxxxxxxxxxx
xxxxxxxxxxxxxxxxxxxxxxxxxxxxxxxxxxxxxxxxxxxxxxxxx.

Figure 2–2

3. WHAT IS THE DIFFERENCE BETWEEN A PARAGRAPH AND A COMPOSITION?

A paragraph is a part of a composition. Just as a group of related sentences composes a paragraph, so a group of related paragraphs makes up a composition. A group of compositions, in turn, can be the chapters that constitute a book. A book, then, is the largest unit; it covers more ground and is more complex than any one of its chapters. A chapter or composition is broader and says more than any one of its paragraphs. A paragraph is generally shorter, less complex, and expresses a great deal less than can a composition. Figure 2–3 may be helpful in showing how a paragraph and composition are related.

Notice that the subdivisions of the book, which are indicated by increasingly smaller circles, each within the other, have been extended to the smallest unit of all, the word. Thus the paragraph, as well as the book and composition, can be subdivided.

In your college courses you will need to develop skill in writing composi-

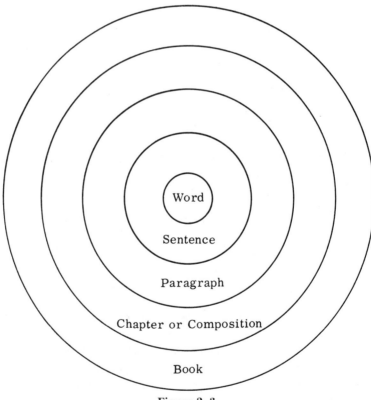

Figure 2–3

tions; therefore, it will be useful to keep in mind the relationship between a paragraph and a composition.

4. HOW LONG IS A PARAGRAPH?

If the idea of the paragraph is simple, the paragraph will usually be rather short. If the idea is complicated, the paragraph will probably be somewhat long. You should keep in mind this principle: *The paragraph should be neither so short that the subject of the paragraph is underdeveloped and insufficiently explained, nor so long that it tends to break down into too many subtopics that would be better organized into separate paragraphs.*

Paragraph length varies according to place and purpose as well as idea. In a newspaper, for example, where the column of newsprint is narrow, one-sentence paragraphs are common. Because comparatively few words can be contained in each line of newsprint, several lines are often necessary to print one sentence. To provide breaks or resting spots that make reading easier, newspapers indent or paragraph frequently. Purpose also determines the length of a paragraph. Newspapers, novels, textbooks, and college compositions each have particular purposes, and they use paragraphs accordingly.

Your paragraphs for the exercises in this book should be approximately *eight to twelve sentences long*, depending on sentence length and complexity. In some cases, your paragraphs should be longer.

5. HOW IS A PARAGRAPH ORGANIZED OR DEVELOPED?

All paragraphs have one basic aim: to communicate a single idea clearly and effectively. All paragraphs, however, are not organized in the same way. *How* they communicate depends on *what* they wish to express. You will face various types of "what" and "how" decisions in the exercises that follow.

Although all paragraphs are not exactly alike, they all nevertheless have some things in common. Consider some of the factors that should be present in any paragraph.

A. THE PARAGRAPH SHOULD CONTAIN ONLY ONE CENTRAL IDEA

A paragraph with more than one central idea is usually overworked and tends to break down under the strain. *Limit* the paragraph. Limiting the paragraph is something like taking a snapshot with a small camera. You should not try to get everyone in your hometown into your picture. Even your own family

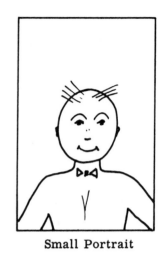

Home Town   Family   Small Portrait

Figure 2–4

is too large or too interesting for your paragraph-sized camera. You had better settle on one member of your family, and keep in mind that you cannot tell everything about even one person in a single paragraph of eight to twelve sentences. Make your picture a small portrait. See Figure 2–4.

Like a small portrait, the paragraph should be limited to one part of a subject, although the subject is probably much larger than the single aspect discussed in the paragraph. To illustrate this idea, suppose you are asked to write something about your house in a paragraph. You cannot tell all about your house. The subject is too big. Even your living room may be too large a subject to discuss in a single paragraph. You need to select a part of the room, such as your fireplace or your favorite chair. Examine the following paragraph.

EXAMPLE

My favorite chair is ugly, but I love it. It is a recliner. Because it is shapeless, heavy, and covered with horrible material, it is an eyesore in my living room. However, it is so comfortable that I would not trade it for the finest piece of furniture I might ever hope to own. There is nothing quite so delightful after a hard day at work as sinking my weary body into that chair. With my back eased into it and my feet eased up from it, I am in heaven. I notice other people like that chair, too. Whenever I have company, the first chair everybody heads for is my ugly, lovely recliner.

Limiting the paragraph is not an exact matter, but a useful rule of thumb may help you determine its approximate limitation: *the more deeply you go into a subject, the more the paragraph must be narrowed down or limited.*

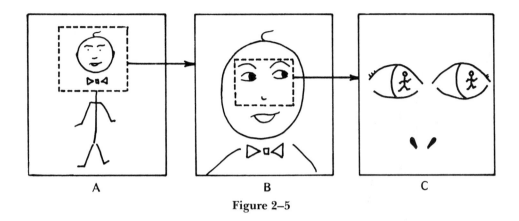

A   B   C

Figure 2–5

A comparison of a paragraph to a camera is useful again. This time think of the process of enlargement. Suppose you take a picture of a standing figure. Then you decide that the expression in the face is good and that you want to see it in more detail. You decide to have that portion of the picture enlarged. Then you decide that there is something in the eyes that is fascinating (perhaps you see a mysterious figure reflected there) and that you want to enlarge that portion of the face. The closer you get to the subject, the more you see in it. Similarly, the closer you get to the subject in the paragraph, the more you see to discuss, and consequently the more the subject must be narrowed if you want to discuss in one paragraph all that you see.

Figure 2–5 may clarify the rule of limitation.

As Figure 2–5 indicates, the paragraph must narrow down or limit its subject to the degree that it concentrates on it or any part of it. Figure 2–5A shows the whole subject, but at some distance. Such a paragraph, although it may give an overall view, cannot go into much detail. Figure 2–5B represents a paragraph that, by limiting itself, can develop its subject more fully. Figure 2–5C shows further limitation that makes further or closer examination of its subject possible.

Although some of the paragraphs that you write may be like Figure 2–5A, your main aim is to develop skill in writing paragraphs like Figure 2–5B, or, in some cases, like Figure 2–5C.

Focus the paragraph. First, decide what the center of interest in your paragraph is and then make sure it is central and unmistakably clear. The following paragraph is focused.

EXAMPLE

My father's face is rough. His complexion is leathery and wrinkled. There are large pores in the skin that covers his nose and cheeks. His nose, broken twice in his life, makes him look like a boxer who has lost too many fights.

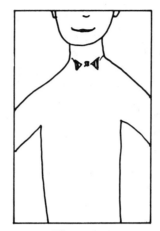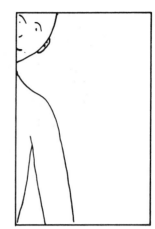

Figure 2–6

His mouth, unless he smiles, looks hard and threatening. His chin is massive and angular. Shaved or not, my father's face is rugged.

The following paragraph is out of focus.

EXAMPLE

I want to talk about my father. He is strict with his children, especially me. He won't let me out of the house unless I've done all my homework. He is a tall and rather skinny man. Some people say he is good-looking. He has a nice streak of gray in his hair. He laughs a lot and enjoys life. My father is interesting.

The second paragraph fails to focus on a particular aspect or make a main point about its subject.

Focusing the paragraph is also like taking a good picture. Like the picture, the paragraph must have a center of interest that is obvious and unmistakable. Bad paragraphs are sometimes like the pictures in Figure 2–6, fuzzy or off-center.

B. THE PARAGRAPH SHOULD HAVE UNITY

Unity means that the paragraph should be of one piece, a distinct unit that has one fundamental purpose. Remember that even though the paragraph is a subdivision or part of a larger unit, it should be complete in itself.

The example given previously of a paragraph that is focused serves also as an example of a unified paragraph. Notice that although the paragraph discusses only one part of a much larger subject, the part discussed is complete in itself and does not need the larger unit to be understood. The paragraph could fit easily into a whole composition entitled, "My Father." Other paragraphs would be needed, of course, to give a complete picture of the larger subject, and they would each need to be distinct units also.

A paragraph should *not* be a *fragment*. It should not be like part of a conversation that is overheard but not quite understood because the complete conversation has not been heard, nor should it be like a piece from a jigsaw puzzle with shapes or colors that confuse the mind. It should be a whole, complete unit, understandable whether it stands alone or is combined with other parts to form a larger whole.

Remember to *stick to the subject*! One of the easiest ways to destroy the unity of a paragraph is to skip from subject to subject, as in the following example.

EXAMPLE

My father is very strict with his children, especially me. He won't let me out of the house unless I've done all my homework. Frankly, I don't care whether I go to school or not. School is such a waste of time. There aren't any good jobs, anyway. My mother doesn't agree with my father. They quarrel a lot. Sometimes I wish they would get a divorce, but then who would I live with?

The preceding paragraph lacks unity because it jumps from subject to subject. (Although it has psychological interest, partly because of its lack of unity, the lack is a definite fault in a paragraph.)

Stick to the subject. If you begin a paragraph about dogs, don't switch the subject to parakeets in the middle of your paragraph unless, of course, you must talk about parakeets to clarify what you want to say about dogs.

C. THE PARAGRAPH SHOULD HAVE COHERENCE AND CONTINUITY

The terms *coherence* and *continuity* are closely related. Coherence means that the parts of the paragraph should be logically arranged and connected. Continuity means that the connection of the parts should be smooth. To make a comparison, a coherent paragraph is like a motor that is properly assembled; with all the parts in the right places, the motor can run. Continuity is like an oil that lubricates the operation, making it smooth and preventing the motor from burning out.

To be coherent, the paragraph must have *order* or *sequence*. The particular

order or sequence needed depends on the subject. For instance, people are usually described from head to toe rather than vice versa. On the other hand, photographs are most often discussed from left to right. Recipes usually begin with
ingredients and end with the oven. Dressmaking starts with the selection of a
pattern rather than the final ironing process. (These subjects illustrate the idea
of order or sequence, though some of them are too large to be contained in a
single paragraph.) The order or sequence that is logical depends on the nature
of the subject to be discussed. The following paragraph is coherent because it
has order or sequence.

EXAMPLE

   To get the most out of his textbooks, a student should follow several
steps carefully. He should make a survey of each book to get a general idea
of what the book contains. He should read for understanding and formulate
questions. He should make notes of the major points of each chapter. He
should test himself to be sure that he can answer questions likely to be
raised in class and in examinations. He should review his notes and reread
any parts of the book that are unclear to him.

   The previous paragraph is coherent, but it is not as smooth as it might be.
Let's look at the paragraph again, with added continuity.

EXAMPLE

   To get the most out of his textbooks, a student should follow several
steps very carefully. First, he should make a preliminary survey of each book
to get a general idea of what the book contains. Second, he should read for
deeper understanding and formulate questions as he reads. Next, he should
make notes of the major points of each chapter. After that, he should test
himself to be sure that he can answer questions likely to be raised in class
and in examinations. Finally, he should review his notes and reread any parts
of the book that are unclear to him.

   Continuity is added by the underlined words, which provide *transition*. Transitional words or phrases are like passwords. They permit easy passage throughout the paragraph by showing the relationship between one sentence or thought
and another. They make the sequence of ideas within the paragraph clearer, and
they make the paragraph as a whole more flowing.
   A good paragraph is a joy to read. It is not something stumbled through

with great labor. It does not stop and start and turn around. It is not jerky. Coherence and continuity, working together, make a paragraph clear and easy to read. For a fuller discussion of coherence and continuity, turn to Chapter 5, beginning on page 55.

D. THE PARAGRAPH SHOULD BE ADEQUATELY DEVELOPED

That is, it should do fully what it sets out to do. It should not leave the job half done. The degree of development depends on the aim or purpose of the paragraph. For example, if the purpose of the paragraph is to explain how to build a bookcase, do not leave the bookcase unfinished. It will probably need paint or stain before you can put books in it, and the paragraph is not complete until it mentions the final part in the building of the bookcase. Do not just end the paragraph—complete it!

Most paragraphs have three basic parts: a beginning, a middle, and an end. These parts are often called the *introduction,* the *discussion,* and the *conclusion.* In the introduction, which may be simply the topic sentence, you should indicate what you will talk about in the paragraph. In the discussion, you talk about the topic. In the conclusion, you complete your discussion, often referring to your main point stated in the introduction. Sometimes, the conclusion takes the form of a summary or brief restatement of the main ideas of the paragraph.

To be adequately developed, the paragraph must have *proper proportion* in its three main parts. That is, each part should be a certain length or size. The approximate size of each part is shown in Figure 2–7.

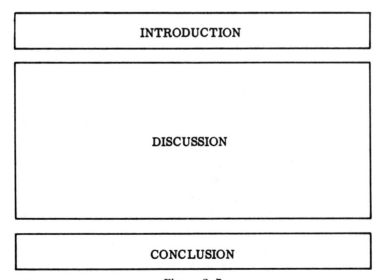

Figure 2–7

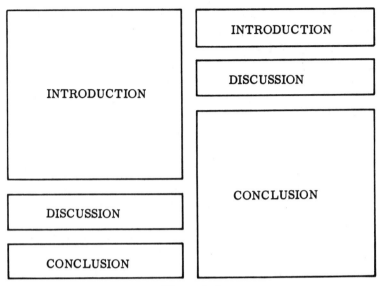

Figure 2–8

The discussion is the biggest part of the paragraph. The introduction and the conclusion are smaller.

Bad paragraphs are sometimes poorly proportioned, as shown in Figure 2–8.

The following paragraph is poorly proportioned. As stated in the topic sentence, the main purpose of the paragraph is to tell about a bad automobile accident. However, most of the paragraph is spent on introducing the subject. The discussion, which is underlined, consists of only two sentences.

EXAMPLE

I had one of the worst experiences of my life when I witnessed a terrible automobile accident a little over a year ago. I was on my way to a party with my boyfriend. It was about eight o'clock at night, and it was raining. Though we were in a hurry to get to the party, my boyfriend was driving slowly because of the poor visibility. We were happily looking forward to seeing our friends, gossiping about some of them, listening to music on the car radio, and humming some of the tunes. We were stopped for a red light at an intersection when the accident occurred. _A car in the lane next to us sped through the red light and crashed into a truck, which was just pulling into the intersection from the cross street. There was a terrible crush of metal, splintering of glass, and screaming and moaning of people_. We didn't feel much like going to a party after that.

The preceding paragraph has interesting (if horrible) possibilities and could be improved by correcting its proportions. The introduction should be shortened, and the discussion should be expanded.

Expanding the paragraph is not simply a matter of making it longer. Never pad a paragraph. *Do not* just *write* more; instead, *say* more. A paragraph should *not* go *on and on;* it should go *in and in.* That is, it should be developed by going more and more *into* its subject.

The best way to develop a paragraph is to be *specific rather than general.* In other words, discuss one thing in definite, exact, precise detail. Do not discuss many things vaguely. Although your paragraph may begin with a statement that is to some extent (within the limits of the paragraph) broad or general, you should develop it by becoming more and more specific, narrowing down your subject, and saying exactly what you mean. Your paragraph should do what is done in the diagram in Figure 2–9, *not* what is done in Figure 2–10.

A general statement should not be developed with a series of further generalizations. A *generalization* is a statement about *all* or *most* of a group or category. It is not definite, not particular, and sometimes not accurate, because it does not allow for exceptions. Moreover, it is vague. It says everything about everything but nothing about anything in *particular.* Your objective in developing the paragraph is just the reverse. You should develop the one central idea of the paragraph with particulars or details that make the idea clear and meaningful.

Realizing that detail is necessary in your paragraph, you may still wonder *how much detail* is needed. Reconsider the rule of limitation given earlier: The more deeply you go into a subject, the more the paragraph must be narrowed down or limited. Now, add to that rule the following: *The more narrowed down or limited the paragraph is, the more it must go into detail.* Remember that when you stand back from a subject, you see it in less detail, but when you move in close to it, the detail you see in it can become so fine as to be almost microscopic.

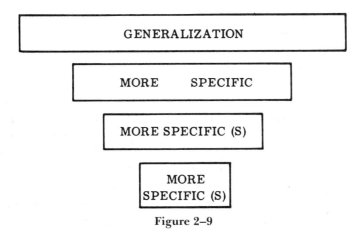

Figure 2–9

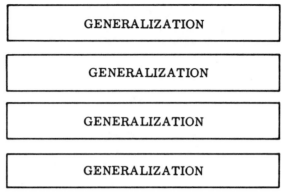

Figure 2–10

Consider the following example of a paragraph that stands back somewhat from its subject, giving an overall view of it. Although it gives some specifics, it does not go into great or fine detail.

EXAMPLE

City College should have a new campus for three major reasons. First, the present campus is badly overcrowded and there is absolutely no space left for additional expansion. Second, the campus is an ugly improvisation of old high school buildings and flimsy, boxlike portables that fail to create a collegiate atmosphere. Third, the equipment in such departments as science, art, and physical education is completely inadequate for the needs of college students. There are other strong arguments for a new campus, but these are three of the most outstanding.

In the next example, the paragraph moves in a little closer to its subject, making more detail possible and necessary.

EXAMPLE

City College is completely overcrowded. The lack of space is apparent in all parts of the campus. The classrooms are so jammed that students feel like sardines, and some of them have to sit on the floor. The library and study rooms are so packed that many students must study in the halls and stairways. The cafeteria so bulges with bodies that students often go hungry or lose their appetites. Every inch of the campus is so overcrowded that it looks more like a bargain basement than a place for higher learning.

In the next example, the paragraph moves in still closer to its subject than either of the preceding two examples. Because it narrows down or limits the subject further, it must discuss the subject in greater detail.

EXAMPLE

The cafeteria at crowded City College is one of the most overworked places on the campus. The service line is frequently so long that a student gives up the idea of eating altogether. If she is patient enough to wait for food, she is lucky if she can find a place to eat it before she wears it. If she is particularly agile, she may work her way through the masses to a spot where she can eat it before it's cold. Once seated, however, she is likely to find the atmosphere so choked with other bodies, noise, and dead air, that she loses her appetite. She cannot easily slip away at that point, either. Wedging her way out of the cafeteria, she discovers, is as miserable a matter as working her way in.

You should keep in mind that the closer you move into or go into a subject, the more the paragraph should be narrowed down or limited and that, likewise, the more the paragraph is narrowed down or limited, the more it must go into detail.

As stated earlier, some of the paragraphs that you will be asked to write may be like the first of the three preceding paragraphs; however, most of your effort should be spent in learning to write paragraphs like the second two.

SUMMARY

Your paragraph will be clear and enjoyable to read if you follow the directions summed up here. First, remember to indent the paragraph—once only! Second, remember that the paragraph should be neither too short nor too long; make it approximately eight to twelve sentences in length. Third and most important, organize and develop your paragraph carefully. Remember that the paragraph should contain one central idea only, that it should have unity, coherence, continuity, and adequate development. If you follow these directions, your paragraph should be as good as or better than this one.

PART 1

Practicing
the Paragraph

The Topic Sentence

1. WHAT IS A TOPIC SENTENCE?

A *topic sentence* indicates what the paragraph is about, what it will describe or discuss. It is often the first sentence in the paragraph. The following are examples of topic sentences.

Owning a car is expensive.

Going to college requires much more self-reliance than going to high school.

Television is (not) rightly called an "idiot box."

Spring is the most pleasant season of the year.

Parents should (not) spank their misbehaving children.

2. WHAT IS THE DIFFERENCE BETWEEN A TOPIC SENTENCE AND A TITLE?

Since a topic sentence tells what the paragraph is about, it is a little like the title of a composition. Because the topic sentence serves that function, *the para-*

graph needs no title. In other ways, a topic sentence and a title are different.

There are several differences between a topic sentence and a title. First, a topic sentence is a sentence *within* the paragraph, *not set off from or above* it, as a title is set off from the main body of a composition. Second, a topic sentence is always a complete thought, whereas a title is frequently a fragment or part of a complete thought. Consider the following examples:

A.   **Title:**   The Art of Changing a Tire
   Topic sentence: Too few drivers appreciate the art of changing a tire.

B.   **Title:**   In Case of a Flat
   Topic sentence: All drivers should know what to do in case of a flat.

Notice the difference in capitalization in the title and in the topic sentence. Several words of a title are capitalized, but only the first word of the topic sentence is capitalized. In addition, of course, if the topic sentence (or any sentence) contains proper nouns, they are also capitalized. Be careful, however, that you do not form the bad habit of capitalizing whenever you feel in the mood for it. Do not go capital-crazy!

Another important difference between a topic sentence and a title is that a topic sentence *limits* the paragraph, whereas a title *expands* the composition. Reexamine Figure 2–3 and the explanation given on page 22. You can see that a whole composition covers more ground than a single paragraph. The title of a composition also includes more, suggests more, is broader than the topic sentence of a paragraph. A title of a composition has the effect shown in Figure 3–1. A topic sentence has the effect shown in Figure 3–2.

A topic sentence must not only indicate what the paragraph is about, it must also make clear what the paragraph is *not* about. It must narrow down or limit the paragraph to an exact point. A good topic sentence controls the paragraph. It sets very clear and definite limits to the topic as well as telling what the topic is.

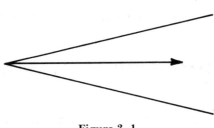

Figure 3–1

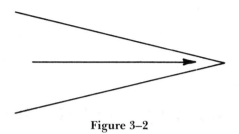

Figure 3–2

3. IS THE TOPIC SENTENCE ALWAYS THE FIRST SENTENCE IN THE PARAGRAPH?

At first, you should pretend that the topic sentence always begins the paragraph, even though it may not. Advanced or professional writers state the topic at various places in the paragraph. Some writers do not state it at all but rather suggest it with other parts of the paragraph. However, you are a beginning rather than a professional or advanced writer; therefore, the first sentence you put on paper should be your topic sentence, to remind you as well as to tell your reader what your topic is.

Be sure your first sentence is your topic sentence. Be sure you take a good look at your topic. Be sure you stick to it!

SUMMARY

Begin your paragraph with a topic sentence rather than a title. Be sure that your topic sentence indicates what your paragraph is about, that it is a complete thought, and that it limits your paragraph.

4

Practicing the Topic Sentence

REQUIREMENT 1. BE COMPLETE

The minimum requirement of any topic sentence is that it be a complete sentence. That is, the sentence must contain at least one complete thought. In fact, if it does not contain at least one complete thought, it is not a sentence at all but rather a sentence fragment or part of a sentence.

The first problem in writing a topic sentence is to learn to *write a complete sentence, not a fragment.* Study the following:

1. **Fragment:** How to change a tire
   Complete: Anyone can learn how to change a tire.

2. **Fragment:** To change a tire
   Complete: A motorist can learn to change a tire without much difficulty.

3. **Fragment:** Changing a tire
   Complete: Changing a tire is simple.

4. **Fragment:** If a driver has a flat tire
   Complete: If a driver has a flat tire, he or she should be able to change it.

5. **Fragment:** When a driver changes a flat tire
   Complete: When a driver changes a flat tire, he or she should observe three important safety rules.

6. **Fragment:** A safe way to change a tire
   Complete: There is a safe way to change a tire.

7. **Fragment:** One of the most important steps in changing a tire
   Complete: One of the most important steps in changing a tire is to set the brake first.

8. **Fragment:** Five easy steps in changing a tire
   Complete: Five easy steps in changing a tire should be followed by all drivers.

EXERCISES

The following are fragments that might become sentences if properly completed. As in the preceding examples, these fragments can be completed in more than one way. Try to figure out one or more of the ways in which to make them complete.

1. Teaching a child good manners
2. How to carry a gun safely
3. Learning to like grammar
4. If a person wants to be popular
5. To fight the fragment
6. How to avoid an argument
7. If a person wants to learn to style hair
8. Exceeding the speed limit
9. To make elderly people happy
10. Knowing how to select shoes
11. To be a good neighbor
12. When a skier learns to fall properly
13. One of the most important steps in learning to drive
14. To learn to fish
15. If a person wants to learn to dance
16. How to hem a dress
17. If a student wants to pass a course
18. One of the most important steps in learning to swim
19. If a teenager disagrees with his or her parents
20. Learning to draw or sketch

21. Five easy steps in making an
    interesting flower arrangement
22. When an individual feels lost in
    a crowd

23. Three easy ways to get
    acquainted with strangers
24. To learn to write a paragraph
25. A sensible way to select a career

REQUIREMENT 2. BE CLEAR

In addition to being complete, the topic sentence must also be clear. Bear in mind that the topic sentence announces the idea to be developed in the paragraph and that the paragraph must contain only one central idea. Therefore, the topic sentence should not confuse the reader with two or more possible meanings. Instead, it should state the one idea of the paragraph in a manner that is easy to recognize, definite, and unmistakable. It should make the topic plain and obvious. The following are examples of topic sentences that fail to be clear.

1. Street and highway construction in California is a debatable subject.
2. To play any kind of instrument, one needs to know something about
   the instrument.
3. House painting should be approached with caution.

Each of the three preceding sentences fails to make one clear and unmistakable statement. The first sentence gives only a hint of its meaning, and the hint suggests many possible topics rather than just one. The second sentence is also vague and says almost everything about nothing in particular. The third sentence, like the other two, is unclear rather than plain and obvious.

The three sentences might be made clearer and more definite in a number of ways. Consider the following:

1. Street and highway construction in California is a debatable subject.

Possible corrections:

Many people in San Francisco argue that the Embarcadero Freeway is
    ugly and obscures the view.
Doyle Drive, the approach to the Golden Gate Bridge, is extremely dan-
    gerous, but people do not agree on how to solve the problem.
All three-lane highways in California should be abolished.
Highway construction in California may diminish or even stop because
    of the increased cost of gasoline.
Redwood Highway is a lovely but dangerous drive.

Panoramic Hill in Berkeley, an area with a relatively high fire risk, has only one narrow and twisting road.

2. To play any kind of musical instrument, one needs to know something about the instrument.

Possible corrections:

To play any kind of drum requires a good sense of rhythm.

To play a French horn with a mellow tone requires extremely skillful breath control.

To play a cello, one must learn to read the bass, tenor, and treble clefs.

To play a violin, one needs a good ear.

To play a piano, one needs to spend much time practicing finger exercises.

To play a trumpet, one needs to develop a strong lip.

3. House painting should be approached with caution.

Possible corrections:

House painting should not be attempted by the average, unskilled person.

House painting can be an interesting family project if carefully planned.

House painting should be attempted by an amateur only in the case of single-floor dwellings.

House painting in the hands of the layperson is usually sloppy work.

House painting is an expensive but necessary part of home maintenance that must be carefully budgeted and planned for by homeowners.

House painting is a career that more people should think about going into.

EXERCISES

The following topic sentences are like the three examples just given. They fail to make a single idea easy to recognize, definite, and unmistakable. Instead, they give hints only, or they suggest many topics rather than just one, or they are vague and mysterious. Try to determine their faults and then correct them in one or more ways.

1. To play a sport, a person needs to know something about it.
2. Going to college should be approached with caution.

3. Taxes are debatable.
4. To be an artist, a person needs to know something about art.
5. The rise in crime is worrisome.
6. Learning to cook requires some knowledge and skill.
7. Unemployment is hurting the economy.
8. To repair a car, a person needs to know something about auto mechanics.
9. A career in music should be approached with caution.
10. Women should have rights equal to those of men.
11. Everyone should know something about computers.
12. People who operate day-care facilities need to know something about children.
13. Motorcycles should be approached with caution.
14. A person needs to have some knowledge of sex before experiencing it.
15. To appreciate old people, one needs to know something about them.
16. Television can be harmful to children.
17. Drugs should be approached with caution.
18. Before people get married, they need to know something about their prospective mates.
19. Writing takes knowledge and practice.
20. The nuclear age requires caution from people in power.

REQUIREMENT 3. BE SPECIFIC

Besides being complete and clear, the topic sentence must be specific. The third requirement of the topic sentence is closely related to the second and can even amount to the same thing. When a sentence is sufficiently specific, it tends to be clear. When a sentence is too broad or too general, it tends to be unclear as well.

Being specific, however, is not exactly the same as being clear. Being clear is a matter of making obvious statements rather than giving hints, of meaning one thing rather than several. Being specific means limiting the topic to the size suitable for a paragraph.

It is important to keep in mind the limitation of a paragraph when considering the topic sentence. The topic sentence must not be so broad or so general as to require a whole composition or even a book to do it justice. The topic sentence must control the paragraph. The shoe should pinch a little, so to speak, for the topic sentence to fit the paragraph. As a matter of fact, the topic sentence must come to a rather narrow point to be specific.

The following are examples of topic sentences that fail to be sufficiently specific.

1. Following the Ten Commandments is difficult.
2. A college student should know how to write a good composition.
3. The Irish have terrible tempers.

Each of the three preceding sentences is much too broad or general to be suitable as a topic sentences that can be developed in a single paragraph. The first sentence may be too large a topic even for a book or a set of encyclopedias. The second sentence calls for many paragraphs rather than just one. The third sentence is the sort of sweeping generalization that should not be written at all.

The three sentences might be made more specific in a number of ways. Consider the following:

1. Following the Ten Commandments is difficult.

Possible corrections:

The commandment to rest on the seventh day should not be interpreted as meaning *only* the seventh day.

Thou shalt not kill is a commandment the state breaks every time it executes a criminal.

Many young people fail to keep the commandment to honor their parents.

The parent of a starving child is sorely tempted to break the commandment regarding stealing.

"Keeping up with the Joneses" can easily be related to the commandment regarding coveting.

The commandment to work six days a week is out of date.

2. A college student should know how to write a good composition.

Possible corrections:

Writing an outline is an aid to organizing a composition.

Word choice in a composition should be both exact and imaginative.

Sentence length and structure should be varied in a composition.

The paragraphs of a composition must be related to each other.

The thesis sentence of a composition is comparable to the topic sentence of a paragraph.

The title of a composition should provoke the reader's interest and give him an idea of what the composition is about.

3. The Irish have terrible tempers.

Possible corrections:

Some of the Irish people who live in my neighborhood get angry quickly.

Many of my Irish friends at school are easily angered.

Most of my Irish classmates engage in very heated discussions.

My Irish business partner gets mad easily but forgets his anger just as quickly.

Although my best friend is of Irish, English, and Scottish descent, he blames only his Irish ancestry for his quick temper.

James Malloy calls himself a mad Irishman at home, but when he travels to a foreign land, he is just another American tourist.

EXERCISES

The following topic sentences are like the three examples just given. They fail to be sufficiently specific for a paragraph. Instead, they are too broad or too general. Try to determine their faults and then correct them in one or more ways. In addition, feel free to give up on some and call them hopeless cases. For example, a sentence such as the following is hopeless:

The Decline and Fall of the Roman Empire by Edward Gibbon provokes thought.

The preceding sentence refers to a work that is far too long and complicated to be considered in one brief paragraph. If you decide that one of the following sentences is hopeless, be able to state your reasons. You will probably find that most of the sentences can be repaired. Do not give up on all of them!

1. It is easy to learn to swim.
2. A police officer has many responsibilities.
3. Being a good parent is difficult.
4. It is exciting to experience live performances by some of the great rock groups.
5. Teenagers have trouble finding good jobs.
6. Pleasure and accomplishment can both be acquired in building a thermonuclear reactor.
7. Professional athletes make lots of money.

8. Inflation is easy to experience whenever anyone shops for anything.
9. Latins love to dance.
10. One can acquire a good education by simply studying *The Great Books*.
11. Gourmet foods are French.
12. Compact cars are replacing standard-sized cars.
13. The field of nursing offers a variety of job possibilities.
14. Learning a foreign language is difficult.
15. All college students should take courses in ethnic studies.
16. It is becoming increasingly difficult to understand and come to a conclusion about some of the most important national and international problems threatening the world today.
17. Unemployment hurts people in a number of ways.
18. Medical insurance is becoming an absolute necessity in view of the rising cost of health care.
19. Some of the most imaginative cooking in the world is soul food.
20. Contact sports can cause serious injuries.

REQUIREMENT 4. FIND THE RIGHT WORD

The fourth requirement of the topic sentence, like the first three, is really a requirement of any good sentence. Because the topic sentence is the first sentence you will write and because it has the important responsibility of introducing the subject of all other sentences in the paragraph, it is given special consideration here. But bear in mind that what is said here and elsewhere about the topic sentence applies to all the sentences you write.

To the first three requirements—being complete, being clear, and being specific—a fourth requirement of finding the right word should be added. Finding the right word or choosing words well is probably the most difficult requirement of the topic sentence. Building a good vocabulary from which to select the right word takes time and lots of practice in using words. You should be prepared to put extra effort into expanding your vocabulary and sharpening your ability to find the right word.

First, you should understand that the *right word* is the word that best communicates your meaning. It is the word that is most exact in saying what you mean. For example, the words *painting, drawing,* or *photograph* are more exact that the word *picture*. The words *play, opera,* or *motion picture* are more precise than the word *show*. You should pay close attention to the exact thought you wish to express and then express that thought with the exact word you need. You may need to ask yourself, "What am I trying to say?" You should then ask, "How can I say that exactly?"

Second, the right word should be *vivid*. That is, it should be strikingly alive or full of life, lively, colorful, bright, intense, vigorous, fresh, spirited, strong and distinct, imaginative (all synonyms of the word *vivid*). Your aim in writing, once you have mastered the first three requirements of being complete, clear, and specific, is to be exciting. You should aim not merely to express yourself but to express the best of you.

You should form the habit (the compulsion, if need be!) of using two important sources of the right word. Whenever you write, you should have at your fingertips: (1) a good, up-to-date dictionary and (2) *Roget's Thesaurus,* a book of synonyms and antonyms. It is likely that the right word, the exact and vivid word you need, is waiting to be discovered by you in one or both of these sources.

Further, in your pursuit of the right word, it may be helpful for you to be able to distinguish between the words *denotation* and *connotation*. The denotation of a word is its precise or explicit meaning that you or anyone else can easily find in a dictionary. For example, the denotation of the word *home* is "dwelling" or "place where one lives." People generally agree about what a word denotes because they accept the dictionary definition that reflects their usage. The connotation of a word, on the other hand, is what the word suggests to each person as a result of his or her experience or emotional association with the word. Because people differ in their experiences or associations with words, a given word may connote one idea or feeling to one person but have quite a different connotation to another. Consider the word *home* again. It may connote security, love, and protection to one person but instability, neglect, and indifference to another, depending on the experiences associated with the word. If people are to understand each other, they must become aware of these differences in connotation and make them known to each other.

While you are thinking about finding the right word, you should realize that you have had much more practice speaking than you have had writing, and you should understand that speaking and writing are different. When you speak, you can express a great deal without words through the sound of your voice, the expression on your face, and body movements. Anger or grief, for example, can be communicated without a word when you are face to face with someone. Writing a letter on either subject, however, takes great effort. How much easier it is to console someone who is mourning the death of a loved one by holding hands in silence or by a hug than it is to write a letter of sympathy.

Keep in mind that writing is different from speaking. You must fully say in writing what can be half said in speech. When you write, you do not have your voice, your face, or a gesture of your hand to help you. You have only words on a page with which to express yourself. Choose those words well!

You will need to strike a balance between being afraid to write anything and writing too much. This balance requires first courage and then discipline. At first you must have the courage to try out new words, to experiment, to expand your vocabulary; you will probably make some mistakes that may embarrass or frustrate you but from which you will unquestionably recover. As your writing skill develops, on the other hand, you may fall so deeply in love with words that you may tend to use too many of them. Your ultimate goal is to be neither wordless nor wordy but to achieve a balance with just the right words.

The following are some exercises in finding the right word. Preceding each exercise is a brief discussion of a problem to be studied and then dealt with in the exercise. The exercises by no means exhaust the subject of finding the right word, but they introduce some of the problems you will face as you learn to choose words well.

PROBLEM A—AVOIDING CHEAP SUBSTITUTES

Some words are not words at all, really, but substitutes for words. They are like grunts, and in speech rather than writing they can be meaningful. In writing, though they may be used as crutches, they cripple rather than support communication. The underlined words in the following sentences are cheap substitutes for exact or precise words. Find the words that are needed in place of the underlined words. Rewrite the sentences, eliminating, if possible, words that may become unnecessary when the exact words are found.

1. The *thing* that makes the car go faster is not easy for an inexperienced foot to control.
2. Those big pointed *things* in Egypt were all built by slaves.
3. He *sort of didn't want* to jump from an airplane.
4. He pulled the *thing* and up billowed his parachute.
5. She didn't want to make a ring on the table with her glass, so she asked for a *thing* to put her glass on.
6. If a person doesn't know what a word means, he should look it up in that *deal* in the back of the book.
7. The stranger handed him a paper *thing* that said he had to go to court.
8. He *kind of* wanted to go on the trip and he *kind of* didn't want to go.
9. The rooster-*deal* that shows which way the wind is blowing fell off the roof of their house.
10. The house was getting too warm, so he lowered the *thing* on the wall that regulated the temperature of the heater.

PROBLEM B—AVOIDING TIRED SUBSTITUTES

Some words or expressions are simply worn out or tired from too much use. These words or expressions are called *clichés*. They lack freshness and vitality now, though they may have been quite imaginative when they were first used.

Now they fail to challenge the imagination. Instead, they say the same old thing in the same old, tired way.

Clichés are often comparisons; that is, expressions that show similarities or differences between one person or thing and another. Although fresh comparisons can be useful in clarifying ideas, comparisons that are clichés are about as helpful as tired blood. They produce dullness and boredom rather than inspiring interest and understanding.

Rewrite the following sentences, replacing the underlined clichés with fresh comparisons or expressions. This is a difficult exercise. As you work with it, you may come to appreciate how original the clichés once were!

1. You *can't tell a book by its cover*.
2. That man is *as strong as an ox*.
3. Stretched out in the sun, the old dog looked *dead as a door nail*.
4. The little girl ran off *happy as a lark*.
5. In this warm sleeping bag, I feel *snug as a bug in a rug*.
6. He sat on his hat and smashed it *flatter than a pancake*.
7. The children were *good as gold* all day.
8. Her *eyes are bigger than her stomach*.
9. *Last but not least,* capital punishment is bad because it is so final.
10. She looks *as cool as a cucumber*.

PROBLEM C—AVOIDING WEAK SUBSTITUTES

Similar to clichés are words or expressions that simply lack force and exactness in saying what they mean. They *kinda, sorta* say it, but they do not say it precisely. These inexact expressions might well be replaced by comparisons (but not clichés) or by exact measurements or clear descriptions.

Find more forceful and exact ways of expressing the underlined statements that follow.

1. It is *very hot* today.
2. That man is *good-looking*.
3. Everybody likes her because she has so much *personality*.
4. That movie is *just great*.
5. We had a *nice* time at your party.
6. That is an *interesting* book.
7. Yesterday was *cold*.
8. He waited a *short* time and then left.

9. She was *sorry* she had lost the contest.
10. That award was a *really big* surprise.

PROBLEM D—AVOIDING WORDINESS

Your search for the right word is a special kind of treasure hunt. You should not look for a pot full of the fanciest words in the dictionary. Instead, you should hunt for the one perfect gem you need to express your thought. Look for quality, not quantity.

Keep in mind that the purpose of language is to communicate, not to call attention to itself. The reader should not notice the words you use but rather what you say with them. Do not decorate! Communicate!

Eliminate the repetitious or unnecessary words in the following sentences. If needed, rewrite the sentence, using words that express the idea with greater force or exactness.

1. He was certainly a very old man, and he never went out in his little boat with anybody at all but rather always went fishing alone way out in the Gulf of Mexico off Cuba, and he had spent all of eighty-four long days now without catching any fish at all, not even one fish. (The first sentence of Ernest Hemingway's *The Old Man and the Sea* illustrates his economy of words as well as his exact though simple word choice: "He was an old man who fished alone in a skiff in the Gulf Stream and he had gone eighty-four days now without taking a fish.")
2. She was a funny little old lady who had no sense of humor at all but was still funny or strange or something because she never came out of her house in the day at all but rather she came out of her house only at night to go to the store or to go to see people or to go anyplace.
3. He was really very tired and weary of working or going to work and he planned to quit or stop working and retire.
4. He couldn't think of the word he needed even though he needed that word and not some other word he didn't need.
5. That painting of Picasso is really very unusual, but then it doesn't really look like what it is, or what it is trying to be, or what I think it is trying to be, if I understand what it is trying to be, and I'm trying.

PROBLEM E—AVOIDING "THIS, THAT, AND IT" ERRORS

One weakness in word choice might be termed the *"this, that,* and *it"* problem. Although the weakness is actually a grammatical error, it is frequently the result of careless word use. As a general rule, *this* and *that* (and *these* and *those*) are words that should not stand alone but should be attached to other words. Most often *this* and *that* are used as modifiers—that is, as adjectives and adverbs— and should be combined with the nouns or other words they modify.

Examine the following sentences to determine how errors in the use of *this* and *that* make meaning vague and sometimes impossible to understand.

1. Advertising associating smoking with the freshness of ocean surf and forest glen is questionable. *This* increases sales desirably but misleads the public.
2. Home buyers are becoming younger despite the enormous cost of real estate. There are two reasons for *this*.
3. Too many clothes are made from synthetics rather than cotton or wool. *These* are harder to find.
4. Some people think of animals only as objects designed to feed them, clothe them, and amuse them. *That* is gross.

Possible corrections:

1. *This method of advertising* increases sales desirably but misleads the public.
2. There are two reasons for *this trend*.
3. *These fabrics* are harder to find.
4. *That attitude* is gross.

It is also often abused or misused. When there is no noun or noun phrase in the same sentence or in the sentence preceding the one in which *it* is used as a substitute, what *it* refers to is either unclear or may even be nonexistent, as in the following example.

Athletes and top sportsmen are used by advertising companies. *It* is giving the public a false impression of the product.

Possible correction:

Athletes and top sportsmen are being used by advertising companies. *Endorsements and testimonials* by athletes are giving the public a false impression of the products advertised.

As seen in the correction given, what is often needed in place of the pronoun substitute *it* is a noun or noun phrase that makes clear what *it* really is! Unless *it* has a clear reference, use an exact noun. Avoid *it* whenever *it* is confusing.

Other pronouns such as *they* and *them* also are often abused. As in the case of the pronouns already discussed, care must be taken in using *they* and *them* to make certain that the nouns for which these pronouns substitute are obvious and clear.

Rewrite the following sentences, using nouns with or in place of the under-lined *this, that,* and *it* errors.

1. When the value of the dollar rises, the price of gold tends to go down. There must be a reason for *this*.
2. He argued with me, insulted me, and then he tried to hit me. *That* did not make me happy.
3. Stella yawned as she looked at the ruby ring, the pearl necklace, and the diamond bracelet. *These* bored her.
4. Dogs chase cats and cats chase mice. Sometimes *they* catch *them*.
5. Why are the children running into the house, screaming at the top of their lungs, and then running out again, slamming the door? I don't like *it*.
6. He was told to rewrite all of his compositions. He didn't like *that*.
7. She liked the short man better than the tall man. However, *they* didn't know *it*.
8. He failed the examination but was admitted to the college anyway. *It* was a good thing.
9. During winter Dennis has to stay inside the house much of the time or wear very heavy clothing when he goes outside. He gets tired of *it*.
10. A person can lose a lot of time worrying about nothing. *This* is not good.

PROBLEM F—BEING CAREFUL OF MANY MEANINGS

Words are slippery. They can mean many different things to people. A word intended to be a compliment can result in being insulting. A word intended to convey one meaning may result in suggesting another or several others. You must be aware of the ambiguous nature of words—that many words have two or more possible interpretations—in your search for the right word.

A single word can stand for many different things, such as the word *show,* for example, which can mean a play, a review, an opera, a motion picture, and so forth. On the other hand a single thing can be referred to with many different words. A *couch,* a *sofa,* a *davenport,* a *chesterfield* are examples of different words that refer to the same thing.

When different words can be used to refer to the same thing, the particular word chosen sometimes reflects an attitude or feeling the user of the word has about the thing. The same play, for example, can be called a *triumph* by one person and a *flop* by another. Words can be classified into three categories: neutral, positive, and negative. When someone has no strong feelings one way or another about a thing, he refers to it with a neutral word. If he likes the thing, he uses a positive word for it. If he dislikes the thing, he refers to it with a negative word. Consider the following:

Neutral	Positive	Negative
1. policeman	officer of the law	cop
2. thin	slim/slender	skinny
3. jail	confinement facility	slammer

Being aware of the neutral, positive, and negative effects that some words can have is vital to successful communication. Obviously, if you want to communicate in a positive manner, you cannot achieve success by using negative words. Neither can you succeed in being negative by using neutral or positive words. Imagine complaining about an unfair bill in positive words or writing a letter to a prospective employer using negative words!

Consider the following words. Determine their various meanings and decide whether they are neutral, positive, or negative. Be prepared for discussion and disagreement concerning this exercise.

1. work	11. family	21. flag
2. party	12. divorce	22. computer
3. budget	13. fidelity	23. apology
4. debt	14. home	24. beauty
5. arrest	15. parent	25. vacation
6. convict	16. chef	26. soul
7. music	17. waiter	27. joke
8. student	18. fashion	28. news
9. average	19. college	29. fat
10. military	20. friend	30. poor

SUMMARY

The four requirements of the topic sentence are that it be complete, clear, specific, and well worded. These requirements apply not only to the topic sentence but to all good sentences. Remember that words used well are the material from which good sentences are made. Good sentences, in turn, make good paragraphs if the paragraphs are properly organized and developed. With these considerations in mind, you should be ready to practice writing the whole paragraph.

5

Coherence and Continuity

1. PICTURE A PUZZLE

Picture a smooth, wooden ball just a little larger than a tennis ball. As you look at the wooden ball more closely, you can see that it is a puzzle, composed of interlocking pieces that can be taken apart. Bound together, the pieces form a single entity, a perfect little ball that is a pleasure to hold in the hand. When the ball is taken apart, each separate piece looks unique, and it is a challenge to reconstruct the ball, which is the point of the puzzle. You are guided in that effort by the fact that each piece of the puzzle is unmistakably a part of the ball. Though notched and angled differently, the pieces are all made of the same wood, and each piece is curved so that you can see in it some part of the round ball. Keeping the shape of the ball in mind, you begin to fit the pieces together again.

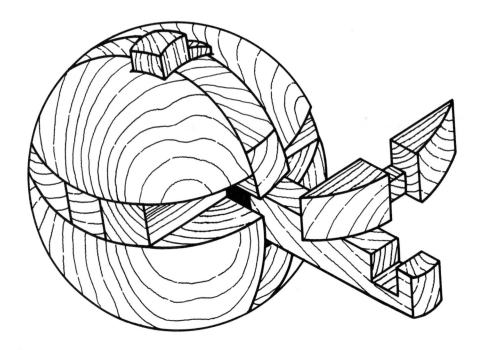

2. COMPARE THE PARAGRAPH AND THE PUZZLE

A well-organized paragraph is like that puzzle. It is a *unified* whole, a single entity, made from interlocking pieces. Its purpose gives it its distinct shape, like the roundness of the ball, and all its parts or sentences are formed and fitted to that purpose. When they are properly assembled, the sentences have *coherence* and can lock together into one *continuous* unit.

3. MAKE THE PARAGRAPH COHERENT

A coherent paragraph is one that hangs together because it is planned and arranged deliberately to have *order* or *sequence*. First things come first, second come second, and so on. To create this order within your paragraph, you must plan your course with care, deciding first what the main topic of your paragraph is. Then you may wish to make a simple list of main ideas and supporting points of your discussion, which at first need be no more complicated than the kind of list you take with you to the grocery store. However, when you make your grocery store list, as a rule, you jot things down as they occur to you, at random. You may do the same with your paragraph list, too, at first, so that your mind is free to wander and snag ideas as they pop into your head. Ultimately, however, you must impose *order* on this list. After all, even when you go to the grocery store or supermarket, you do not actually follow your random list, scrambling back and forth through the store picking up things as you have listed them. The store is organized, even if your shopping list is not, and you proceed through the store in an orderly manner, selecting what you need from each of its departments. When you return home from the store and think in terms of the dinner you will serve, you organize your thoughts in yet another way. Compare the following two lists and decide which is the random list you might take to the store and which represents the dinner as you might serve it.

I. Dinner for friends	II. Dinner for friends
cake	A. salad
asparagus	1. lettuce
tomatoes	2. tomatoes
coffee	3. cucumbers
lettuce	4. scallions
ice cream	B. main course with wine
wine	1. roast
cucumbers	2. asparagus
roast	3. potatoes
potatoes	4. rolls
rolls	C. dessert with coffee
scallions	1. cake
	2. ice cream

It is quickly apparent that the first list is one made at random. Obviously, the meal will not begin with cake and end with onions! The order of the meal is shown in the second list. You may notice another difference in the two lists. The second is organized into categories with main headings (A, B, C), and under them are subheadings (1, 2, 3) that show what each category contains. This systematic scheme makes the second list a clearer plan or *outline* than the first, and as a result, the total meal as well as its component parts can easily be seen. As you begin to think about your paragraph, you may start by making the first kind of list, but you should end by organizing your thoughts into the more coherent form shown by the second list or outline.

4. MAKE A SIMPLE OUTLINE

Your sense of order will likely sharpen as you work on your outline, and you will probably begin to see how to organize not only your main ideas or headings (A, B, C, and so on), but how to arrange their supporting points or subheadings (1, 2, 3, and so on), as illustrated in the following example. Notice that the subheads indicate both *content* and *order.*

(TOPIC) Giving a good party
    A. Early evening
        1. Welcome guests at door
        2. Attend to introductions
        3. Serve and maintain beverages
        4. Circulate among guests
    B. Middle evening
        1. Begin buffet dinner by 8:00 P.M.
        2. Serve dessert and coffee about 9:30 P.M.
        3. Present special event such as musical performance
        4. Play parlor games if guests in mood
        5. Serve after-dinner drinks and offer more coffee
    C. Late evening
        1. Depending on mood of party, dance, sing, or converse
        2. See guests to door

If your topic is a process that takes place within a time period, as in the preceding example, you will probably want to organize your outline *chronologically*; that is, to arrange the events within the time period in the order in which they occur. The main headings of your outline can show the major divisions of the time, and subheadings can indicate specific activities within each major division as well as the order of their occurrence. If your topic is *spatial* or *geographical*, then your main headings will likely divide that space in some way such as north, south, east, west, or left, right, top, bottom, and so forth. Examine the following outline, which is organized geographically.

(TOPIC) My messy study
    A. West side of room
        1. Cluttered desk
        2. Dirty windows
        3. Mishmash of cards and pins
    B. North side of room
        1. Disarray of books
        2. Crowded collection of toys, other objects
        3. Paper, letters falling to floor
    C. East side of room
        1. Closet doors busy with posters, photographs, museum magazine
           cover, cartoons
        2. Old thermometer jammed next to door to room
        3. Door to room almost concealed by posters
    D. South side of room
        1. Books, artifacts stacked every which way
        2. Bed, table, chair covered with books and papers
        3. Typewriter table overcrowded with papers

Notice that the room that is outlined is divided into four geographical sections. However, the purpose of the outline is not simply to describe the room but to show that the room is messy. Therefore, the subheadings select only those aspects of the room that focus on that topic. Thus, although the main headings of the outline are *geographical*, the subheadings are *topical*. That is, they all support the (messy study) topic. You will often experience just such a mixture of structures, but try not to be confused by it. Your topic and supporting points or subheadings are always closely related, regardless of how your support is "packaged" by main headings or divisions of the support. Remember that your primary aim is to make your thoughts hang together or cohere, and that objective may require an outline that is "purely" chronological (organized by time), strictly geographical, completely topical, or that uses some other structural scheme that is entirely consistent. Or, you may need to use some combination such as the preceding example.

The following outline is *topical*. That is, it is organized by topics. The order or arrangement of ideas in a topical outline depends on both the subject and the writer's approach to the topic. As with the chronological and geographical outline, related ideas are generally grouped together. For example, an outline on birds might group water birds under one main heading and shore birds under another. However, a particular writer might approach the subject of birds in terms of his or her favorites, beginning with those liked best—hawks, for instance—and then proceeding to others that are not as well liked. Examine the following outline, which divides the topic simply into two main headings (see p. 93 for the paragraph on this topic).

(TOPIC) Why I don't want to be in college
  A. What I want
    1. To lie around
    2. To shoot pool, work on the car, watch television
    3. To relax and have a beer with friends
    4. To avoid struggle
  B. What college makes me do that I don't want
    1. To work and compete to get good grades
    2. To look at myself and worry about my future
    3. To grow up
    4. To become a useful citizen and real person

You may have been exposed to outlining before and therefore know that it can be much more complicated than the examples given to you in this chapter. However, these outlines are enough to help you think through your paragraphs in a coherent manner. They will permit you to organize your paragraphs, to line up your ideas from beginning to end.

5. STUDY TWO PARAGRAPHS BASED ON OUTLINES

When you have completed your outline and are ready to write your paragraph, you should keep in mind that your outline is your *plan*, the skeletal *basis* of your paragraph. Be sure to *follow* your plan as you put flesh on these bones! The two paragraphs that follow do just that. They are based on the first two outlines (giving a good party, my messy study) in this chapter. Study the examples and compare them to the outlines.

EXAMPLE 1

When I give a party, I try to make it a good one by being both careful and casual. As the evening begins, I am careful to meet guests at the door and welcome them, not just let them slip into my house unnoticed and unsung. If some of my guests do not know each other, which is possible, as I believe new faces help to spark a party, I see to introductions next. After that, I serve my guests beverages and then keep an eye on their glasses to see that no thirsty person lacks refreshment. Before dinner, I try to circulate among my guests, sharing their interests, breaking the ice, and doing what I can to generate lively conversation and good will. By eight o'clock most people are hungry, and I serve them dinner then, which I like to make a casual buffet. My guests select what they like, and they arrange themselves, having got acquainted by that time, in informal groups around my living room. After a leisurely dinner, we have dessert and coffee around nine-thirty, and then one of my guests might entertain the group with piano music for a brief period, which I hope gives the evening a quiet focus and a change of pace. Next, if the mood of the guests is agreeable, we play charades or some other parlor game, which I follow with after-dinner drinks and more coffee. Later in the evening the mood of the party often peaks with dancing and singing, but sometimes it simply mellows out with more conversation. I don't push the party in any particular direction. I like it to flow wherever it goes naturally. The party ends as it began, at the door of my house, where my guests and I part with much reluctance and with promises to "do it again soon."

EXAMPLE 2

My study is an almost uncontrollable mess everywhere I look. Beginning on the west side of the room, where I sit at my cluttered desk and look through dirty windows to a tangle of trees that almost conceals the beautiful bay, I can also see a mishmash of picture postcards tacked to the wall and

Curtain

buttons declaring such mottos as "Support Your Right to Arm Bears" attached to the drapery above the desk. Turning north in this smallish room, I can view one of the two floor-to-ceiling bookcases the room contains. Besides a disarray of books, the bookcase is crowded with antique toys, paperweights, bottles, seashells, and photographs. Reams of paper, assorted envelopes, bills, and old letters are also stuffed into the bookcase, though they are almost falling to the floor. The east side of my study contains closets, and the closet doors are busy with old Dutch shipping posters, the photograph of a French cathedral, the cover of a museum magazine picturing reclining Holstein cows, and some of my favorite cartoons. An old thermometer is jammed next to the door to the room, also located on the east side, and the door itself is almost concealed by museum posters. The south side of the room contains the second bookcase, where the only semblance of order is in the uniform rows of encyclopedias and Great Books. Otherwise, books are stacked every which way, together with assorted artifacts such as a teddy bear squashed against two volumes of folklore, a bud vase leaning perilously, and the figurine of "Speak No Evil, Hear No Evil, See No Evil" about to sail out at me where I sit at my typewriter. There are also a single bed, a low table, and a canvas chair on the south side of the room, all covered with books and papers. The one sometimes clear space in my study is a second chair that I now occupy, turned to the typewriter table next to my desk. As I type this paragraph, I must constantly reassemble the papers beside my typewriter lest its movement jiggle them to the floor.

6. COMPARE THE OUTLINE AND THE PARAGRAPH

As you can see, the paragraph *follows* the outline and is a "fleshed-out" version of it. The main ideas and supporting points in the paragraph are approximately the same as those in the outline, and the order or sequence in each is identical. However, the outline only *suggests* what the paragraph must fully *explain*. Therefore, the paragraph contains more words than the outline and sometimes even some supporting ideas that do not appear in the outline. In addition, the paragraph begins with a topic sentence. Although a topic is given at the beginning of the outline, it does not (though it may) contain a topic sentence. That is, no sentence in the outline indicates what its exact point will be or what will be said about the topic, only what the topic is. Another benefit of the outline is that, by writing it, you may discover exactly what you want to say in your paragraph; that is, what your topic sentence is. On the other hand, if your topic sentence is clear to you from the beginning, then you may as well use it at the beginning of your outline.

As you may have noticed, there is a striking difference between the outline and the paragraph in their *written style*. The outline is often written with fragments and in a telegraphic style—that is, in the concise style of a telegram, including only the most essential words—whereas the paragraph is written with standard sentences and complete wording. There are also marginal differences. The left margin of the paragraph, as you know, moves down the page in a straight line except for the indentation with which it begins. However, the left margin of the outline begins without an indentation for main headings (A, B, C), but beneath these headings are subheadings (1, 2, 3), which are indented, as in the repeated example that follows.

EXERCISES

Think about the following topics. As you let your mind wander, thinking of ideas at random, make up a "grocery store" list of the thoughts that occur to you. When you are ready, organize this list into an outline with main ideas or headings (A, B, C) and under them supporting points or subheadings (1, 2, 3) that indicate both the *content* and *order* or sequence of that content. Use the following example to guide you. (Notice that the example makes use of the first topic but that this topic is therefore by no means "used up" but can be used over and over with different results, depending on the opinions or tastes of the particular writer.)

(TOPIC) Giving a good party
    A. Early evening
        1. Welcome guests at door
        2. Attend to introductions
        3. Serve and maintain beverages
        4. Circulate among guests
    B. Middle evening
        1. Begin buffet dinner at 8:00 P.M.
        2. Serve dessert and coffee about 9:30 P.M.
        3. Present special event such as musical performance
        4. Play parlor games if guests in mood
        5. Serve after-dinner drinks and offer more coffee
    C. Late evening
        1. Depending on mood of party, dance, sing, or converse
        2. See guests to door

1. What does a good party, one that you give or attend, contain? How should the party proceed from beginning to end? Organize your outline chronologically.
2. Describe a room in your house, organizing your outline spatially or geographically.

3. What is your idea of a good date or a perfect evening out? What does it require and what should it include? Organize your outline chronologically.

4. You have a beautiful day off, and there are many things you would like to do with it, but there are also commitments you have made to study, do chores around the house, pay bills, visit a sick relative or friend in the hospital, and so forth. Organize your outline chronologically into three parts, morning, afternoon, and evening; divide each part topically, showing first what you would like to do, but second, what you will do instead.

5. People who are important to you are coming to your area for the first time, and it is your job to show them around. They will be with you for only one day, and you want them to see the most striking sights and most interesting places. How do you plan the day to make the most of it? Organize your outline chronologically, indicating what you will do with each part of the day.

6. Is your diet wholesome? On a typical day, what do you eat for breakfast, lunch, and dinner, and if you snack, what do you normally consume? Organize your outline topically, indicating what each meal consists of, and then decide if your diet is nourishing or primarily junk food.

7. Recreate the high points of a film, play, or concert that has impressed you. What were the most memorable features? Organize your outline topically or chronologically.

8. Describe an outdoor area with which you are familiar, such as the yard around your house, a nearby park, or your college campus. Organize your outline geographically.

9. Recreate a frightening, embarrassing, maddening, or amusing moment in your life. For example, have you experienced a burglary; had your car, purse, or wallet stolen; been clumsy or fallen down in front of a lot of people; waited in a long line and failed to achieve your goal; been the perpetrator or target of a practical joke? What happened and how did you handle the experience? Organize your outline chronologically.

10. Are you and your best friend alike or different? Consider such points of comparison as appearance, personality, activities, and interests, and use these or other subjects to organize your outline topically, deciding how you and your friend should be described in each category.

Having tried your hand at outlining at least one of the preceding topics, you may now want to write a paragraph based on your outline. Remember to *follow* your outline, to keep main ideas and supporting points in the same order or sequence; however, keep in mind that in your paragraph you must fully explain what may be only suggested in your outline.

EXERCISES

Think back (or see pp. 55–56) to the comparison of the puzzle with which this chapter begins. When the ball is taken apart, as already stated, it can be a challenge to reconstruct it. However, that is the point of the puzzle. It is also the purpose of the exercises that follow. The paragraphs have been purposefully mixed up or jumbled. Your task is to assemble them again in their correct order. Rewrite the paragraphs so that they have *coherence*. It may help you to locate the topic sentence and then to proceed from that point. There are no superfluous sentences. Each sentence is "a part of the ball," so to speak. In other words, each fits somewhere in the paragraph. (Note that the sentences, though they are numbered for easy identification and classroom discussion, are *not* in the correct order.)

A. [1]As soon as her dog hits the night air, his automatic response is to howl and bark, which he does for a full half hour. [2]An example is my neighbor's dog across the street from me. [3]My neighbor lets her dog out for about a half hour every night around midnight. [4]If there's one thing I dislike, it is dogs that bark late at night. [5]I want to be a good neighbor, so I try not to complain too much, but I am getting very tired of that midnight serenade. [6]Instead, barking seems to be his form of nightly exercise. [7]He does not seem to bark at anything in particular.

B. [1]Pressing my remote control, I survey the available channels, looking for my "sleeping pill." [2]I begin that process generally around eleven or so at night, right after the news. [3]I must, of course, reject the most action-packed movies, though their repetitious violence is often monotonous enough; however, car crashes, gunshots, and scream-filled stabbings do not make the best background "music" for my tentative trip to Nod. [4]I perversely try to follow the speaker for at least ten minutes before my eyelids get in the way, my mind grinds down to zero, and I gradually flunk the class. [5]Instead, I must find something more tranquil. [6]If I am lucky, I discover someone droning on about a topic in which I have little interest or aptitude, such as one of the finer points of auto repair, a complex mathematical problem, or some subtle insight into stocks and bonds. [7]One way I use television is to put myself to sleep.

C. [1]Cars weren't locked, either. [2]After that, I go up the stairs to my car, where I use one key to turn the alarm off before I insert another to open the car door. [3]I have joined the paranoid ranks of Americans who, of necessity, have become fully security minded, but I did not grow up that way. [4]It was not uncommon to leave the key in the switch, where it was handy and ready to go. [5]With what nostalgia I think of those sweet old days as I leave my house in the city now, after first pressing out the code on the panel of my electronic security system and double-locking the front door. [6]I drive off to work, remembering the sounds of lowing cows grazing in fields, as yet another neighbor's house alarm rings out, fire, fiend, or false alarm! [7]In fact, I doubt if anyone had a house key, though one might have existed and been lost somewhere in a drawer full of old string and rubber bands. [8]Where I grew up in the country, nobody in my family ever thought of locking our front door.

D. [1]Related to the problem of energy are other crucial environmental issues such as clean air and water, the preservation of the wilderness, and endangered species. [2]However, they are working hard to change the apparent fate of the earth. [3]Another problem concerning environmentalists is man's dependence on nonrenewable energy sources and his need to develop alternative energy programs that will preserve the natural ecosystems on which his survival depends. [4]Perhaps the most threatening is the danger of nuclear war. [5]Mankind is beset with profound environmental problems. [6]According to a report by one environmental organization, there are fifty thousand nuclear warheads stored in silos, submarines, bombers, and warehouses around the world. [7]These and other problems worry conservationists, who feel that time is running out. [8]The touch of a button or the turn of a key could end the world as we know it.

E. [1]You want to get a head start on the day, so you leave home early in the morning, but that is a mistake because you must contend with rush-hour traffic on the freeway. [2]By noon you are exhausted and hungry, and you line up at a restaurant where, afterwards, you line up again to pay your check. [3]The pressure of increasing population is easy for anyone to feel in both auto and pedestrian traffic. [4]Suppose you plan to leave your suburban home (where there are more houses than there used to be) to spend a day in the city. [5]In the afternoon you think of going to a movie, but the line is so long that you decide to line up for your car instead, to get a jump on the evening traffic going home. [6]Even with car pools, the morning and evening freeway "rush" is a bumper-to-bumper snarl that is tedious and time-consuming. [7]Once again you edge your car into the bedlam of the city streets, but when at last you find the freeway, you are appalled by how many others have had the same idea as you and are also very slowly heading home. [8]Finally parked, you wend your way through crowded streets into crowded department stores, where you elbow your way to what you want and then wait in line to pay for it. [9]You feel worn out before you reach the city, and when you get there, you must devote more exasperating time to finding a parking space.

7. GIVE THE PARAGRAPH CONTINUITY

Turn your thoughts again to the puzzle with which this chapter begins. Imagine that you are holding the smooth wooden ball in your hand. You can, of course, feel that there are slight spaces between the interlocking pieces that compose the ball, but the pieces are so well fitted together that the narrow spaces are hardly noticeable. So it should be with your well-organized paragraph. A *coherent* paragraph, although made of a number of pieces or sentences, hangs together as one unified piece that has continuity; that is, it moves without interruption in one unbroken course.

To have continuity, the puzzle and the paragraph must first have the right pieces in the right places. Imagine trying to assemble the puzzle with a stray piece in it or with a piece in the wrong place. The puzzle couldn't cohere and would most likely fall apart. Similarly, if an unrelated idea is introduced into the paragraph or if its ideas are jumbled or out of order, it falls apart for lack of unity, or it becomes incoherent. If the paragraph is neither one unit nor an orderly progression of ideas, it lacks continuity as well. Continuity is the result, in large measure, of both unity and coherence. These essential elements move the paragraph in one continuous direction (not stop and start and turn around) and make it easy to follow.

8. USE TRANSITIONS

If your paragraph is put together well with all its pieces or sentences in their right places so that it hangs together as one coherent unit, it may nonetheless have slight spaces or gaps, as with the puzzle, between its sentences. Even though these gaps may be hardly noticeable, you may want to bridge them to ensure that continuity is not lost or to reenforce it. You can bridge these gaps with *transitional* words or phrases that permit easy passage from one sentence or idea to the next. A transition is a little like a road sign that alerts a motorist to what lies ahead along the road, if there is a curve coming up or a downhill grade, for instance. Although you may not have been as aware of transitions as you will now become, you probably depended on them to help you reassemble the mixed-up paragraphs in the exercises beginning on page 64. You may remember (or want to look back at) such expressions as *an example, but, instead, after that, another,* and *finally,* which helped you see the correct order of the sentences in those paragraphs. Of course, you relied still more on figuring out the logical progression of ideas within the paragraphs, but these transitional expressions helped you do that. Transitions help to point the way, to keep the direction clear, to reenforce the continuity of the paragraph.

Transitions are frequently used at the *beginning* of a sentence, to link or relate that sentence to the one that precedes it, but they are also used *within* a sentence, especially one that is a bit long or complicated, to relate ideas within it to each other. There are a number of ways transitions relate sentences or ideas. Some of them are (1) they may show that something is being *added, repeated,* or *intensified*; (2) they may *compare* or *contrast* two things or *contradict* something; (3) they may show a *time* or *space* relationship; (4) they may *limit* something or prepare for an *example*; (5) they may signal *cause* or *result*; (6) they may assert that the *truth* of something is *obvious* or *grant* an *opposing* argument or position. The following list is by no means comprehensive, but it includes some of the most commonly used transitions. (Note that some of the words in one category may also be used in another and that there are some duplications to suggest these various uses.)

1. Transitions that *add, repeat,* or *intensify*:

and	moreover	first, second, and so on
also	indeed	to conclude
in addition	in fact	to sum up
besides	as a matter of fact	again
too	to put it another way	once again
another	nevertheless	usually
in other words	finally	habitually
further	after all	anymore
furthermore	to repeat	

2. Transitions that *compare, contrast,* or *contradict*:

similarly	unlike	in spite of,	on the contrary
like	on the other	despite	nevertheless
likewise	hand	but	nonetheless
in like manner	however	yet	then again
by comparison	though	whereas	to put it
as	although	even when	another way
as well as	regardless	rather than	in fact
as, as if			

3. Transitions that show a *time* or *space* relationship:

before	earlier	beside
now	at first, last	between
next	then, just then	beyond
after that	until	across
after so much time	soon	over
in time	the next day, night	at
later	while	from, to
following	meanwhile	into
finally	then	outside, inside
eventually	from then on	up, down
since	during	near, far
ever since	beginning, ending	within
even when	still	

4. Transitions that *limit* or prepare for an *example*:

if	that is
unless	namely
when	for example
provided that	for instance
in case	to illustrate
in particular	such as
that	

5. Transitions that signal *cause* or *result*:

because	thus
for	so, so that
for this, that rea- son	as a result
therefore	consequently

6. Transitions that *assert obvious truth* or *grant opposition*:

no doubt	of course	in fact
doubtless	naturally	granted that
undoubtedly	surely	conceding that
without a doubt	certainly	

EXERCISES

Underline the *transitional* words or phrases that help to give the following paragraphs *continuity*.

A. [1]The two old friends were happy to meet again after such a long separation; however, the meeting was a strain for both of them. [2]It was an effort, after so much time, to find common ground for comfortable, easy conversation. [3]In addition, they had not parted on the best of terms, so that they each needed to labor to rise above old wounds. [4]At first they stuck to "safe" topics such as the weather, the health of those they knew, and ordinary events in each of their lives. [5]At last they approached the problem that had led to the break in their relationship. [6]How painful it was to stir that up again. [7]In fact, they experienced the same old impasse, but they discussed the subject for about an hour before they gave it up, both frustrated by the effort to communicate. [8]Finally they parted, each one wondering what had become of their friendship.

B. [1]I am suspicious that anyone who uses the expression "women's lib" is not very liberated. [2]To illustrate, there was an article in the newspaper the other day that asked if women were better off before "women's lib." [3]Of course, the way the question was put evoked biased answers. [4]For example, one woman said, "Women shouldn't be allowed to be boss. That's what women's lib comes down to . . . being the boss or equal. It's not right. The man is supposed to be the head of the house." [5]Although that woman may be happy with her husband, she is nonetheless denying herself full citizenship and rights equal to his. [6]However, if she had been asked if she enjoyed being a second-class citizen, her consciousness might possibly have been raised enough to answer differently.

C. [1]One of the reasons the violin is difficult to learn to play is that its fingerboard contains no visual or tactile aids to help the beginner acquire competence in fingering. [2]Unlike the banjo or guitar, for instance, the violin has no frets, that is, no small metal bars or ridges to guide the fingers. [3]Therefore, the novice must learn exact positions and literally feel her way, unaided, from position to position up the fingerboard of the instrument. [4]That precise process is demanding and painful to the fledgling violinist, who must contort her fingers and her arm into unnatural and unfamiliar angles while pressing the strings at the correct places and with enough force to get a clear tone. [5]If she is a hair off, the note will be sharp or flat, that is, sour. [6]Until the novice develops skill, many of her notes are painfully out of tune.

⁷Even when her skill increases, she may still sound off key unless she has a good ear and can hear when she is off. ⁸Thus, not only does the novice suffer, she can also torture those listening, as many a stoic parent or sacrificial sibling can affirm.

D. ¹What a drab place the culinary world would be without onions! ²In fact, losing any member of the onion family would be an international disaster to the world's great chefs, the gourmet cooks, the slingers of hash, and the heaters-up at home. ³For instance, how could the Dutch manage without leeks? ⁴What would the French do for onion soup? ⁵How would the Italians make spaghetti sauce? ⁶Moreover, how could any part of the world get along without garlic? ⁷Regardless of the tears shed over these bulbous plants, the smells that are endured, the deodorants and mouthwash that are spent on them, onions and their kin are vital to the gustatory pleasures of this world. ⁸Surely fine restaurants would lose their stars without the onion family, and great chefs would lose their flair. ⁹The zing would go out of even hamburgers and hot dogs, as well as the freedom of those hard choices one must make when ordering them. ¹⁰Besides, think of holidays and children growing up without the familiar smell of turkey stuffing wafting from the oven; and who would have the heart to toss a salad anymore? ¹¹Indeed, it would be a depressed and dreary world without onions.

E. ¹Most people like to talk, but few people like to listen, yet listening well is a rare talent that everyone should treasure. ²Because they hear more, good listeners tend to know more and to be more sensitive to what is going on around them than most people. ³In addition, good listeners are inclined to accept or tolerate rather than to judge and criticize. ⁴Therefore, they have fewer enemies than most people. ⁵In fact, they are probably the most loved of people. ⁶However, there are exceptions to that generality. ⁷For example, John Steinbeck is said to have been an excellent listener, yet he was hated by some of the people he wrote about. ⁸No doubt his ability to listen contributed to his capacity to write. ⁹Nevertheless, the results of his listening did not make him popular. ¹⁰Thus, depending on what a good listener does with what he hears, he may pay a price for his talent or go unappreciated in his lifetime.

EXERCISES

Write in the blank spaces the *transitional* words or phrases you think are needed or appropriate in the following paragraphs to help give them *continuity*. Note that your choice of transition will depend on how you interpret the statements in the paragraphs and that there may be more than one way to fill in the spaces correctly. Therefore, prepare to explain or defend the transition you choose.

A. ¹The problem with an old car is that it is always needing something replaced or repaired. ²_____, about the time the fourth tire is replaced, the first one begins to wear thin again. ³_____, if the front brakes are renewed, _____ the rear brakes start to go. ⁴_____ common problem is that some kind of pump is always breaking down and needing replacement. ⁵_____ the air pump may develop trouble, _____ the fuel pump may go bad, and _____ the water pump may give up. ⁶These pumps _____ require new hoses. ⁷_____, everything under the hood seems to need a new hose or a new valve. ⁸_____ the car needs a new transmission or a new engine. ⁹There seems to be no end to the trouble and expense of keeping up an old car.

B. ¹The homes of the two friends are very different. ²One is situated in the United States on a hill in Berkeley _____ the other is located in The Netherlands by a canal in Amsterdam. ³There is a generous yard around the hill house, _____ there is no space at all around the canal house _____ canal houses are built right next to each other, wall to wall. ⁴The Berkeley house has only one floor, _____ some of its rooms are spacious; _____, the Amsterdam house has five floors, _____ most of its rooms are small. ⁵The differences in these homes _____ reflect differences in life-style. ⁶The American house is casual, and being in California, opens to a patio for outdoor living. ⁷_____, the Dutch house is more formal, and _____ of hard winters, is closed against the cold outside. ⁸_____ the two homes are different, each one suits its location.

C. ¹Some of my older relatives amaze me with their vitality. ²_____, one of my cousins is in her eighties; _____, she has the vitality of someone much younger and is as active and interested in what goes on around her as anyone I know. ³Her quick wit, _____, is a match for only the sharpest, most alert of people. ⁴_____ illustration is my aunt, who is in her nineties. ⁵_____ she recently broke her hip and suffered a small stroke, she is _____ still driving her car _____ playing cut-throat bridge. ⁶_____ my cousin, my aunt is _____ a dynamo. ⁷_____, these two ladies put some of their younger relatives to shame with their vigor.

D. ¹Most people who live in the San Francisco Bay Area appreciate the night and morning fog. ²_____, they like the fog _____ it controls the temperature naturally, keeping the nights and mornings cool _____ disappearing _____ for the day to warm to a comfortable degree, _____ in the sixties or low seventies _____ the summer months. ³Just a few miles _____ the Bay Area, suburbanites may be sizzling in temperatures ranging _____ the mid-eighties _____ the upper nineties and higher _____ people near San Francisco keep their cool in the mild climate of the Bay. ⁴The _____ reason San Franciscans and their immediate neighbors like the fog is _____ its beauty. ⁵They love to see it tumbling _____ the hills, enveloping the Golden Gate Bridge, and _____ creeping _____ the Bay itself _____ it touches its eastern shore, where it climbs _____ the hills again. ⁶Few people dislike the fog. ⁷_____, most people depend on it and admire it.

E. ¹Frustration is the life blood of daytime dramas. ²All story lines in *All My Children*, _____, depend on the characters' inability to fulfill their hearts' desires. ³_____, one of the main characters is Palmer Courtland, who can't be happy with his young wife, Natalie, _____ she has had an affair with Palmer's son Ross. ⁴Ross is still in love with his wife, Ellen; _____, she has given up on their marriage _____ of his repeated infidelity. ⁵_____, she is in love _____ with her former husband, Mark, _____ they can't be reunited _____ he, a recovering drug addict, may have AIDS. ⁶Julie, Ross and Ellen's adopted daughter, is desperate to keep the disintegrating family together. ⁷_____, she longs to be with her boyfriend, Charlie, _____ he has gone away to college. ⁸All these characters yearn for something they can't have. ⁹_____, their frustrations keep *All My Children* alive.

SUMMARY

A well-organized paragraph is a single entity, a unified whole made of a number of parts or sentences so well ordered and fitted together that they cohere or hang together in one continuous unit. If you make a simple outline of the main ideas and supporting points of your paragraph before you write it, you will more likely achieve the order needed to make your paragraph coherent. In addition, if you make good use of transitional words or phrases when you write your paragraph, you will ensure that it has continuity as well.

6

Elementary Problems of Form and Organization

The paragraph models in the exercises in this chapter are fairly rigid in their form and organization, which may prove frustrating to you in the beginning. You may wish to express yourself more freely than the exercises permit. Your thoughts may be forced into patterns of organization with which you are unfamiliar or that may seem unnatural to you, and you may suffer at first the way a dancer suffers learning the fundamentals of dance. Yet it is impossible to dance without knowing the steps; or swim without knowing the strokes; or play tennis, football, chess, or anything requiring skill without laboring through the necessary training period. Similarly, it is impossible to communicate in writing without learning form and organization.

The strict order of the exercises in this chapter is aimed to block your worst impulses, not your best. It is to correct your tendency to be formless and disorganized, not to murder your imagination. It is to give you a sense of the form and order necessary to communication. Once you get used to using the organizational patterns discussed in Chapter 6 and the more advanced patterns presented in Chapter 7, you should then be ready to go on to the exercises in Chapter 8 that encourage you to express yourself with greater variety and imagination.

The particular patterns of organization used in this chapter are not the only acceptable forms through which to communicate, but they have proved to be among the best for the beginning student. You will find that they are clear and not too difficult to imitate. They make your subject obvious from the beginning. They should also help you to stick to the subject and develop it to a conclusion.

Keep in mind that the emphasis in Chapter 6 is on form and organization. That is, your primary aim here is to be orderly and clear. However, you should also make every effort to be imaginative and thoughtful. To stimulate your imagination as well as to assist you with structure, you may find it helpful to precede each of the following exercises with clustering. Return to Chapter 1 if you need to refresh your memory regarding the clustering process.

EXERCISE 1. EXPLAIN HOW TO DO OR MAKE SOMETHING

Directions

Write a paragraph in which you explain how to do or make something; that is, clarify a process, step by step. Organize your paragraph chronologically, following the structure in the example that follows. Notice how the transitional words that are underlined show sequence and provide continuity within the paragraph.

EXAMPLE*

(Topic Sentence) To wash your dog properly, you should follow several steps with the utmost care. (Discussion) *First,* you should make sure that your dog knows nothing, in advance, of your plan to wash him. *After* quietly preparing his tub of lukewarm water, you should plunge him into it tenderly but firmly. *Then,* keeping his head well above water, you should soap his whole body, proceeding from his neck to his tail. Work the soap throughout his hair and skin until it lathers and saturates his body. *After* your pet is completely covered with soap, be sure to rinse him thoroughly. For your dog, being washed is an experience that cannot end soon enough. (Conclusion) *Therefore,* as soon as possible, you should both enjoy the *final* step of his bath—the vigorous sport of drying him.

*Note that in most situations in formal college writing, the second person *you* is not preferred or acceptable. It is easy to substitute a noun for the pronoun *you,* for example, *an owner, a person, a builder.* There are some cases, however, such as when giving specific instructions, as in Exercises 1 and 2, when this form of direct address is permissible and may be called for. Further note that it may be wise to avoid the subject of recipes in Exercise 1, unless they are carefully written in complete sentences, because recipes are often written in fragments.

EXERCISE 2. EXPLAIN HOW TO CONSTRUCT OR MAKE SOMETHING

Directions

Write a paragraph in which you explain how to construct or make something. Follow the pattern of organization given in the following example, which is chronological. Notice that the necessary equipment and materials must be discussed before the process is described. Be careful to describe the process in the correct order, using transitional words such as those italicized and underlined to make the sequence clear.

EXAMPLE

(TOPIC SENTENCE) To construct a simple cat door in a standard door of your house, you need only follow these directions. (DISCUSSION) *First*, you should acquire the necessary tools and materials, which are a pencil, a ruler, a drill, a saw, two small hinges, a hook and eye, and a screwdriver. *Second*, select a door, such as your kitchen door, that can be sacrificed for your pet. *Begin* your operation with your pencil and ruler, marking a square the approximate size of your cat in the lower-middle of the door just above its hard bottom frame. *Next*, keeping in mind that the square to be cut out must be usable for the cat door, carefully apply the drill to an upper corner of the square, making a hole large enough to insert the saw. *After* the sawing is complete, remove the square cut from the door, fasten the hinges to it at the top, and reattach it to the door. *Then* fasten the hook and eye at the bottom of the square and to the door beneath to permit the cat door to be locked if necessary. (CONCLUSION) Your cat door is complete. *Now* call your cat!

EXERCISE 3. EXPLAIN HOW YOU GOT YOUR NAME

Directions

Write a paragraph in which you explain how you came by your given (first) name. You may need to talk to parents or other relatives to learn the details needed to do this exercise. For example, you may have been named according to some tradition in your family or in the area where you were born and raised, or you may have been named to honor a relative or a famous person or event, or there might be a simple story behind your name, as in the example that follows. It is likely that you will need to organize your paragraph chronologically, as in the example. You may also wish to indicate, as in the opening and closing parts of the example, how you feel about your name.

EXAMPLE

(Topic Sentence) I have always been grateful that my parents decided to change their name for me from Mary to Kathleen. (Discussion) Their original plan had been to name me after my father's mother, who was born and raised in Ireland. Like so many other colleens, my grandmother had come into the world with the name of a saint, and hers was a favorite, Mary, mother of Jesus. However, the night before I was born was a long one, apparently, and as my mother and father waited it out at the hospital, they listened to music on the radio. They were taken aback when one of their favorite songs was played. It was "Kathleen Mavourneen," an Irish song that so touched them at that moment that they decided to change their plans and name me after it. Their rush of sweet sentiment left me with a name that was hard for me to pronounce as a child, but I later learned to love it because it was distinctive and musical. I was glad I had not been named Mary because every other little girl I knew, it seemed, was called by that name. It would have been a hard name to live up to, as well. (Conclusion) Indeed, although Mary is a fine and reverent name, I'm thankful for the musical inspiration that changed mine to Kathleen.

EXERCISE 4. DESCRIBE SOMEONE'S FACE

Directions

Write a paragraph in which you describe the face of someone, preferably someone you do not know well, so that you have not formed prior impressions of the person but must observe him or her carefully for the first time and record exactly what you see. A likely candidate for your small portrait is a classmate you have just met or someone in class you turn to for the purpose of this exercise. Look at your subject carefully (he or she may be doing the same with you simultaneously) and begin to make quick notes at random of what you see. Note your overall impressions and then look for details that will sharpen your portrait. Next, organize your observations spatially or geographically into a paragraph. Perhaps the easiest procedure is to work from the top to the bottom of your subject, as in the following example, although you may find other ways to proceed. Try to be objective. Do not flatter or insult your subject. Just write about what you see. You may wish to draw a tentative conclusion about your subject at the end of your paragraph. If so, be sure your discussion supports your conclusion. Do not introduce a new or unrelated idea at the end of your paragraph. Note the use of the name John Smith in the example and replace it with the name of your subject.

EXAMPLE

(TOPIC SENTENCE) John Smith's face is distinctive and interesting to observe. (DISCUSSION) He has a thin, oblong face. Under his light brown hair, which is thick and straight, his forehead is smooth, tanned, and slightly sun-burned. His heavy eyebrows are darker than his hair, but they have reddish blond tips, as if bleached by the sun. His eyes are a pale sky blue, fringed with short brown eyelashes. One eye looks a little smaller than the other from habitual squinting. His long, straight nose is sunburned and peeling. There is a large mole on the right side of his high-boned, tanned cheeks, about midpoint between the tip of his nose and his short sideburns. There is also a noticeable scar on his upper lip just under his nose. His mouth is fairly wide, but his lips are thin, and they smile slightly, even in repose. He has a clean-shaven, chiseled chin. (CONCLUSION) John Smith is apparently an out-doors man.

EXERCISE 5. DESCRIBE A ROOM IN YOUR HOME

Directions

Write a paragraph in which you describe a room in the house or building where you live. You may select any room that interests you or that you think you can describe well, such as the living room, dining room, kitchen, bedroom, or hall. Study the room carefully. As you look at it, what overall impression does it give you? Find a theme or central idea around which you can focus your description, as in the following example, which shows that the room is messy. Other such themes might show that a room is formal or informal, warm or cold, colorful or drab, ugly or beautiful, orderly, large, small, congested, spacious, airy, sunny, or dark. Regardless of your approach, the basic structure of your paragraph will need to be spatial or geographical. Decide on what point in the room you should begin your description, and proceed from there around the room. If the ceiling and floor are remarkable, you may want to include them in your paragraph as well.

In this exercise be careful not to make your paragraph a mere listing of what the room contains. Your objective here is not to take inventory but to make the room interesting. Begin by making the theme or central idea clear, and build interest as the description proceeds. Try to find a lively or novel way to end the paragraph.

EXAMPLE

(Topic Sentence) My study is an almost uncontrollable mess everywhere I look. (Discussion) Beginning on the west side of the room, where I sit at my cluttered desk and look through dirty windows to a tangle of trees that almost conceals the beautiful bay beyond, I can also see a mishmash of picture postcards tacked to the wall and buttons declaring such mottos as "Support Your Right to Arm Bears" attached to the drapery above the desk. Turning north in this smallish room, I can view one of the two floor-to-ceiling bookcases the room contains. Besides a disarray of books, the bookcase is crowded with antique toys, paperweights, bottles, seashells, and photographs. Reams of paper, assorted envelopes, bills, and old letters are also stuffed into the bookcase, though they are almost falling to the floor. The east side of my study contains closets, and the closet doors are busy with old Dutch shipping posters, the photograph of a French cathedral, the cover of a museum magazine picturing reclining Holstein cows, and some of my favorite cartoons. An old thermometer is jammed next to the door to the room, also located on the east side, and the door itself is almost concealed by museum posters. The south side of the room contains the second bookcase, where the only semblance of order is in the uniform rows of encyclopedias and Great Books. Otherwise, books are stacked every which way, together with assorted artifacts such as a teddy bear squashed against two volumes of folklore, a bud vase leaning perilously, and the figurine of "Speak No Evil, Hear No Evil, See No Evil," about to sail out at me where I sit at my type-writer. There is also a single bed, a low table, and a canvas chair on the south side of the room, all covered with books and papers. The one sometimes clear space in my study is a second chair that I now occupy, turned to the typewriter table next to my desk. (CONCLUSION) As I type this paragraph, I must constantly reassemble the papers beside my typewriter lest its move-ment jiggle them to the floor.

EXERCISE 6. DESCRIBE A PICTURE IN A MAGAZINE

Directions

Write a paragraph in which you describe a picture or photograph you find in a magazine. Before you choose your picture, look through several magazines so that you realize the tremendous variety of possibilities for this exercise. Then narrow down your choices to a few with which you feel most in touch or that you think you can describe well. You might choose something quite simple or touching, a picture that is amusing, dramatic, strange, poignant, tragic or horrifying, something ugly, fashionable, plain, or beautiful. You may want to try writing about two or three different pictures before you settle in your final choice, which should be interesting but not too complex to cover well in a single paragraph. The example that follows describes a fairly small (approximately 3 × 5 inches) though relatively complex photograph; you may want to choose a less difficult subject. Look at your final choice very carefully and decide, first, what it is "saying," so that you can make that point clear in your topic sentence and carry it throughout your paragraph. Next, plan your discussion so that you describe the picture spatially or geographically, moving from left to right, top to bottom, or in some clear arrangement, such as in the example.

EXAMPLE

(Topic Sentence) At first glance the scene looks picturesque, a study in dramatic contrasts, exciting and colorful at its focal point, where a great bomb or rocket is exploding, but the photograph in *Time* magazine is of West Beirut, a city being destroyed by war. (Discussion) The upper portion of the picture shows a cloudless, blue-gray sky, but just a little below, massive clouds of smoke billow across the city and rise hundreds of feet into the air. The smoke surges to its highest point on the left side of the photograph, and under that mass the tops of the buildings in closest camera range are barely visible, while much of the city nearby has disappeared from view. Arid ground slopes down from the buildings on the left to cliffs that dip abruptly into the blue-green shore of the Mediterranean, and this lower left corner of the picture is its only calm area on land. From left to right, the lower half of the photograph is shared by land and sea, the land being so devastated that the vibrant sea beside it seems out of place, an intruder frolicking upon a tragedy. Just right of the picture's center, the eye is struck by a huge building located by the shore. It might be a large tourist hotel, for the view of land and sea from its many stories of balconies and picture windows must normally be breathtaking. However, the view is now the panorama of the war exploding almost everywhere in the city, and the great flash that is the focal point is not more than about a mile down the coast, to the right in the picture. The upper-right corner of the photograph, balancing the lower left, is filled with placid-looking sky, the fresh air no doubt blowing from this direction, carrying the smoke to the center of the city, where it appears to be most dense. (CONCLUSION) Alas, what a lovely old city this must have been without a war, the sea skirting its length, its buildings looking out on the water and catching the breezes as they climbed the hills behind. Now strangely illuminated by fire and setting sun, what is left of the battered city is fast becoming rubble.

EXERCISE 7. DESCRIBE AN INTERESTING INCIDENT

Directions

Write a paragraph in which you describe an interesting (exciting, funny, tragic) incident or moment in your life. The incident you write about is one that must have taken place in a matter of minutes or hours, not in days, weeks, or months. Do not try to tell the story of your life in this one paragraph! Limit yourself to one brief event in your life. Study the example that follows. Notice that the topic sentence gives three important informational cues—the age of the writer (or time period) when the incident occurred, a characterization of its impact (frightening), and an indication of what happened or almost happened (suffocation). Your topic sentence should give these cues without giving away the entire incident, and thus it will serve not only its usual function as a topic sentence, but it will also become a "teaser" to interest the reader. In addition, notice that the chronological discussion is in two parts. Observe the function of each part.

EXAMPLE

(Topic Sentence) One day when I was a little girl about nine years old, I had a frightening experience during which I almost suffocated. (Discussion 1: *set scene, give background, introduce characters*) The incident occurred on the ranch in California where I grew up. Pestering the hired hands working there, my brother and I had been playing in the barn where baled hay was stored, stacked high for winter feed. Between the bales there were sometimes spaces, like tunnels, which my brother and I liked to explore. (Discussion 2: *present problem, develop action*) That day I discovered an unusually long, dark hole in the haystack and crawled into it. I had crawled several feet into the hole when I realized, with a shock, that I could not get back out. I was trapped in the middle of the huge haystack! I screamed for help. My brother and the hired hands ran to my rescue, but it was some time before they could discover where the small voice in the haystack came from. After a seemingly endless period of waiting in the dark and dusty spot where I was caught, I was finally dug out by my rescuers. (Conclusion) I shall never forget the first clear breath of air or the wonderful sight of summer sunshine I experienced when I was lifted from my tomb.

EXERCISE 8. SUPPORT A GENERAL STATEMENT WITH PARTICULARS

Directions

Write a paragraph in which you make a general statement and then support it with particulars, examples, or illustrations. Organize your paragraph topically. That is, decide on the topic of your general statement, and then think through or outline a number of subtopics or particulars to support the general statement. Finally, arrange that support in your paragraph in the manner you think most effective. You might present your strongest support first, and having "won" your audience, add other points that are also convincing. On the other hand, you might begin with moderately convincing points, then "top" them by placing your strongest support last; or you may discover some other effective way to proceed. In addition, you may use illustrations from particular situations you have experienced, or you may wish to invent or create illustrations that are representative or typical of your general experience, as in the example that follows. Among the general statements you might use for this exercise are these: Applying for a job can be frustrating; telephone solicitations are annoying; people in supermarkets can be pushy; waiting in line is tiresome; people can (not) be trusted; doctors are not gods; high school is (not) a waste of time; it is not safe to be out alone at night; parents are not perfect; children grow up too fast; crime does (not) pay; no one takes pride in his or her work anymore; women are (not) underpaid; the pen is mightier than the sword; discrimination is (not) a thing of the past.

EXAMPLE

(TOPIC SENTENCE) Some people go crazy when they get behind the wheel of an automobile. (DISCUSSION) For example, to save a few seconds, an otherwise sane person may race through city streets as if he were competing at the Indy 500. He may also run red lights and ignore stop signs, putting pedestrians in jeopardy or even hitting them. When traffic is congested, a temporarily insane driver may lean on his horn, as if its blast could clear his way instead of making everyone around him miserable. On the freeway, a mad driver can be a dynamo, supreme in first one lane and then another, swerving in front of other cars, never looking back or signaling, getting ahead of the pack at any cost. Heaven help the car that blocks his way, for his specialty is tailgating at high speeds, even if he must lock bumpers with the car ahead of him. On the other hand, with an out-of-town guest in his car, a daffy driver may travel very slowly in the fast lane, oblivious to the traffic snarl and near accidents he may be causing in back of him as he gestures toward some interesting vista. When it comes to parking, such a driver is short on manners and a star at stealing base. (CONCLUSION) However, when this crazed person steps out of his vehicle, he magically becomes his docile self again.

EXERCISE 9. DISCUSS YOUR NEIGHBORS

Directions

Write a paragraph in which you discuss your neighbors. Since you cannot write about all of your neighbors in a single paragraph, select one family or house that is most interesting, enjoyable, difficult, or obnoxious. Be selective in your discussion, also, deciding on your neighbors' most remarkable features and limiting your discussion to only those qualities or points. You may also want to discuss your relationship with your neighbors, as in the example that follows. Organize your paragraph topically, after first deciding on your main topic and making a list or outline of the subtopics or supporting points that you will present in your discussion.

EXAMPLE

(Topic Sentence) The neighbors closest to my house are my favorite people in the neighborhood. (Discussion) He is a retired carpenter, but she is still working for the nearby university. They are both musicians, she a cellist and he a violist, and they frequently have friends over, who play in the major symphony in this area, to play quartets and trios with them. It is particularly enjoyable to wake up on a Sunday morning to the sounds of their musical sessions, which are really quite impressive most of the time. However, I also love to hear them crack up laughing when they make mistakes or something off-beat happens to amuse them. Besides music, carpentry is still his main interest, and most days he is outside in his work space creating a marvelous heavy wooden door or making a fascinating piece of furniture. Since both of them are friendly, outgoing people, numerous friends are always dropping in on them, and these people are usually very interesting, poets, painters, professors, craftspersons, and other lively people I enjoy meeting when I visit. My neighbors are ideal to live next door to, however, because although they can be very helpful if I need them, they don't intrude on me, and I generally behave with them in the same way. We have helped each other out with numerous emergencies such as fire, theft, and an auto accident that damaged both our properties, and we cooperate with each other in little ways such as bringing in the mail when one of us is away. We also meet sometimes to walk the hill where we live or to share some special occasion such as the Fourth of July, when we watch the fireworks display together. (Conclusion) Otherwise, we simply live next door to each other, peacefully, side by side.

EXERCISE 10. DISCUSS YOUR HOBBY IN A SPECIAL WAY

Directions

Write a paragraph in which you discuss one of your hobbies or pastimes in a special way. That is, try to discover why you need the hobby or what it does for you psychologically, not simply why you "like" it. Look beneath the surface and discuss your hobby honestly, with feeling and insight. After you decide on your main topic, dig into it and list or outline what you find, and then develop your paragraph topically. Use the example that follows to guide you.

EXAMPLE

(TOPIC SENTENCE) I like to garden under most circumstances, but gardening when I am upset emotionally is particularly therapeutic. (DISCUSSION) When my day has been particularly hectic, when I have been frustrated, when people have hurt me or made me mad, then, especially, I like to work in the yard. When I weed, I not only clean up my garden, I clean away the ugly parts of my day. When I dig, I imagine what I would like to have said to some people but didn't or couldn't. Sometimes I pulverize the soil with my thoughts! Releasing my pent-up energy of the day on weeds and soil, I am ready to recreate it with bulbs or new plants. I relax completely when I water my garden and then sit and look at it. (CONCLUSION) I see in my weedless, freshly dug, newly planted garden my day as I wish it had been or the next as I hope it will be.

7

Advanced Problems of Form and Organization

Having mastered the more elementary exercises in form and order in Chapter 6, you are now ready to go on to the more complex patterns of organization in this chapter. The exercises that follow pose special and more advanced problems, which will require extra concentration for you to master them. In addition, you may find it useful to practice clustering before you write your paragraphs. Each exercise is preceded by a discussion designed to help you through the exercise.

DISCUSSION OF EXERCISE 11

Your main purpose in Exercise 11 is to discuss or describe something *in detail*. Earlier in this book you considered the need to develop the paragraph by being specific. This exercise is designed to emphasize that point. Here you should concentrate most on going into detail, on being specific or particular (these terms have basically the same meaning).

Being specific is a matter of degree, as mentioned earlier, and you may wonder what degree is required of you in this exercise. Figure 7–1 may make the degree clear to you.

The illustration begins with a generalization or general category and proceeds by degrees to specifics. As noted previously, your paragraph in this exercise should begin at the fourth level or degree of being specific and should progress still further into details. In other words, you should be very, very specific in this exercise.

Your choice of topic for the exercise should be guided by the degree of detail you are asked to discuss. The "food" level, for example, is much too broad or general a topic for the exercise, nor can you discuss "vegetables," nor even the third level, "carrots." You must narrow down to one specific such as a single, particular carrot, and discuss or describe it in detail.

Organize your paragraph *geographically* or *topically*, or you might mix the two schemes, as in the example that follows, which focuses on simplicity and age as it describes an antique clock from top to bottom.

Other topics you might use for this exercise include man-made objects such as a lamp, table, chair, plate, flowerpot, hat, ring, shoe, gate, or birdbath, or natural objects such as a rock, flower, or branch of a tree.

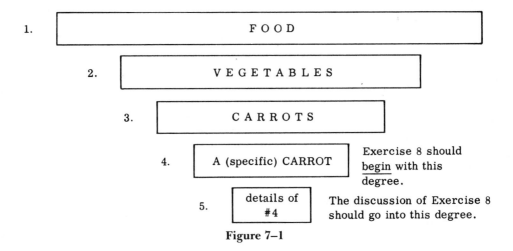

Figure 7–1

EXERCISE 11. DISCUSS SOMETHING IN CLOSE DETAIL

Directions

Write a paragraph in which you discuss an object in close detail. Because you must go into detail, be careful to limit your topic. Use the following example as a guide.

EXAMPLE

(TOPIC SENTENCE) The antique clock I recently purchased for my living room is appealing to me primarily because of its simplicity and age. (DISCUSSION) It has a plain, round oak case and a large, easy-to-read face. It has black, handpainted Roman numerals, and its brass hands are also handmade. Protecting the face of the clock is a simple glass cover that is opened once a week when the clock must be wound. A plain, unencased pendulum of brass, fastened to a short piece of wood, swings from beneath the face of the clock. From a distance, the clock appears to be in perfect shape, but when I approach it closely, I can see that time has worn away some of its original appearance. The hands are bent a little out of shape, the white of the face is cracked, and the black numerals are chipped in several places. (CONCLUSION) The old clock was once a school clock, and as I watch the slow-swinging of its pendulum and listen to its regular ticktock, I can imagine how it must have lulled the pupils of some country school to sleep a century ago.

DISCUSSION OF EXERCISE 12

As you will realize, Exercise 12 is something like the preceding Exercise 11, for you are again asked to discuss or describe an object in close detail. There are, however, two differences in this exercise. First, Exercise 12 calls for a fresh and more immediate response to the object. Two requirements of the exercise are (1) that you complete the whole exercise within a fairly restricted time limit such as a class period or an hour or so, and (2) that you make careful observations of an object that you have *never studied before.* The second difference is that Exercise 12 should provoke a more complete sensory reaction. That is, you will need to observe and write about not only what you *see* but also whatever you are able to *touch* or *feel, hear,* and *smell* about your object. (The sense of *taste* is omitted only for reasons of health and safety. If it is safe to do so, taste your object also.)

You should begin the exercise with a ten- to twenty-minute walk around the campus of your college, preferably, perhaps, in the vicinity of your classroom. Take a pen or pencil and a notebook with you to jot down ideas before you return to your classroom to write your paragraph, or if space and weather permit, you may even want to write your paragraph outside the classroom wherever your object, especially if it is not portable, is located.

Look around you carefully as you walk. Stand and stare at something. Touch it. If possible, pick it up. Turn it over. Smell it. Rub it. Crinkle it. Listen to it. Notice how it catches or reflects the light. Get in tune with it (or be jarred by it). Study it. If it bores you, put it down or go on to something else. "Try out" objects until you find one that you can really relate to, one from which you get the right "vibrations."

Record your impressions. You might begin by making miscellaneous notes about your object. As you proceed to write, you will probably come upon some scheme by which to organize your paragraph. For example, you might write about your object as you perceived it in time; that is, what you noticed about it first, then second, and so on. You might organize your observations according to what your senses dictate. Your sense of smell may be most powerful, and after that your sight, and then your touch. You might give your overall impressions and then proceed to details. You might also let your imagination wander a bit, as in the example that follows, finding comparisons between your object and other objects that may be surprisingly like it.

Your choice of subject matter will, of course, vary with your own taste and with what is available in your surroundings. You might choose a natural or a man-made object, including anything such as the following: a blade of grass, a stone, a leaf, a door, a windowsill, a section of a wall with or without graffiti, a section of pavement, a faucet, a doorknob, a gum wrapper, a paper cup, a can, an apple, a feather, a handful of sand, a hubcap, a nail, a seed, an ocean wave, a coin, a drainpipe, a piece of candy, a piece of string.

EXERCISE 12. DESCRIBE YOUR SENSORY REACTION TO AN OBJECT

Directions

Write a paragraph in which you describe your fresh and immediate sensory response to an object you have never studied or thought about before. The object may be natural or man-made. Use the preceding discussion and the following example to guide you.

EXAMPLE

(TOPIC SENTENCE) The fresh new leaf that I hold in my hand I have just picked from a nearby oak tree. (DISCUSSION) The leaf pricks my palm with its jagged edges that curve in tight, symmetrical swoops to short, stiff points, like tiny needles or delicate cat claws. Veins lead back from each of the points to the center stem of the leaf. When I hold the leaf up against the sky by the end of the stem, I can see that the shape of the leaf is like the shape of the tree from which it came, the stem like the trunk of the tree, the veins its branches. When I turn the leaf over, it becomes a little boat. The veins are the ribs of the boat, the stem an inverted keel. The leaf is not dark green and brittle, like the old growth on the tree, nor have caterpillars crawled over it, leaving holes. It is a bright, avocado color, unspoiled in any way, a light and pliant little boat such as a child might play with on a pond. (CONCLUSION) It smells faintly like an acorn.

DISCUSSION OF EXERCISE 13

In Exercise 13 you are asked to discuss your biggest problem in college. Your problem may or may not be the one discussed in the model paragraph that follows, though you may organize your discussion in a similar way and should give details like those in the model.

Suppose your biggest problem is a particular subject you are taking, such as mathematics or biology or English. If you are having trouble with everything about the class, you will need to select two or three representative problems to discuss, because you cannot write about everything without making your paragraph too long or without destroying its unity. After selecting the two or three representative problems, you will need to connect them in some way, such as showing a common difficulty you have with them. Also, be sure to give specific examples or details to make your discussion clear.

If you are having trouble with only one part of a class, such as speaking before it or participating in class discussions, you will need to discuss the problem with quite a bit of detail. You might first give instances in which the problem generally exists, and then you might settle on one particular example in which it has occurred, telling what happened and how you felt about it.

Perhaps your problem is not knowing how to study or being easily distracted from your studies. You discussion should make clear, then, what your study habits, or lack of them, are. You might describe the environment in which you study, telling about distractions such as television, phone calls, family traffic, street noises, and the like.

Your problem may be adjusting to some aspect of college life, such as learning to think for yourself, meeting new people, getting along with your instructors and classmates. Make clear what you are used to, what is unfamiliar, what is painful or confusing. Give an example or illustrate your thoughts.

Your problem may be something personal that interferes with your academic life, such as illness in the family, financial worries, a part-time job, a hobby that consumes much of your time, or an overactive social life. Take stock of what it is and discuss it realistically. Make your discussion meaningful by giving particulars.

You may decide that your problem is that you are immature, that going to college is a responsibility you are not quite ready to face. The model paragraph that follows discusses this kind of problem. To see the paragraph that follows in outline form, turn to page 59. As indicated there, the paragraph is organized *topically*.

EXERCISE 13. WRITE ABOUT YOUR BIGGEST PROBLEM IN COLLEGE

Directions

Write a paragraph defining or discussing your biggest problem in college. The example that follows may be helpful as a guide.

EXAMPLE

(TOPIC SENTENCE) My biggest problem in college is that I don't really want to be here. (DISCUSSION) What I really want to do is lie around all day and, somehow, become a screaming success by magic. I want to shoot pool, work on the car, or watch television. I want to relax. I want to have a beer with my friends. I want no struggle in my life, no strain. College makes me leave all of this life and go to work. College makes me compete, forces me to think about getting ahead, about beating the next fellow, about getting good grades. College nags at me, embarrasses me, makes me look too clearly at myself and my future, makes me worry. If it weren't for college, I might never have to grow up and become a useful citizen and maybe, even, a real person. If it weren't for college, I might be happy. (CONCLUSION) I might grow old instead of up; I might vegetate instead of live.

DISCUSSION OF EXERCISE 14

In Exercise 14 you are asked to define an important word by first giving its dictionary meaning and then discussing your interpretation of it. The first part of the exercise is easy, but the second part is not. In the second part you may move from a consideration of what the word *denotes* to what it *connotes* (see p. 48)—that is, you may need to think about your experience or emotional association with the word. Your paragraph should not be a mere parroting of the dictionary or other sources outside yourself (remember to use quotation marks wherever quoting, and take care that your quotation(s) do not become too long). You must do some original work in this paragraph. Put your "personal stamp" on it. To do the second part well will require quite a bit of thought and effort on your part.

As stated earlier in this book, words are slippery and can have many different meanings, depending on who speaks them and to whom they are spoken. After you have selected your word for this exercise from the list on page 95 or from suggestions your instructor may give you, and after you have looked it up in one or more dictionaries, you should formulate a plan by which to make your own special study of the word. This study should result in your discovering many meanings and applications of the word that you may never have thought of before.

Your plan for studying the word might first consist of going to written sources in addition to the dictionary. For instance, you might consult an encyclopedia, or you might ask your librarian to help you find essays, newspapers, magazine articles, or books that discuss the word. After you read about the word, or while you are reading about it, you should also discuss it and listen to other people who discuss it. You may learn enough about the word by using it in casual conversation with various people you know. If not, your plan may require more of a system.

You might systematize your plan by working up an interview with people concerning the word. You should interview as many people as possible and people from as many walks of life as possible. Interview your family, your friends, your neighbors, your instructors, even the person on the street, whom you may not know. Your interview might include the following questions:

1. What does (the word) mean to you?
2. When and how do you use the word?
3. Do you like the word? Do you think it is complimentary, insulting, or neither?
4. Whom do you hear using the word and where and how?
5. Does the word mean to you today what it did in the past?

If you have followed this procedure carefully, you have generated some ideas of your own and have shared them with or tried them out on people you have interviewed, in order to test your perception of the word. Little by little, or in a flash of realization, you should come to a plan or an approach to the second part of the paragraph, your original statement or personal stamp. This is the more interesting part of the paragraph, the part your reader is looking forward to and will weigh more heavily. In it you will reveal your feelings or share your ideas about the word as they have evolved during the course of your study.

Your study of the word should result in your having too much to say about it for one paragraph. You will need to boil down what you have discovered and thought about the word or you will need to select what you consider to be the best possible statement you can make about it. Remember that you can develop only one central idea.

List of Words

self-confidence	sex	mythology	vanity
parapsychology	complex	growth	sports
conservative	merger	sensitivity	intelligence
suicide	profit	senior	respect
style	strike	valid	advertising
farmer	premoni-	bravery	motor
hero	tion	reckless	fate
heartbreak	sales	trust	astrology
liberal	career	culture	flight
addiction	love	rhythm	photographer
monogamy	husband	guilt	wedding
hostage	wife	bicycle	neurotic
sexism	lover	prerogative	business
racism	maturity	optimism	mortgage
education	poverty	teacher	computer
revenge	wealth	champion	ambition
war	ageism	thoughtful	pollution
laughter	athlete	ritual	meditation
critic	citizen	artist	wilderness
reactionary	planet	collector	slang
election	earth	justice	nucleus
space	crime	law	hypothesis
friend	punishment	obedience	graffiti
masculine	political	control	poetry
feminine	expert	gossip	charisma
time			

EXERCISE 14. DEFINE AND DISCUSS A SIGNIFICANT WORD OR TERM

Directions

Write a paragraph in which you define a significant word or term according to its dictionary meaning(s) and then proceed to an original discussion of its meaning(s) or applications. Your discussion should reveal your personal feelings or ideas about the word. The following example may help to guide you.

EXAMPLE

(Topic Sentence) The word *tolerance* is an ambiguous term that, I believe, is worth thinking about. (Discussion) To tolerate someone, according to *The American Heritage Dictionary,* means, on the one hand, to recognize and respect him, his beliefs or practices, without necessarily agreeing or sympathizing with him. On the other hand, the word can mean to put up with or bear with someone, though you may despise him, because some force, such as the law, requires that you do so. It seems to me that people often pretend to use the first meaning of the word when they really have in mind the second meaning. In such cases, people are hypocritical when they use the word, and I do not admire them. They pretend respect for someone, but in reality they are merely putting up with him. It is as though they were saying: behave yourself and I will be gracious enough to permit you to exist. Has anyone the right to be that gracious, I wonder? The idea can be expressed in another way: if you will accept my superiority, I will tolerate you. With such an attitude, the word *tolerance* implies a sense of inequality that is unacceptable to me. (Conclusion) Because the word is ambiguous and often used in a hypocritical if not an insulting manner, I often wonder what people mean when they use it, and I sometimes think we would be better off without the word.

DISCUSSION OF EXERCISES 15 AND 16

In Exercises 15 and 16 you are asked to make comparisons. In Exercise 15 you must show how two things are similar. In Exercise 16 you need to contrast two things or show how they are different.

Think about what a comparison (including the idea of contrast) is. The word *compare* comes from a Latin word that means "to pair" or "to match." Keep this meaning in mind when you think about and try to decide on topics you will use for comparison. The two things you choose to compare must have enough in common to make them comparable. You cannot compare, or pair, an antelope with a rock, for instance. There is insufficient common ground, if any, between the two. The two things you compare or contrast must be matchable or mis-matchable rather than totally unrelated to each other.

Examine Figures 7–2A and 7–2B, which are overlapping circles. The circles in Figure 7–2A overlap (see the shaded area) more than those in Figure 7–2B. That is, they have greater common ground. Figure 7–2A represents two things that should be compared to show *similarity.* There is less common ground (but enough in common to make the two circles comparable) in Figure 7–2B. This figure represents two things that should be compared in terms of their *differences.*

One of the primary problems in making a comparison is *sustaining both parts* of the comparison. That is, you must discuss equally the two things being com-pared, keeping a balance between the two. A paragraph that promises (the topic sentence is a promise that must not be broken!) to compare *two* things must not end in discussing only *one.* You must not merely mention one of the two things and then spend most or all of your discussion on the other, nor should you spend the first half of the paragraph all on one thing and the second half all on the other. The first mistake is a matter simply of failing to fulfill half of your prom-ise. The second mistake causes your paragraph to split into two parts, thus de-stroying its unity. Exercises 15 and 16 should look like Figure 7–3, not like Fig-ures 7–4 or 7–5.

Before you write your paragraph for either Exercise 15 or 16, it may help you to make a preliminary list summarizing the similarities (differences) you see in your comparison. This list will then serve to guide you in the development of your paragraph. You might work out a scheme or plan similar to either of the two examples on the top of page 98.

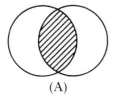 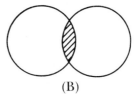

(A)   (B)

Figure 7–2

Mary and Anne are alike as follows:

1. girls/sisters
2. similar age/teens
3. look and act alike
   a. tall/slender
   b. brown hair/eyes
c. olive complexions/warm smiles
d. dress alike
e. talented/friendly
4. popular

Standard cars and compact cars are different as follows:

	Standard	Compact
1. purchase price:	higher	lower
2. operating expense:	higher	lower
3. repairs/maintenance:	higher	lower
4. comfort/room:	greater	lower
5. maneuverability:	less	greater
6. power/performance:	greater?	less?
7. prestige:	?	?
8. safety:	?	?

Suggested topics for Exercises 15 and 16 include the following: two people, famous or otherwise; two sports; two types of food; two neighborhoods; two ethnic customs; two kinds of music; two kinds of dance; two different times or periods in the same place (see the example in Exercise 16); two cars; two jobs; two trees; two ways of walking; two college classes; two teachers; two kinds of weather; two buildings; two characters in fiction; two kinds of crime; two pieces of furniture; two hobbies; two types of tires; two tools; two objects of art; two ways of relating to people; two forms of greeting or leave-taking; two attitudes.

```
                                                             X O X O X O

                                                             X X X X X X

                                                             X X X X X X

X O X O X O              X O X O X O                          X X X X X X

X O X O X O              X X X X X X                          O O O O O O

X O X O X O              X X X X X X                          O O O O O O

X O X O X O              X X X X X X                          O O O O O O
  Figure 7–3               Figure 7–4                           Figure 7–5
```

EXERCISE 15. MAKE A COMPARISON BY SHOWING SIMILARITIES

Directions

Write a paragraph in which you show that two things are similar. Because your comparison will be about similar rather than identical things, inevitably you will notice differences as well as similarities; but your purpose is to focus on the likenesses, not the differences. Because you do not want to lie or distort the picture, you must choose your comparison carefully, selecting two things that have more in common than they have at odds with each other. Use the preceding discussion and the following example to guide you.

EXAMPLE

(TOPIC SENTENCE) My two cousins Mary and Anne are similar in many ways. (DISCUSSION) In fact, some people think the two girls are twins rather than sisters because they are close in age, both of them in their early teens, and because they look and act a good deal alike. They are both tall for their age and slender, and they both wear their dark-brown hair long and straight. Mary, who is fifteen, has stunning large brown eyes with long, dark eyelashes; and Anne, who is fourteen, also has beautiful dark eyes. They both have lovely olive complexions, and when they smile, they radiate warmth and happiness. They even dress alike. Mary sews almost all of her own clothes, and Anne is also learning to sew. Because they are almost the same size, the can borrow each other's patterns as well as each other's clothes. What is most noticeable about the two girls is that they are both talented, outgoing, and friendly. Mary is the vice president of her class and active in dance and drama. Anne, who is also a good student, is a star member of the tennis team as well as an accomplished guitarist. (CONCLUSION) As might be guessed, my two cousins are both very popular.

EXERCISE 16. MAKE A COMPARISON (CONTRAST) BY SHOWING DIFFERENCES

Directions

Write a paragraph in which you contrast two things or show how they are different. Because the two things you choose to write about must have something in common to be comparable, you will recognize that they have similarities as well as differences, but your aim in this paragraph is to concentrate on their differences. Select your subject matter carefully so that it is easy, without distorting the facts, to focus on differences. The example that follows is a discussion of two different times or periods in the same place. Other suggested topics are given in the discussion preceding Exercise 15. Use that discussion and the following example to guide you.

EXAMPLE

(Topic Sentence) Orinda is a different town today from what it was a few years ago. (Bridge to Discussion) Many changes have taken place. (Discussion) In just a few years Orinda has been transformed from a small country village where everyone knew each other to a large suburban community where people who rush home each night from city offices barely have time to get acquainted. Just a few years ago the children of Orinda walked to one small school through pear orchards and tomato patches. Now they ride to several schools in cars and buses, driving past well-trimmed lawns and swimming pools. Orinda used to be a quiet, rural town. Now it is bustling and sophisticated. The rocking chair has been replaced by the aluminum recliner. Community suppers have given way to country club parties. The horsedrawn plow has been replaced by the tractor and rototiller. The two-lane road through town has moved aside for a wide new freeway. (Conclusion) There are a few oldtimers left in Orinda who probably wonder whether all the changes that have taken place rightly deserve to be called progress, but most of the people are caught up in the new life and seem to be satisfied with it.

DISCUSSION OF EXERCISE 17

The purpose of Exercise 17 is to summarize a short story or, as in the case of the model exercise that follows, a short novel. You should think about a few of the problems posed by this exercise before you begin to write.

First, you should realize that your purpose is simply to give the plot or to tell what happens in the story. To do this task well, you must be objective. You must keep your own ideas or opinions out of what you write. Whether you like the story or not is not the point of the exercise. No personal comments should appear in your paragraph.

Perhaps the most difficult part of this exercise is to condense, or boil down, the story to approximately *ten* sentences, which you must do in your paragraph. The complete story is probably many pages long, but you must tell it in one short paragraph. The paragraph will thus test not only your ability to write clearly, but also your understanding of the essential parts of the story. You can give only the skeletal outline of the story in one paragraph. You must leave out much in the way of incidental background, minor points in the plot, and minor characters in the story.

Be careful as you shave away the story to its barest minimum that you do not distort the story or misrepresent it. Do not fall in love with one part that, though it may be a meaningful sidetrack, is not essential. Do not blow it up and out of proportion. You must spend your ten sentences most carefully to represent the story fairly and clearly in summary form.

You should also realize that a story, if it is fiction, neither lives nor dies but is always present whenever you read it or discuss it. Therefore, when you write about it in your paragraph, you should use the simple present tense. That is, you should write, first, this *takes* place, then such and such *happens*, after that something else *occurs*, and finally the story *ends*. In most cases no other tense is needed. To use the model paragraph that follows as an example, the main character *fishes* alone rather than *fished* alone. Though the story itself may be written in the past tense, when you talk *about* it, your discussion is present and requires the present tense.

This exercise, though difficult, is worthwhile. Being able to boil down a story in your own words (you should use few quotes, if any) gives you a better understanding of the story as a whole. Once you have mastered this exercise, you will be ready to go on to the next, in which you will be asked to give your opinion of the story. Because of this exercise, you will be in a better position to do the next.

EXERCISE 17. SUMMARIZE A PLOT

Directions

Write a paragraph summarizing the plot of a short story or novel. Remember that your object is to condense the story. Try to tell it in no more than ten sentences. Use the following example to guide you.

EXAMPLE

(Topic Sentence) *The Old Man and the Sea* is a short novel by Ernest Hemingway. (Discussion) The novel is about an old Cuban fisherman, Santiago, who fishes alone in the Gulf of Mexico. Friendless except for a young boy named Manolin, Santiago has only one remaining purpose in life, to catch a big fish in order to prove to Manolin and to himself that he is still a good fisherman. After eighty-four days of unsuccessful fishing, on the eighty-fifth day Santiago goes far out into the gulf, where he hooks a giant marlin. He struggles with the fish for two days and nights and finally kills it. Lashing the fish to his skiff, he sails for home. Soon sharks appear and attack his prize. The old man fights them off with all his strength but fails to protect his catch. (Conclusion) Only the skeleton of the great fish remains as proof of Santiago's courage and endurance when he returns with it to the harbor in Havana.

DISCUSSION OF EXERCISE 18

For Exercise 18 you should select a character from a short story or novel to discuss in a paragraph. You know, of course, that the paragraph must be limited and that any interesting character is too complex to be contained fully in a single paragraph. Therefore, you must focus on *one limited aspect* of the personality or appearance of the character.

Although your paragraph will be *your view* of the subject, you must be careful to base your discussion on what the *author tells you* about the character. Examine the evidence in the story before you draw your conclusions. Notice the details the author gives about the appearance of the character and observe the cues given about the character's behavior, thoughts, fears, and desires. Note how the character interacts with others in the story. Pay attention to what he says and how he says it.

If you study the character carefully, you will probably become fascinated with some special facet of personality or appearance. Something in particular will catch your eye. Having studied the character (and story) as a whole, you will begin to form an opinion about the particular aspect of the character that interests you most. You will then be ready to try to express your opinion or conclusion in the topic sentence of your paragraph.

Remember that your topic sentence must be sharply focused and your paragraph limited. Suppose that you conclude that the character you choose to write about is a cruel, bitter person. It will be impossible for you to deal with every aspect of the character's cruelty and bitterness. Instead, write about one part; for example, the way in which he mistreats his animals. If you think your character is appealing, say, because she is a sincere and thoughtful young girl awakening to the complexities of adult life, you might demonstrate one aspect of this larger theme by showing that her relationship with her mother is questioning rather than totally submissive and obedient. If the appearance of your character strikes or repels your fancy, you will need to restrict yourself to some particular feature such as the character's fashionable dress. Discuss one part rather than the whole of what you see in your character.

Your topic sentence is a conclusion, a claim or assertion that you make about the character. How will you support, substantiate, or prove your claim in your discussion? You will need to cite the evidence in the story that justifies your interpretation of the character. You will need to build a convincing case, something like a lawyer in court, that proves your position. You must present the evidence and interpret the evidence so that your reader will view it your way and respect that view.

Bear in mind that it is essential to keep a *sharp focus* in the development of your discussion. Do not be sidetracked or lured away from your primary objective. You may need to discuss fragments of the story to get your point across, but

do not become immersed in the storytelling. Move quickly from the story fragment to the point you are making with it. Brief quotations, as in the example
that follows, may help to clarify your position, but keep them brief. Do not allow
your paragraph to turn into a summary of the story (you have already done that
in the preceding exercise) and do not let it become one long quote. *Your* ideas
are what matter here. Develop *them.* Be in control of your paragraph. Keep an
eye on your topic sentence. Let it remind you of your objective, and stay on
course!

EXERCISE 18. DISCUSS A CHARACTER IN A STORY

Directions

Write a paragraph in which you discuss one limited aspect or element of a character in a short story or novel. Notice that the following example examines a very small part of the character. Limit your paragraph accordingly.*

EXAMPLE

(Topic Sentence) The laughter of the tinker in John Steinbeck's short story "The Chrysanthemums" is one sign of his deceitful personality. (Discussion) When the tinker first meets Elisa, the main character of the story, he appears to appreciate the humor she sees in the cowardly behavior of his mongrel dog. He echoes her laughter with his own. His attitude changes abruptly, however. "The laughter had disappeared from his face and eyes the moment his laughing voice ceased." The fact that his expression becomes suddenly so humorless suggests that there is something false about his laughter or that there is little humor in him in reality. The moment in which Elisa has been caught up has not really involved him. Perhaps he has merely turned on (and off) the required social response needed to gain Elisa's approval. Similar behavior can be seen a little later when Elisa tries to rekindle the wit she believes they have shared. He smiles "for a second" before artfully shifting the subject. (Conclusion) The tinker's laughter and his fleeting smile convey the impression that, although he is a skillful salesman, he is underhanded and dishonest.

---

*This exercise can be expanded into a short composition if two or three aspects of the character or the character as a whole is discussed.

DISCUSSION OF EXERCISE 19

In Exercise 19 you are asked to propose some change in the existing state of affairs on the local, national, or international scene. In other words, you must present an argument.

The discussion part of Exercise 19 poses a special problem in logic and in presenting proof in support of the topic sentence or proposal. Notice the verbs used in this paragraph. *Should be* is used only in the topic sentence. In the supporting sentences in the discussion, the verbs *is* or *are* should be used.

Correct Verbs in Discussion: *is* or *are*
                    Incorrect: *should be, would be, might be, could be*

The purpose of the discussion part of Exercise 19 is to give *partial* support of the topic sentence by discussing the evils, faults, or flaws of *present reality*. It is *not* to guess about the *future*. Whenever anyone proposes a change in the way things *are*, he must *first* show that there *is* something wrong with the way things *are*. Naturally, also, it is wise to look ahead and wonder what would happen, or might happen, or could happen if the proposed change become a reality in the future. But pondering the future is not the task of the discussion part of Exercise 19.

To provide more complete support of the change proposed in the topic sentence of exercise 19, a fairly long composition would be needed. In the long composition it would be necessary to show, for example, the benefits of the proposed change, that the proposed change is the best among possible changes, that the change would not bring about additional problems, that the change would not be too expensive, and so on.

You should think of Exercise 19 as only *part* of an argument. In fact, it is a *summary* of part of an argument. The example in the exercise is not a typical paragraph, nor is it an especially good paragraph, because it is quite general rather than specific. Its main purpose is to give an overall view in summary form. You will see that it is a means to an end rather than an end in itself. Exercise 19 is really a condensed composition. Before writing a composition, it is wise, first, to write an outline or summary to guide the organization of the composition. Exercise 19 serves this purpose.

Notice that the exercise does not go into much detail in the discussion but rather gives only main ideas with a few supporting clues. Later, in Exercise 20, you will be asked to go into more detail. Here in this exercise only a few details are needed.

You should think about the order or sequence of ideas that is best to use in the discussion of Exercise 19. Most often, it is best to present the strongest supporting idea (or reason for the proposed change) first and to present ideas of less importance after that. In some cases, it is more dramatic or effective to begin with the weakest support and then to build to the strongest. Think about your topic carefully before you decide on the order that is best for your paragraph.

Your choice of topic for this exercise, as indicated in the directions, is broad. You should, however, choose a topic about which you are informed. If you are not well informed about topics of international or national importance, then you had better write about a problem close to home.

The topic of the model paragraph that follows is billboard advertising. This topic may or may not be a problem where you live. Look around you. What needs a change? Is there a curfew in your town you think is unreasonable and would like to see abolished? If so, show the faults of the curfew. Is there a course at your school that you are required to take that you feel has little value? If so, you might propose that it should not be required, and in the discussion part of your paragraph, you should shown what is wrong with the course. Do your parents impose a rule on you that you think is unjust? Propose a change and discuss the injustice of the rule. Is your school badly in need of a new campus? See the arguments regarding this topic on pages 32–33 of this book.

While you search for a proposal to write about in this exercise, bear in mind that you must be reasonable. Do not propose that your allowance should be raised to a thousand dollars a week, unless your parents can afford it, or that you should get As in all your classes unless you merit them. Your proposal might be debatable, but it should be capable of being debated by reasonable people.

You will see that the model paragraph in Exercise 19 does not have a conclusion. Keep in mind the special nature of the exercise, that it is a *summary* of *part* of an argument. No conclusion, therefore, is possible. The whole argument would need to be presented, and that would require many paragraphs before it would make sense to come to a conclusion.

EXERCISE 19. PROPOSE A CHANGE IN THE EXISTING STATE OF AFFAIRS

Directions

Write a paragraph in which you propose some changes in the existing state of affairs on the local, national, or international scene. Your paragraph should contain two or three reasons in support of your proposal. Follow the pattern of organization given in the following example.

EXAMPLE

(TOPIC SENTENCE) Billboard advertising should be abolished along public highways. (BRIDGE TO DISCUSSION) There are three reasons billboard advertising should not be permitted near public highways. (DISCUSSION) First, billboards are ugly and hinder the enjoyment of natural roadside beauty. Second, billboards are a distraction and therefore, I believe, a danger to the motorist, who should keep his or her eyes on the road. Third, the purpose of billboards is to promote private business; therefore, they do not belong along public, tax-supported highways.

DISCUSSION OF EXERCISE 20

Look at the topic sentence of the model paragraph of Exercise 20 and then look back at the first sentence of the discussion part of the model paragraph of Exercise 19. You will see that they are the same except that the first four words of the sentence in Exercise 19 have been dropped in Exercise 20. The sentence in Exercise 20 is as follows:

Billboards are ugly and hinder the enjoyment of natural roadside beauty.

From this sentence, you should be able to conclude that the purpose of Exercise 20 is to illustrate or explain the first point made in the discussion part of Exercise 19. You need not be restricted in your paragraph to the first point, but you should limit your paragraph to *one* of the points made in Exercise 19.

You might organize Exercise 20 in one of two ways. One way is through illustration. The model paragraph that follows should guide you if you elect this method. Another way to organize the exercise is by explanation. If you choose this method, you might turn back to pages 32–33 of this book for guidance. The paragraph beginning "City College is completely overcrowded" should be particularly helpful.

Using either method of organization, you should develop Exercise 20 with as much detail as possible. Your experience with Exercise 11 in which you discussed something in close detail should be of value to you here. In fact, it might be worthwhile for you to turn back and review the discussion of that exercise before you begin this exercise.

You should see that Exercises 19 and 20 are related to each other, and you might also consider how they could be used as exercises preliminary to writing a short composition. A composition usually consists of several paragraphs that are related because they discuss the same subject. The subject of the example paragraphs in Exercises 19 and 20 is billboard advertising. Exercise 20 develops the first argument given in Exercise 19 against billboard advertising. If the two remaining points against billboard advertising made in Exercise 19 were also developed into paragraphs, the result would be three paragraphs that could form the main body or discussing part of a short composition. To complete the composition, two additional paragraphs, one an introduction and one a conclusion, would be needed. The total of five paragraphs would comprise a short composition that might be titled, "What's Wrong with Billboards?"

Figure 7–6 illustrates how Exercise 19 might be expanded into a short composition if Exercise 20 were used three times, each time developing one of the three points made in the discussion part of Exercise 19.

Your instructor may ask you to write Exercise 20 three times rather than once to prepare you to write the short composition. Whether you write it one or

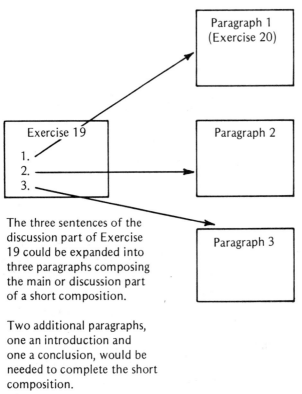

Exercise 20 is an expansion or development of the first point of the discussion part of Exercise 19; hence, it could serve here.

Exercise 20 could be used again to develop the second point of the discussion part of Exercise 19; hence, it could serve here.

Exercise 20, if used to develop the third point of Exercise 19, could serve here.

The three sentences of the discussion part of Exercise 19 could be expanded into three paragraphs composing the main or discussion part of a short composition.

Two additional paragraphs, one an introduction and one a conclusion, would be needed to complete the short composition.

Figure 7–6

more times, the exercise should help you see the relationship between one paragraph and another and between a paragraph and a composition.

Exercise 19 and 20 are among the most difficult exercises that you will encounter in this book and have therefore been placed last among the exercises that emphasize form and organization. Though difficult, the exercises should prove useful in helping you to think and to organize your thoughts about countless topics of importance to you.

EXERCISE 20. GIVE ONE REASON IN SUPPORT OF YOUR PROPOSED CHANGE

Directions

Write a paragraph in which you illustrate or explain one reason in support of a proposed change in the state of affairs on the local, national, or international scene. Use the following example as a guide.

EXAMPLE

(Topic Sentence) Billboards are ugly and hinder the enjoyment of natural roadside beauty. (Bridge to Discussion) To illustrate this statement, an experience that is common to many people must be brought to mind. (Discussion) Suppose a person is tired of the city—the smog and the hurry—and he decides to get away for a while. He gets into his car and travels away toward freedom and relaxation. Along the way, he pulls over to the side of the road to enjoy the quiet beauty of a country scene. What does he see? Billboards! One billboard shows giant dice dripping dirty motor oil; another billboard displays huge slices of bread falling on an immense plate; still another shows pastel toilet tissue, spelling out the name of the product he should buy. These and numerous other billboards are ugly substitutes for what he is seeking. (Conclusion) They spoil his enjoyment of natural roadside beauty.

Problems of Variety
and Imagination

The paragraph models in the exercises in this chapter are organized in a variety of ways. Although some are the same as or similar to those in Chapters 6 and 7, others are quite different. For example, in some of the models that follow, the topic sentence is the first sentence. In others, the topic sentence appears elsewhere. In still others, the topic is not stated at all but is implied or suggested by other parts of the paragraph.

There are other differences in organization in the paragraphs that follow. One of the most noticeable, perhaps, is the lack of obvious form in some of them. Freer form, however, does not mean formlessness or disorganization. You should remember that all paragraphs must contain unity, coherence, continuity, and the other essentials discussed earlier. Without these ingredients, a paragraph cannot communicate.

You will see that no parenthetical guides to organization like those in the exercises in Chapters 6 and 7 are given in this section. It is assumed that by now you will recognize the form in the exercises that follow or that you will have achieved the sense of form that is needed in the exercises. You are free now to use the models only as cues rather than as exact patterns of organization to imitate. You should read them primarily to stimulate you to form your own ideas.

If you have learned to discipline yourself in writing a paragraph, by now you should be free to do as you wish.

The emphasis here is to encourage you to express yourself with variety and imagination. Here you will be asked to be creative and to express your feelings. Expressing your feelings with imagination and clarity, as you may know, is not easy. How many times have you said, even to your closest friends, "I know what I mean, but I can't express it"? Understanding that you have difficulty expressing yourself to those who know you well, you can imagine how much harder it will be to write the paragraph in this chapter, which will be read by your instructor, who probably knows relatively little about you. How will your instructor, a comparative stranger, know what you mean?

Think about how you are going to make your feelings clear. Strangely enough, you cannot come right out with your feelings. You cannot write, for example, "That night it was very quiet." Your instructor, reading your paragraph, will wonder what you mean by "very quiet." *Like what?* he or she will wonder. To make the quietness clear, you will need to tell your reader what you could hear or not hear that very quiet night. Shakespeare had this problem in the beginning of his play *Hamlet,* and he solved it by writing, "Not a mouse stirring." It was so quiet that even the tiniest of nighttime creatures, mice, could not be heard. With such exact detail, Shakespeare made the quietness of the night clear.

To make your feelings clear, you must write about the *cause* of your reaction, *not the result.* You should not write "I felt afraid." Instead, you should make the cause of your fear so clear that the reader too can feel the horror. When you can make the reader feel what you have felt, then you can communicate your feelings successfully.

Your job, then, is to recreate your experience in order to convey your feelings about it. Examine the following paragraph.

EXAMPLE

Often during my young life I had galloped my horse down hills, chasing cows, and I had never been afraid. Suddenly I experienced a moment that terrified me. I was on a narrow ledge of rock on one of the highest points of the ranch, and I could see the treetops on the plateau below, like tiny shrubs, racing beneath the hoofs of my horse. The cow was getting away from me! I urged my horse to go faster and then, to gain distance, I made him jump to a steep slope below. He skidded in the winter mud to the edge of the slope and hung for an instant, balanced precariously, half falling into the deep canyon hundreds of feet below. Miraculously, he got his footing again. Shaking with fright, I got off him and sat down in the wet grass, trembling with the thought of what had almost happened. Then, slowly and carefully, I led my horse back down the steep hill, wondering how we had ever got up so high in the first place. "Somebody else is going to have to get that cow," I said to my father. "I'm not going up there again."

The experience described in this example is one of sudden and unusual fright. Very little is said about the emotion inspired by the experience. Instead, the paragraph recreates the experience in such a way that the emotion can be felt without discussing it outright.

Consider how the example expresses the feeling of fear. First it discusses height, fearsome to most people, not only by talking about it but by giving a comparison of the trees to small shrubs, which makes the sense of height clearer. It also relates speed of movement not only to height but also to a minimum of space that suggests the risk involved in the experience. At the moment of greatest fear in the experience, the emotion is not discussed at all. Rather, the action is given—"skidded . . . half falling"—causing the reader to use his or her own imagination, to draw back from the edge of the slope and balance precariously, too.

You must get readers to participate in the experience you write about, to share it with you, if you wish to express your feelings to them. To cause their participation, you must *appeal to their senses.* You must make it possible for them to see what you have seen, hear what you have heard, taste what you have tasted, touch what you have touched, smell what you have smelled, and in every way have the same experience that you have had. When you appeal to readers' senses, you must be as *exact* as possible. If they cannot quite see what you have seen, for example, they will be unable to participate in your experience, and hence you will have failed to convey your feelings.

Being exact requires finding the right words, and it might be worthwhile for you to review the section on words beginning on page 47 before you begin to write the exercises here. Remember, when you write the exercises that follow, to have a good dictionary and also *Roget's Thesaurus* at hand. Remember, also, to avoid cheap, tired, and weak substitutes for the right words you need, to be neither wordless nor wordy in expressing yourself, and to be careful of the many meanings some words have.

Remember the value of comparisons and use them whenever they will make your meaning clearer. Be creative in your use of comparisons. Avoid clichés. Find your own fresh comparisons. Surprise readers with your imagination. Make them sit up and notice you. Show them who you are, what you have experienced, and be so clear as well as clever about it that they cannot help but appreciate your effort. Above all else, make readers understand your experience as you do; every reader should be able to say, after reading your paragraph, "I know what you mean."

Finally, think about the difference between well-expressed sentiment and gushing sentimentality. Sentiment, when expressed well, consists of feeling or emotion that is both powerful and controlled. It is neither overstated nor understated. It is just right when it is sincere and when it leaves a little to the imagination of the reader. Do not pour it on! On the other hand, do not be afraid to show your feelings. If they are imaginatively expressed and carefully restrained, they can be the most beautiful statements you are capable of making.

You should notice that at the end of this chapter there are notes on each of the exercises. These notes should be helpful to you in writing the exercises.

Remember that these exercises may be easier and more enjoyable to do if you practice clustering before you write the paragraphs.

EXERCISE 21. DESCRIBE AN UNPLEASANT SENSORY EXPERIENCE

Directions

Write a paragraph in which you describe an unpleasant sensory experience that you have had. In other words, tell about something that has happened to you that has involved, in an unpleasant way, your sense of taste, touch, sight, smell, hearing, or any combination of these senses. Choose an experience that you know or remember well, and write vividly, selecting words that will make the reader feel what you have felt. The example that follows may be a helpful guide.

EXAMPLE

When I reached the front door of the nursing home, I thought I had pre-pared myself for the heat, the lack of air, and the odors, but I was never ready. It was always a shock, something to get past, that opening of the door. I tried to hold the door open as long as possible to let in a little fresh air, but someone usually called out, "Close the door! It's cold!" When it closed, the door seemed to seal out freshness, and everyone inside became hot-house plants, shielded from anything resembling weather. I understood the chill of the patients with their thin skin clinging delicately to bony arms and legs, but what about the nurses? How could they stand the close atmosphere, much less work in it? I took off my sweater and walked toward the nurses' station, adjusting as I went to the odd mixture of smells that permeated the place. The noonday meal was being prepared, but its aroma was overpowered by the pervading odor of disinfectant doing battle with incontinence. The charge nurse looked up and smiled and said "hello," and I could tell by her expression that she had long since withdrawn from the outside world and was satisfied with the way things were running.

EXERCISE 22. DESCRIBE A PLEASANT SENSORY EXPERIENCE

Directions

Write a paragraph in which you describe a pleasant sensory experience. The directions are the same here as for the preceding exercise except that in this case there is a change from an unpleasant to a pleasant experience. Notice that the difference between a pleasant and unpleasant experience is not necessarily in the subject matter itself but in the way it is viewed by the writer. For example, the experience in the following example might easily be regarded as unpleasant by some people, but the writer does not present it that way.

EXAMPLE

The smell of alfalfa in the tightly packed bales of hay I sat on was strong and fresh. With my knees tucked up, my arms curled around my legs, I watched the cows come into the open barn for their evening meal. It was twilight, my favorite time of day. The summer air was quiet. The burnt hills were turning from dark amber to a darker grayish brown, becoming faintly magenta where the last sun streaks had recently left them. When the cows had settled into their stanchions, the only sounds left were the shiftings and breakings of dry hay as twenty-five big tongues reached out and wrapped up large mouthfuls to chew, and then the chewing itself, which was strangely peaceful to watch and listen to. I sat as though mesmerized, and only dimly did the day's struggles or my life's ambitions enter my mind. When thoughts did come, they came effortlessly, like the gentle rustling of the birds in the nearby trees, and they were as comfortable as the birds, sleeping peacefully, with room to spare in the generous oaks for all of them. I could easily have sat on top of the haystack for the rest of the night, but then the dinner gong sounded in the distance. I got down from my perch in the cow barn and walked back to the house, reluctant to close the front door on the sights and sounds I had been enjoying outside. It seemed a shame to me that people lived in houses on summer nights, and I thought that maybe after dinner I would take my sleeping bag back down to the barn and sleep there.

EXERCISE 23. DESCRIBE AN EXPERIENCE
IN FLASHBACK FORM

Directions

Write a paragraph in which you tell about an experience in flashback form. Begin with the conclusion in which you state the most outstanding feature(s) of the experience and then proceed to tell what happened leading up to the conclusion. Use the following example as a guide.

EXAMPLE

What I remember most is running down the driveway to our house, clutching my back and screaming with pain, and then feeling the agony of my hands soaked in iodine. This experience was the result of my habit as a child of collecting stray dogs and bringing them home. It began one dusty day in the middle of summer when I introduced a stray dog to our family of five dogs, calling the five by name, petting the stray, and trying to make everybody feel at home. Nobody was very happy about the situation but me, and soon a fight started, with my hands on the stray dog in the middle of it. In seconds my hands were riddled with dog bites. Because the shock was so great, I did not feel the pain at first in my hands. Instead, my back jerked out of shape, and I ran down to the house humped over, like an old lady. My frantic mother looked to see what was wrong with my back as I screamed to her, "No! My hands! My hands!" Blood gushed from the punctures the dogs had made. My mother ran for the medicine chest, grabbed a bottle of iodine, and poured the whole bottle over my hands.

EXERCISE 24. DESCRIBE A MOMENT WHEN YOU FOUND OR LEARNED SOMETHING NEW

Directions

Write a paragraph in which you describe a moment in your life when you found something or learned something you had never known about before. Use the example that follows to guide you.

EXAMPLE

It was a rainy day and there was nothing for a child my age to do, so I went down into the basement of our house to investigate some of the mysteries that were stored there. My favorite diggings, a musty old trunk, smelling of camphor and mildew, in which my mother stored old clothes, held no fascination for me that day. Looking for new excitement, I tried on an old raincoat that was hanging on a hook. It was miles too long for me, and I almost hanged myself with it when I fastened the top snap, for the rubber in it had grown stiff with age. Next I read some old magazines that oozed moisture, and it became a game to separate the pages without tearing them. Finally I came across my prize, a book that held me spellbound, primarily because I could barely understand a word of it, yet the words themselves captivated me. "What wild heart-histories seemed to lie unwritten upon those crystalline, celestial spheres," I read. I spent hours reading that book, and I was still absorbed in it, treasuring each word, as I carried it back up into the house. I was like a sleepwalker, moving as in a dream, unaware of existence outside of the biggest discovery of my life, a book of poetry by Edgar Allan Poe!

EXERCISE 25. EXPLAIN HOW OR WHY YOU ASSOCIATE ONE THING WITH ANOTHER

Directions

Write a paragraph in which you explain how or why you associate one thing with another. Perhaps a certain sound or smell calls to mind something you remember at some point in your life. Or perhaps an object, an animate or inanimate thing, reminds you of a particular experience. Use the example that follows as a guide.

EXAMPLE

I have always associated the stone turquoise with my first trip to Lake Tahoe. I can still see myself as I was then, eight years old, sitting next to my brother in our family sedan. My mother and father had been talking about the Donner party, and as we approached the summit, my brother and I imagined we could see skeletons in the shadows of the tall trees. The sharp granite cliffs and brisk air of the mountains seemed in sharp contrast to the heat and haze of the Sacramento Valley, through which we had passed not long before. My father stopped the car somewhere near the summit, and we went into a shop that sold Indian things. It was like walking into a jewel box, it seemed to me. Everywhere I looked I saw the sky-blue stone. It was in rings and bracelets inside glass cases; it was in necklaces hanging from hooks; it was in other ornamental objects spread out on brightly colored blankets. My mother went up to the shopkeeper and asked the price of something she had seen in one of the cases. It was a tiny silver cross with a little round turquoise stone set in the center of it. "How would you like that?" she asked me. "Oh, could I?" I responded eagerly. Looked at through adult eyes, the event might seem unimportant, but I can remember well what a thrill it gave me when my mother placed the little cross on its silver chain around my neck and how proud I felt as we walked out of the shop and climbed back into the car.

EXERCISE 26. DISCUSS A QUOTATION

Directions

Do you have a saying in your family or is there a famous quotation that you have wondered about or found particularly meaningful? Present it and discuss it in one paragraph. Use the example that follows as a guide.

EXAMPLE

An aunt of mine has often said, "Youth is wasted on the young." This statement has piqued my curiosity for years. People usually smile when she says it, and I have always smiled, too. But I think I'm just now beginning to understand the meaning of the saying. Quite recently I thought how close in meaning it is to a statement Thornton Wilder made in his play *Our Town*. Toward the end of the play, Emily, one of the main characters says, "I didn't realize. So all that was going on and we never noticed! . . . Do any human beings ever realize life while they live it—every, every minute?" Older people, looking back, can appreciate youth, its real meaning and significance, but young people, while they are in the middle of their youth, never fully realize what they have. An older person recognizes his increasing age by making comparisons to his youth. "I'm not as young as I was. Better slow down," he says to himself. The vitality of youth, the energy and excitement of it, is realized, ironically, only after it is gone. Thus, it seem to me, my aunt is right. Youth *is* wasted on the young. Babies should be old and gray-haired when they're born. Only after many years should they be permitted to enjoy their youth.

EXERCISE 27. WRITE WHAT WOULD HAPPEN IF . . .

Directions

Write a paragraph in which you express what you imagine would result if something we all take for granted in our lives were to end, to stop, or to die. For example, suppose there were no more police officers, suppose all the rivers or lakes should dry up, suppose all schools were to close permanently, what would happen? Remember, you cannot discuss everything in one paragraph. Limit your subject. The example that follows may be a helpful guide.

EXAMPLE

Suppose the sun were to die. What would happen then? Could people find a way to survive? Perhaps they could split atoms for heat. Perhaps they could manufacture synthetic foods to eat. Perhaps they could create a new sun. Maybe there would be many new suns, one for each city, and some man-made stars along the freeways so that people could get from one place to another. Just think, the world would fill with people who had never seen the sun. Grandparents would be revered for their tales of what it was like before the sun died. Then they would drop away, like the Civil War veterans, and the reality would become a legend. If the story got into books, would people believe it? Or would they, except for the most devout, believe there had never been a sun at all?

EXERCISE 28. DESCRIBE SOMEONE YOU SEE OFTEN

Directions

Write a paragraph in which you describe someone you see often, but do not know, in your neighborhood, or on your way to school or to work. Describe the aspects of appearance or behavior that cause you to notice this person, and also explain your reaction to the person. Use the example that follows as a guide.

EXAMPLE

Her hair is white, like her face. Her eyes are sunken into her head. They look opaque; I wonder what they see? She mutters to imaginary companions as she wanders about in the garden. Crazy old woman, I think, whom is she talking to? Her legs are frighteningly thin. I wonder how they can carry her to and from the nearby store for groceries. When she walks by my house, I see her hesitate before the tiniest bit of water that spills down onto the sidewalk from my front lawn. She talks to herself for a moment, then moves carefully out into the street, then back onto the sidewalk again. I feel guilty for having turned the water on. This cadaverous creature is my neighbor. She lives in a room and has kitchen privileges in the house next door to me. She has visitors once or twice during the year, I think, for I see her come to the front porch, waving them off with her thin fingers. I stand at a window in my house watching her, and I wonder how pity and repulsion can become so intertwined. There seems so little left of her, so little left for her. This ghost of a woman is a haunting vision.

EXERCISE 29. DESCRIBE A FAMOUS PAINTING

Directions

Write a paragraph in which you describe a famous painting. Discuss what you think is most striking about the painting, and then describe whatever else seems most noticeable to you. Use the example that follows as a guide.

EXAMPLE

The most striking feature about Van Gogh's famous painting *The Bridge at Arles* is the sense of calm it projects. The light blue sky behind the bridge is clear; the nearby trees are straight and unmoving, suggesting that there is little or no wind blowing; and a man in a horsedrawn cart is leisurely crossing the bridge. Even the women scrubbing clothes in the stream beneath the bridge seem to be working contentedly. The half-sunken boat in the foreground invites the mind as well as the eye to a peaceful submersion in the gently rippling water. The colors in the painting are noticeable, too, and contribute to the calmness of the whole. Although all parts of the painting are bright and clear, nothing is glaring. Various shades of yellow strike the eye in pleasant contrast to the blues of the sky and water. A third predominating color, green, is distributed about the painting, mixed with burnt orange in places and flecks of brown. This rural scene, it is easy to tell, was done when Van Gogh lived in Arles, the happiest, most peaceful period in his life.

EXERCISE 30. DESCRIBE YOUR REACTIONS TO ILLNESS

Directions

Write a paragraph in which you describe your physical and/or emotional reactions to injury or sickness. You might discuss a particular time when you have been hospitalized or ill in bed at home. Or you might, as in the following example, describe a recurring feeling that you experience whenever you are ill. See the discussion on page 130, which explains the use of the third person in the example that follows.

EXAMPLE

The most depressing thing about an illness is the sense of being left out or brushed aside by it from the mainstream of living. When a person is ill, he cannot keep up with the world of healthy people. Life begins to occur without him. Even language seems to change. What is said to a sick person does not involve him, and therefore he begins to interpret it differently. He loses touch with the outer, healthy world. "It's affected his mind," the outside world murmurs, shrinking back from him kindly, gently imprisoning him more deeply in his own thoughts. His sense of isolation is increased rather than lessened by the regular visits of the doctor. The doctor labels the sick person's disease and confines him to his special place. With tact and skill, the doctor completes the patient's helplessness and makes final his division from the world of strong arms, sound legs, clear skin, and lungs that breathe deeply. The sick person's only hope is to return to life again, and he clings to the thought of getting well. He thinks of sick people who will not get well, and he thinks of old people who will soon die. He discovers compassion he hopes he will not lose when he is well again, and he feels gratitude that he, unlike some others, will get well.

NOTES ON EXERCISES IN CHAPTER 8

EXERCISE 21

To do this exercise well, you should write at least two or three drafts of it. In your first, or rough, draft, do not worry about organization or mechanics such as grammar, sentence structure, spelling, and so forth. Free your mind of such matters. Concentrate, instead, on remembering the experience just as it happened and getting it all down on paper. Write everything about the experience that you can think of, even seemingly unimportant details. Details are especially important in this exercise. The more exact you are with details, the more reality your paragraph will have. Remember, in this paragraph you must make it possible for your reader to see what you have seen, feel what you have felt, hear what you have heard, and so forth.

When you write your paragraph for the second or third time, you will need to organize it and polish it. Probably you will need to cut parts of your first draft as you get a better idea of what you want to say and how it is best said.

Do not decorate your paragraph. Do not put anything in it that is not real. Tell about the experience just as it happened, and tell it exactly.

Suggested topics: listening to a boring lecture; seeing an accident; being sick; trying to cross a busy intersection; traveling on a crowded bus on a hot afternoon; experiencing severe cold or frostbite; listening to your younger sister practice the cello; feeling stage fright; forcing yourself to eat something terrible or to take bitter medicine; trying to stay awake or to go to sleep; being punished; being hungry or thirsty; trying to diet.

EXERCISE 22

Details are as important here as they are in Exercise 21. It is even more important in this exercise, perhaps, not to decorate. Do not try to "paint a pretty picture." Instead, be exact and real. If you are realistic, the pleasantness of your experience, whatever it is, will be felt by the reader.

Suggested topics: enjoying Thanksgiving dinner; walking in the park or country; sailing; attending a party; dancing the last dance at the senior prom; picnicking on the beach; receiving unexpected money; buying new clothes; traveling; meeting someone famous; buying your first car; seeing an unusually beautiful sunrise or sunset; enjoying a day in spring; hearing, seeing, or tasting something exciting for the first time.

EXERCISE 23

The first sentence should make a clear and definite impression, even though the facts leading up to it are not explained until later. The first sentence would also tease the reader into wanting to know more about the "how," "when," "what," and "why" of the experience to be explained in the paragraph. The paragraph should then proceed to explain everything that must be known to make the first statement fully understood. The paragraph should not leave noticeable gaps in the experience; neither should it become too long.

Suggested topics: narrowly escaping some kind of danger; taking or resisting a dare; missing an important plane or train; saving someone's life or being saved; waking up after an accident or operation; meeting a shark, bear, tiger, bull, mad dog, or thief; being wounded or shocked while hunting or playing a sport; winning or losing a race; running for your life or a political office; having an embarrassing moment; learning a lesson. (Notice that rather dramatic topics are best suited for this exercise.)

EXERCISE 24

Be careful to set the right mood in this exercise. Notice that the mood of the model paragraph is rather playful, indicating that the content is not to be taken too seriously. If you wish to present your discovery more seriously, then you will need to establish quite a different mood. Also, build your paragraph with an element of suspense, carefully leading up to the moment of discovery.

Suggested topics: realizing your parents are human; discovering hidden talent in yourself or someone else; realizing the truth or falsity of an old saying; discovering music or art or beauty in something unrealized before; seeing your first view of a foreign country; feeling strange in familiar surroundings or feeling familiar in a situation that is actually strange; suddenly feeling unafraid in previously fearful circumstances; sensing your own maturity or immaturity; achieving humility.

EXERCISE 25

Allow your mind to be free to make emotional as well as logical associations in this exercise. Consider how you feel, for instance, when you hear a popular song that reminds you of that summer two years ago, or that time you visited Uncle Joe in South Dakota, or that moment you met a very special person. You can make associations with things you see, smell, or taste as well as with things you hear, such as music. Free your mind to be imaginative, to wander at will, to make the association that is needed in this exercise.

You should make a rough first draft of this exercise before you worry about organizing your thoughts into a good paragraph. Your rough draft may consist of nothing more than a series of fragmentary thoughts scribbled on paper. Let your ideas flow freely before you try to give them order.

Suggested topics: chocolate ice cream may remind you of your tenth birthday; the scent of gardenias may call to mind your first formal dance; the odors of an old house might remind you of someone who has died; camel's hair coats may make you think of football in the fall; cole slaw or codfish might bring back a moment of discipline when you were a child; other associations might be made with the following: the smell of newly mown grass or freshly cut lumber; the sight of sunshine on a blade of grass or a gold filling in a smiling mouth; the sound of glass breaking, brakes screeching, or music in a minor key.

EXERCISE 26

"That's life," the saying goes, but what does it mean? In this exercise you should think of an old saying, examine it, and decide what it means, if anything. No doubt you have grown up listening to countless quotations, some of them, perhaps, more meaningful than others. Think of one that stands out in your mind because it has affected you in some way, made you happy or sad, made you wise or thoughtless, or simply because you have heard it used so many times that it might be interesting to study it and write about it.

Suggested topics: "All work and no play makes Jack a dull boy"; "It is better to have loved and lost then never to have loved at all"; "Nothing is right or wrong, but thinking makes it so"; "Judge not, lest you, yourself, be judged"; "Do unto others as you would they did unto you"; "'He's a penny-saver and a pound-loser"; "Take a stitch in time and sane nine"; "A penny saved is a penny earned"; "Shirt-sleeves to shirtsleeves in three generations"; "Turn the other cheek"; "He who hesitates is lost"; "Neither a borrower nor a lender be"; "Familiarity breeds contempt."

EXERCISE 27

Here you can and must be wild. Be as daring in using your imagination as you can be. Look around you and think about the many things you are used to, the many things you count on, the many things you could not do without. Then imagine life without one of them. What would it be like? Your guesses should make some sense, of course.

Suggested topics: suppose there were no more gravity; no more babies born; no more deaths; no more wars; no more birds; no more means of communication such as telephones, radios, television, newspapers; no more entertainment such as television or movies; no more major cities such as New York or Washington; no more grass; suppose people could no longer laugh, or cry, or feel sorry for others; suppose you were the last person on earth; suppose you could find nobody who knew you; suppose you could not suppose.

EXERCISE 28

There are always people at the edges of your life that you notice but do not really know. When you shop in the grocery store, for instance, you begin to recognize faces you see there often, or when you go to school or work, you pass the same people over and over again. You may nod, but you never or rarely speak. Why do you notice one person in particular? Is he or she lame? Do you wonder what that person is thinking? Do you wonder what makes that person happy or sad or what he or she is really like? When you do not see that person for a day or two, do you wonder why? Select one of the people at the edges of your life to write about.

Suggested topics: someone who waits with you for the same bus; someone who drives or walks to school or work when you do; a customer where you work; someone who plays the flute in the symphony orchestra concerts that you attend; someone who walks his or her dog past your house in the evening; an elderly person you see in a wheelchair through a window of a convalescent hospital; a person who looks mysterious, funny, sinister, distinguished.

EXERCISE 29

When you really look at a painting, you see much more in it than you can at a casual glance. The subject matter means more, whether it is exciting, interesting, amusing, or confusing. The composition is more meaningful because of its shapes, colors, contrasts, variety, and so forth. The mood of the painting may be impressive. If the painting is famous, you may wonder why and linger over it to try to find out why so many people admire it.

Your instructor may select a painting for you to study and write about in this exercise, or you may need to make your own choice. Look at the painting carefully. What do you see? What is most noticeable? What else is impressive? Study the painting and then write about it.

Suggested topics: Mona Lisa by Leonardo da Vinci; *The Harvesters* by Pieter Bruegel; *Northeaster* by Winslow Homer; *Stone City* by Grant Wood; *The Flower Vendor* by Diego Rivera; *Vegetable Gardens* by Vincent Van Gogh; *Tahitian Moun-*

tains by Paul Gauguin; *Woman at the Mirror* by Pablo Picasso; *The Dancer on the Stage* by Edgar Degas; any good painting, either old or modern.

EXERCISE 30

Consider your emotional and physical reactions to illness or injury in this exercise. Although you will be discussing your innermost feelings, try to be objective. That is, keep in mind that someone who does not know you very well will be reading your paragraph and that you must make yourself clear to him. You may find comparisons useful. Your reader will understand you better if you can tell him that your reaction was *like* something he knows.

Neither underplay nor overstate your feeling in this exercise. Be sincere. Be as exact as possible.

The model paragraph uses the third person (he, she, they) as a means of objectifying or avoiding sentimentality. This technique is an experiment that you need not use unless you want to. If you find it simpler to use the first person (I), go ahead and use it. The point, however, is still the same, and that is to show feeling without becoming so involved in it that you lose objectivity or discipline.

Suggested topics: feeling like a queen for a day in a hospital after minor surgery; feeling like a prisoner in solitary confinement with a contagious disease; waiting for a cast to be removed; getting bored with ice cream after a tonsillectomy; being embarrassed to have your friends see you with your face swollen from poison oak; sharing an illness with your hospital roommate; not being able to live like others because of some permanent physical disability.

PART 11

Writing the Short Composition

The Short Composition

1. WHAT IS A SHORT COMPOSITION?

A short composition, also called a *theme* or *essay,* has already been partially defined elsewhere in this book. The word *composition* means putting together a whole by the combination of parts. Thus defined, the word applies to art and music as well as to literature. Here the word is applied to a form of writing done by students. It is an exercise in putting together words, sentences, and paragraphs—the parts of the composition that are combined into the whole. The word *short,* of course, is relative. *Short composition* here means a composition of about four to eight paragraphs or two to five pages in length.

2. WHAT DOES A SHORT COMPOSITION LOOK LIKE ON THE PAGE?

The first page of a short composition might look like Figure 9–1. The appearance of the composition on the page depends, of course, on whether it is typewritten or handwritten. Figure 9–1 contains more paragraphs than could probably be handwritten on one page, at least by the average hand.

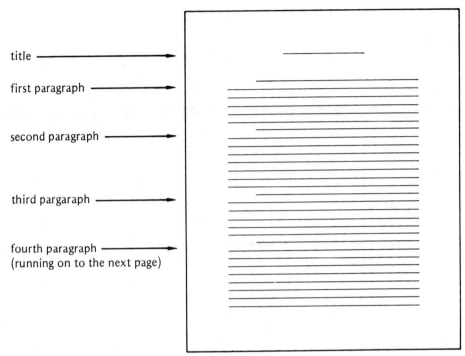

title

first paragraph

second paragraph

third pargaraph

fourth paragraph
(running on to the next page)

Figure 9–1

3. WHAT IS A TITLE?

Notice that the title is the first thing written on the page in Figure 9–1. It is written in the upper part of the page and centered.

A title should do the following:

1. Indicate what the composition is about.
2. Provoke interest in the composition.
3. Be as brief as possible.

A title is often a fragment rather than a complete sentence. The first and last words of a title are always capitalized. Unless they are the first or last words of the title, prepositions and articles are not capitalized, though there is a preference among some people to capitalize prepositions of five or six letters or more. Examine the capitalization in the following titles:

The Grapes of Wrath
A Farewell to Arms
The Return of the Native

The preceding titles are the work of experienced and well-known writers. You might find it helpful to see examples of titles more typical of student compositions.

The Rustic Imagery of Robert Frost

Ban the Billboard!

Looking at a Painting by Picasso

How to Wash a Dog

An Unforgettable Moment in My Life

An Examination of the Word *Tolerance*

An Argument Against Capital Punishment

Are Americans Money Mad?

A Walk in the Country

A Discussion of Proposition 14

4. WHY SHOULD A COMPOSITION BE ORGANIZED?

Understanding "why" can make "how" easier. Appreciating the importance of organization is a key to better organization. Take a quick look at Figure 9–2. How many dots are there in each group? The dots in Figure 9–2A must be counted carefully to determine their number, but you can tell at a glance that there are four groups of three, or a total of twelve dots in Figure 9–2B. There is no readily discernible pattern or arrangement in Figure 9–2A, whereas Figure 9–2B is clearly organized and its pattern is easy to recognize.

A disorganized composition is like Figure 9–2A. The words, sentences, and paragraphs of the composition, like the dots in Figure 9–2A, fly off every which way in no easily recognizable pattern. An organized composition is like Figure 9–2B. The words, sentences, and paragraphs line up easily to form a clear pattern.

"But I like Figure 9–2A better!" you might say, finding it more interesting or imaginative than the seemingly dull and monotonous Figure 9–2B. However, you should keep two points in mind. First, remember that you are a beginner and that your primary objective is to be organized and clear. Second, do not misinterpret the two drawings. Figure 9–2B is intended to represent order, not monotony. Once you can achieve order, then and only then can you free yourself to be imaginative, and your imagination will make sense because it will be organized and clear.

Figure A   Figure B

Figure 9–2

5. HOW IS A COMPOSITION ORGANIZED?

The composition has a central purpose or objective that controls the whole composition. The purpose is expressed in the beginning paragraph of the composition in a sentence called a *thesis statement* or *thesis sentence.* The thesis statement gives the plan for the composition, and the composition must follow that plan. No matter what the thesis or plan of a particular composition is, all compositions have in common three major parts.

The first part of any composition is the *introduction.* In a short composition the introduction is usually quite brief. It may consist simply of the thesis statement, or it may contain additional sentences. (For further discussion of the introduction, see Chapter 14.)

The second part of the composition, the *discussion,* is the main part. In a composition of five paragraphs, for example, the discussion normally consumes the three longest paragraphs. The proportion is similar in longer compositions, the discussion part being three fifths to four fifths of the total composition.

Among the problems that most frequently arise in the discussion part of the composition are the following:

1. Getting the correct order.   The correct order depends on the purpose of the composition. If the purpose is to narrate or tell a story, the correct order might be *chronological.* In other words, you should tell what happened first, what happened second, what happened third, and so on.

If the purpose of the composition is to explain something, the correct order might be *cause and effect* or vice versa. In other words, you should tell first what causes A and describe the results of A, then tell what causes B and describe the results of B, and so on. Or you might show the results first and then the causes.

If the purpose of the composition is to argue for or against something, the correct order is a matter of what is *logical.* For instance, in an argument against capital punishment, the first task would be to show what is wrong with capital punishment. The next job might be to show the benefits of abolishing it. If the purpose of the composition is to show both sides of an argument, then it is logical to discuss first one side and then the other.

If the purpose of the composition is to discuss several related things or a group of things, the order might be simply *topical.* In other words, one topic would be announced and then discussed and then a second topic would be introduced and discussed, and so on with the remaining topics. Of course, a unifying relationship would need to be shown among the topics to maintain the necessary order or organization of the composition. For example, if the purpose of the composition were to discuss dogs, you might divide your subject into the various species of dogs, the various purposes served by dogs, or the various sizes and shapes of dogs. You must make certain that a central purpose controls the whole while you divide the whole into intelligible parts. There must be unity in your topical arrangement.

If the purpose of the composition is to describe something, the correct order might be *spatial* or *geographical*. You might move your description from north to south or from west to east, for example, or from top to bottom or from side to side.

Whatever the correct order is for the particular purpose of the composition, it should be made clear to readers and maintained throughout the composition.

2. Keeping a balance.   Keeping a balance among the parts of the discussion, like putting them in correct order, depends on the purpose of the composition. If the purpose of the composition is to show two sides of an argument, for example, both sides must be shown equally. If the purpose of the composition is to discuss the life work of an author, a poet, or a painter, major events in your subject's life should not be slighted or left out of the composition. Because no composition can fully describe anything or anyone, the limits of the composition are set in the introduction, but the composition must be sure to live up to those limits. You must not fall in love with only one part of your subject, for example, after you have promised to discuss two or three parts. A balance must be achieved, and that balance depends on the purpose that you state in the thesis sentence of the introduction.

3. Providing signals.   You should provide signals to readers at all important points in your composition, particularly at major turning points. These signals, like road signs to the motorist, should help to keep readers moving in the right direction in following your thoughts in the composition. The easiest direction for you to take to avoid losing readers is a straight line, but turns are often inevitable, as well as interesting. Such turns must be announced with phrases like "Going back, for a moment, to 1910" or "In England, as well as in America, the problem exists" or "Ten years from now" or "The argument against this proposition is more reasonable than the one that supports it." Readers will be happy to follow you in any reasonable direction you care to take, but your direction must be made clear to them.

4. Paving the way.   Reading the composition should not be an unpleasant experience for readers. In addition to providing them with signals along the way, you should pave the way for them. Your word choice, your sentence structure, and the organization of your paragraphs should be smooth and readable. You should do everything possible to make the composition a pleasure to read. If readers must struggle to get your point, if they must stumble, go back, read parts over and over again to understand your meaning, if they must, in effect, work harder at the composition than you have, the result is disastrous. Readers become frustrated, irritated, and antagonistic rather than sympathetic with you. On the other hand, if you pave the way for your readers, your composition can provide you both with the exquisite joy that is known as communication.

(For a closer examination of the discussion, see Chapters 12 and 13.)

Finally, the third part of the composition is the conclusion, which, like the introduction, is usually brief. (See Chapter 14 for further discussion of the conclusion.)

10

The Thesis Statement

1. WHAT IS A THESIS STATEMENT?

A *thesis statement* or *thesis sentence* (the terms are synonymous) states the purpose of the composition. It conveys the central or main idea of the composition and often indicates how the main idea will be supported. Ideally, it is a one-sentence summary of the whole composition.

2. WHAT IS THE DIFFERENCE BETWEEN A THESIS STATEMENT AND A TOPIC SENTENCE?

A thesis statement governs the content and structure of a whole composition, whereas a topic sentence guides only one of its parts or paragraphs. Both sentences are signals of what is to come. The thesis statement plans the trip, as it were; the topic sentence shows one of the places that must be passed through to get to the destination.

3. WHERE SHOULD THE THESIS STATEMENT BE PLACED WITHIN THE COMPOSITION?

The best place for the thesis statement is in the beginning of the composition. It should be written in the first paragraph and may be the first and only sentence of that paragraph, or it may follow an introductory sentence or two and then come as the climax of the first paragraph.

4. ARE ALL THESIS STATEMENTS ALIKE IN CONTENT AND FORM?

Thesis statements vary in a multitude of ways with respect to content (who knows how many subjects there are to write about?); they also vary in their form.

In your college courses, you will frequently be called on to formulate thesis statements in response to assigned reading. You will read, and then you will be asked to react in writing. To some degree, therefore, both the content and the form of your thesis statement, which is your reaction in a nutshell, will be determined by your reading and by the nature of your particular assignment. In all cases, however, *a thesis statement* is a statement of *position,* of *belief,* or of a *point of view,* either your own or that of someone else, such as the author of your assigned reading.

The form of the thesis statement is important not only in making a clear statement but in making it in such a way that it governs or controls the organization of the whole composition. A good thesis statement tells not only where the composition is going but how it is going to get there. Much like a good outline, the thesis statement gives the plan for the composition.

One suggestion may aid you in making the thesis statement not only a clear sentence but a good plan. *Divide the thesis statement into two or three parts.* When you divide your thesis statement into two or three parts, you give your reader, as well as yourself, a more precise preview of the composition as a whole than would be possible with an undivided thesis statement.

Compare the following sentences. The first of each pair is an undivided thesis. The thought is expressed in one vague lump that gives no indication of the way in which the composition will proceed or how it will be organized. The second sentence of each pair is divided into two or three parts that suggest the organization of the composition.

1. People who live in the suburbs are alike. (UNDIVIDED)
   People who live in the suburbs are alike in *age, race,* and *politics.*
   (DIVIDED INTO THREE PARTS)

2. Capital punishment should be abolished. (UNDIVIDED)
   Capital punishment should be abolished because it is *useless* and *inhumane*. (DIVIDED INTO TWO PARTS)
3. The essay is a satire. (UNDIVIDED)
   The essay satirizes *younger* as well as *older* people. (DIVIDED INTO TWO PARTS)
4. Pollution constitutes a serious problem to humanity. (UNDIVIDED)
   Air and *water* pollution constitute a serious problem to humanity. (DIVIDED INTO TWO PARTS)
5. Life on this earth may soon be wiped out. (UNDIVIDED)
   Plants, animals, and *people* (the so-called higher forms of life) may soon be wiped out. (DIVIDED INTO THREE PARTS)

The second sentence of each pair is a brief summary that tells not only where the composition is going but how it will get there. Consider the first example: *People who live in the suburbs are alike in age, race, and politics.* One can tell at a glance not only the subject of the composition but also how the composition will be organized. The subject, the similarity of suburbanites (that you may disagree is perfectly all right; the point is that you know the subject), is divided into three parts: age, race, and politics. One knows what to expect in the composition. Your reader knows and you know (if this is your subject). The division is as useful to you as it is to your reader. Suppose you lost track of your subject and the way in which you wanted to present it. Look back. There it is, all spelled out in the thesis.

Keep in mind that *the composition must discuss each part of the thesis in the order in which it appears in the thesis.* The discussion part of the composition about the similarity of suburbanites must begin with *age,* proceed then to *race,* and then turn to *politics.* Of course, you might decide that you prefer a different order in your discussion and therefore rearrange your thesis to agree with it, but whatever you end up with as the order of one, so must be the order of the other. In other words, thesis and discussion must match.

The division of this thesis statement into parts is sometimes simply for the purpose of breaking the thought down into areas or aspects that make the discussion more orderly and manageable. More often, the division is for the purpose of *supporting the thought.* The position, belief, or point of view you present in your thesis statement is more meaningful or convincing when it is supported. *Proof* is needed, in other words. *Why* do you think such and such? What is your *evidence?* What are your *reasons?* When you summarize or outline your major points of proof by stating them in your thesis statement, you straighten out your own thinking and you permit your reader to see in advance of your discussion not only what it is that you want to prove but also how you plan to prove it.

Compare the following pairs of sentences. The first of each pair makes an unsupported claim. That is, no proof, evidence, or reasoning is offered to support the position, belief, or point of view presented. The second sentence of each pair offers support.

1. It may rain today. (UNSUPPORTED)
   It may rain today because there are dark clouds in the sky and my barometer is falling. (SUPPORTED)
2. Mr. X thinks he has a cold or the flu. (UNSUPPORTED)
   Mr. X thinks he has a cold or the flu because he has a sore throat, a headache, and a fever. (SUPPORTED)
3. Ireland is a tourist's delight. (UNSUPPORTED)
   Ireland is a tourist's delight for three reasons: the country is beautiful, the people are friendly, and the prices are reasonable. (SUPPORTED)
4. Rachel Carson's thesis in *The Silent Spring* is that the indiscriminate use of chemical insecticides should be abolished. (UNSUPPORTED)
   Rachel Carson's thesis in *The Silent Spring* is that the indiscriminate use of chemical insecticides should be abolished, as it is unnecessarily poisoning wildlife and as there are better controls, such as the use of natural predators. (SUPPORTED)
5. Real estate, though it promises work and worry, is a good investment. (UNSUPPORTED)
   Real estate, though it promises work and worry, is a good investment in that it is substantial and relatively secure, it generally appreciates, and if offers tax advantages. (SUPPORTED)

The second sentence of each preceding pair, because it gives proof or reasons, is the more meaningful or convincing of the two. As a thesis statement, it would also be a better guide than the first. It would suggest both the content and the order of the whole composition.

5. DO COMPOSITIONS ALWAYS CONTAIN A THESIS STATEMENT?

Compositions that are expository—that is, that explain or discuss ideas and facts—require a thesis statement. Argumentative compositions demand a thesis statement also. These are the two types of compositions you are most often asked to write in college courses; therefore, it is important that you master and learn to think in terms of the thesis statement. For you, the thesis statement is a matter of *almost always*. You should be aware that there are other types of compositions, however, such as narrative and descriptive compositions, and that these types may or may not require a thesis statement. If you learn to write so well that you decide to take a course in creative writing, for example, you should then be in a position to decide whether your composition needs a thesis statement. Meanwhile, assume that it does.

6. IS THE THESIS ALWAYS A SINGLE SENTENCE?

In some cases, it may be simpler or clearer to break the thesis down into more than a single sentence, especially if the main idea of the composition is unusually complex or if the composition is long. In most cases, at least in the exercises in this book, you should be able to state the purpose or main idea in a single sentence because you will not be asked to write compositions that are extremely complicated or very long.

7. IS THE DIVISION OF THE THESIS STATEMENT ALWAYS LIMITED TO TWO OR THREE PARTS OR SUPPORTS?

In a short composition of about four to eight paragraphs, which is the approximate length expected in your compositions, it is a good plan to limit the parts or supports of the main idea to two or three. Additional parts or supports would likely result in insufficient development of each part within the relative brevity of the composition as a whole. In a longer composition, however, the parts or supports might well exceed two or three.

SUMMARY

Begin your composition with a thesis statement that is precise in conveying the purpose or central idea of the composition. It is best to divide your thesis statement into two or three parts, in order to make clear not only what your composition is to be about, but exactly how it is to be organized or developed. You thus give a preview or overview of the entire composition.

11

Practicing the Thesis Statement

Before you begin to practice the thesis statement, it may be helpful for you to consider it in a way that has not yet been discussed. Another way to view the thesis is to see it as a condensed form of the paragraph. See Exercise 19 on page 108, to which you might return after you read this brief discussion of its relationship to the thesis statement. As already stated, Exercise 19 is a special paragraph, in fact a summary in several sentences, capable of being expanded into a short composition. Condensed into one sentence, Exercise 19 could consist of a thesis statement with a three-part support, as follows:

Billboard advertising should be abolished along public highways because it is ugly and hinders the enjoyment of natural roadside beauty, because it is a distraction and therefore a danger to the motorist, and because, since its purpose is to promote private business, it does not belong along public, tax-supported highways.

Just as Exercise 19 can be expanded into a whole composition, so the preceding thesis statement can function in the same way. Notice that the argument in the sentence is supported. An unsupported version of the argument follows:

Billboard advertising should be abolished along public highways.

The unsupported version is useful in that it presents a subject capable of being developed into a composition. However, because of the lack of supports, it does not show how the subject will be developed, argued, or proved. It does not summarize the composition as a whole. Remember that a good thesis statement tells not only where the composition is going but also how it is going to get there. The first sentence, in which the argument is supported, is a far better guide than the second sentence. It makes the total plan of the composition clear.

1. THE MOST COMMON FORM OF THE SUPPORTED THESIS STATEMENT

Probably the most common form of the supported thesis statement is the one that *first states the subject and then presents the supports.* The supports are often introduced by words or expressions such as the following: *because, for, since, as, due to, by, in, in that.* A punctuation mark, the colon (:), may substitute for these words and serve the same purpose.

Examine the following:

1. Deems Taylor calls Richard Wagner a monster <u>because</u> Wagner was conceited, unstable, and selfish.
2. It makes sense to attend a community college, <u>for</u> the quality of instruction is high and the cost is low.
3. Two years in the army provided me with valuable experience, <u>as</u> there, for the first time, I learned the value of discipline, neatness, and respect for authority.
4. Christmas is an exhausting experience <u>due to</u> the extra energy and tension it inspires.
5. *The Forsyte Saga* is an outstanding television experience <u>in that</u> it is a good, old-fashioned story of an English family from 1879 to 1926, the many characters are all various and interesting, and the acting is superb.
6. The profession of law demands three important qualities of mind: the ability to analyze ideas, an interest in people, and patience with details.

EXERCISES

The following are unsupported thesis statements—that is, they contain no proof, evidence, or reasoning to support the position, belief, or point of view expressed. Try to develop them into thesis statements with two or three supports. Use the common forms just given—that is, make the supports *follow* the subject and introduce them with words such as those in the preceding examples or with the colon (:) punctuation mark.

1. The Surgeon General has determined that cigarette smoking is dangerous.
2. It makes sense to drive a compact car.
3. A career in nursing offers rewarding opportunities.
4. Writing a good composition can be an exhausting experience.
5. A good marriage depends on three important qualities in a couple.
6. Daytime television dramas are emotionally draining.
7. Men as well as women suffer from sexual stereotypes.
8. Four years of high school were (not) of great value to me.
9. Being a good police officer demands three important qualities of mind.
10. It is dangerous to be living in this world today.
11. A dictionary is a good book to study.
12. Tennis (football, baseball, and so on) is a challenging sport.
13. It is important to protect whales and other endangered species.
14. It makes sense to cook and eat at home.
15. A good vacation has three important ingredients.

2. OTHER FORMS OF THE SUPPORTED THESIS STATEMENT

The supports or breakdown of the subject sometimes precede it in the thesis statement for reasons of style or for the purpose of emphasis. Examine the following sentences, which illustrate the reverse order the thesis statement can take.

1. The bore, the brag, the flirt—these people typify most cocktail parties.
2. A grain of achievement, an avalanche of failure and frustration, and then the shroud of oblivion—these elements constitute the human condition.

3. To love, honor, and obey—these vows may be altered by circum-
    stances.
4. Hunger and poverty plague a great portion of the world today.

The thesis statement sometimes announces a composition that aims to compare or contrast two or more subjects. Such a sentence requires special consideration with respect to form. Examine the following sentences.

1. Mr. X is short, fat, and outgoing, whereas Mr. Y is tall, slim, and shy.
2. Mr. X and Mr. Y are similar in two ways: They are both rich, and they
    are both married to intelligent women.
3. Suburbanites tend to be conformists because they are similar in such
    ways as age, race, and politics, whereas city dwellers are less likely to
    conform due to their variety in these same matters.
4. Flying in an airplane is fast and noisy, whereas flying in a balloon is
    slow and quiet.

3. COPING WITH PROBLEMS IN WRITING THE SUPPORTED
THESIS STATEMENT

Having begun to practice the most common form of the supported thesis
statement, you may have met with some frustrating problems and wondered how
to cope with them. Indeed, a good thesis statement is a challenge to write for a
number of reasons, but with effort and practice, you should be able to master
the problems.

First, writing a supported thesis statement requires you to think through the
main points of your composition, points that are summed up in the thesis. It
should be easy to sum up the main points once you have actually written the
composition and know what it contains. If you have not written the composition
but are simply practicing the thesis statement to learn its form and to think
through the structure that it represents, then you are on less familiar ground. In
that case, you need to imagine what the composition might contain, what its main
points would be. Hopefully, you will know something about the subject from
your general experience and reading, and you will give it further thought as you
write about it. However, your practice thesis will necessarily be tentative or experimental. You might think of it the way scientists view a scientific hypothesis;
that is, as an experimental conclusion to be tested and proved either right or
wrong. Your instructor may ask you and your classmates to share some of your
practice thesis statements in class to see how well they hold up when examined

and discussed, to see how well they are written, and to pool suggestions from the group for possible improvement. Such workshop sessions can be very helpful, but they are sometimes frustrating as well. You might keep in mind that learning to write a supported thesis statement is a complex, not a simple, matter. It is a process that takes time, effort, and patience. It should prove well worth your energy, however, because it will teach you to think and to organize your thoughts.

Another challenge is to write the thesis statement so that the supporting points, though related, are not repeated or overlapping, two faults that you can recognize in the following examples.

> I avoid fast foods because they tend to be too salty, too high in calories, and too fattening.
> It makes sense to buy a compact car because the purchase price is reasonable, the operating cost is low, and it saves on gas.

In the first example the problem is repetition, in this case saying the same thing in different words. What appear to be three supports are really only two, the second idea stated twice in differently worded versions. In the second example the problem is that the second and third supports overlap. One support is a specific and the other is a general category in which the specific is contained, the cost of gas being a part of the general cost of operating a car. One way to avoid this flaw is to decide in advance of writing your thesis whether your supports should consist of *general categories* or *specifics*. (Besides the cost of gas, other specifics within the general category of operating expense might include lubrication, oil change, tires, and other such expenses.) Whether you organize your supports by categories or by specifics may depend a good deal on how full or rich the subject is or how much you know about it. If you have a lot to say about the cost of gas, for example, and about one or two other related specifics, you might make each of them a main support of your thesis. However, remember that you must develop each support with a full paragraph or more in the discussion part of your composition. Think about it. Could you write a well-developed paragraph on the cost of gas? If not, you need a broader topic; that is, a category with enough specifics to build a good discussion paragraph.

Like the topic sentence studied earlier in this book, the thesis statement needs to be clear and definite, not vague and ambiguous. Consider the following example.

Smoking should be banned in public places because it affects personal enjoyment and creates a safety hazard.

Exactly what is meant in the two supports is not clear. First, the word *affects* by itself is vague. The probable intent is that smoking has an *adverse* effect on someone or something that the words *personal enjoyment* do not make clear. Whose enjoyment of what needs to be spelled out. In addition, the words *safety hazard* are ambiguous. Do they refer to polluted air, fire, or something else? Be careful not to fall into the trap of thinking that you can explain later in the composition whatever the thesis does not make clear. Your readers cannot wait until the second page to understand what they are reading on the first page. You need to make yourself as clear as possible as you go along. The thesis statement must be especially clear. The preceding statement might be improved in a number of ways. Here is one possibility:

Smoking should be banned in public places because it violates the rights of nonsmokers to breathe smoke-free air and it creates a potential fire hazard.

You may discover that the demands of the thesis statement sometimes pull you in opposite directions at the same time. On the one hand, you should make the thesis as concise as you can. On the other, you may find that to make it clear and definite rather than vague and ambiguous requires additional words, as in the preceding example. The improved version added ten words to the original statement. However, it is improved because it is clearer and more definite, not because it is longer. Succinctness is still one of your objectives in writing a supported thesis statement. Say as much as you can, as clearly as you can, in as few words as possible. If these objectives try your patience by pulling you in two different directions at once, it may help to think of the thesis as a complex puzzle that needs to be solved very carefully.

Finally, as you work with the thesis statement, you may need to cope with mechanical problems; that is, problems with such matters as sentence structure, grammar, or punctuation. Among its other requirements, the thesis should be a good sentence. For example, the sentence structure should be *parallel*. In the following example, the structure is *not* parallel.

Jogging is a popular sport because it is good exercise and also for the scenery.

The first support in this thesis is a clause, *it is good exercise,* whereas the second support is a phrase (and not a very clear one), *for the scenery.* This difference in the structure of the two supports makes the sentence bumpy and unbalanced rather than smooth and even. To make the two supports line up better, both must be of the same construction; that is, corresponding words, phrases, or clauses are needed in both. (See p. 207 for another brief explanation of parallel structure.) The preceding thesis could be corrected in several ways. One of them is the following:

Jogging is a popular sport because it provides good exercise for the body and a stimulating variety of scenery for the mind.

For further guidance with other mechanical requirements of the thesis statement or any good sentence, refer to Appendix B, "Correction Symbols," in the back of this book. In addition, you may find Chapter 4, "Practicing the Topic Sentence," useful, for almost all of what is presented there also applies to the thesis statement.

EXERCISES

You will frequently need to formulate your thesis statements in response to questions or problems given by your instructors. The answers or solutions may not come to you easily in the form of good, clear, well-supported thesis statements. You may need to think and struggle over them. However, with effort you should manage to cope very well.

The following are questions or statements designed to give you practice in developing thesis statements in response to questions or problems such as you might meet in some of your college classes. Try to respond to them by writing thesis statements that are divided into two or three parts or supports. Generally you will want to use the most common form of the supported thesis statement, stating the subject first and then presenting the supports, but you may try out any of the forms you think appropriate. Study the following example, and then proceed to the exercises.

EXAMPLE

Question: What well-known person do you admire?
Answer: I admire Shirley Chisholm for her outspoken political independence and her defense of the women's movement.

1. Who should be the next president of the United States? Why?
2. Should children who have AIDS be permitted to attend public schools? Why or why not?
3. What are the primary benefits of a college or university education?
4. Is it good for parents to sacrifice for their children, or should parents look after their own interests first?
5. How do you account for the rise of sports figures as superstars?
6. Discuss the outstanding achievements of Frederick Douglas.

7. With which objectives of the women's movement do you agree or disagree?

8. What is the essence of soul food?

9. Is fidelity important or necessary in marriage?

10. Compare two presidents of the United States.

11. Give arguments for or against abortion.

12. Give arguments for or against divorce when there are young children involved.

13. Navajo weaving (rugs, blankets) is highly prized for many reasons. What are some of them?

14. What famous person, living or dead, do you admire and why?

15. What are the advantages or disadvantages of living in a small town, a city, or the country?

16. Which professional sport is most popular or well attended and why?

17. What does it mean to be poor?

18. What is your idea of an ideal job?

19. What importance do you place on the wilderness and wildlife?

20. If you could travel anywhere in the world, where would you most like to go and why?

21. What arguments can you present for or against marriage, for or against living with a person rather than being married to him or her?

22. Is the space program or the exploration of space important? Why or why not?

23. Is religious training important in the rearing of a child? Why or why not?

24. What do you know or think about the People's Republic of China, the Chinese culture, or the Chinese people?

25. Do you think homosexuals are sick or healthy people? Except for their sexual preferences, are they like or different from heterosexuals?

26. Should every college student be required to study a foreign language? Why or why not?

27. Do you believe or have any faith in astrology? Why or why not?

28. Should euthanasia be legalized? Why or why not?

29. What place has television in your life? Do you prefer watching it to reading a good book or conversing with people?

30. What is your view of the relocation of Japanese Americans during World War II?

31. Do you honor your mother and father? Why or why not?

32. Is there less racism in America now than there was ten years ago?

33. What job, profession, or career do you think holds the most prestige? Why?

34. What is your most difficult subject in college? Why?

35. Explain the popularity of a certain form of music, such as western, rock, or blues.

36. What is the finest sports car on the market today? Explain.

37. Do you have trouble trying to understand or make up your mind about a national or international situation, problem, or conflict? If so, about which situation or problem are you confused, and what is the nature of your confusion?

38. Are rodeos cruel to animals? Why or why not?

39. Which of your talents do you value the most and why?

40. Compare Martin Luther King, Jr. to Malcolm X.

41. What are either the accomplishments or the objectives of Cesar Chavez, leader of the United Farm Workers?

42. Do you think the current president of the United States is doing a good job? Why or why not?

43. What are your greatest fears or hopes about the future?

44. If you could live in some age other than your own, which would it be and why?

45. Women do most of the cooking at home, but most of the world's great chefs are men. True or false? Why or why not?

46. Now that the Equal Rights Amendment has been defeated, do you think the issue is dead and buried? Why or why not?

47. Which bills do you most dislike or resent having to pay? Why?

48. What is your most prized material possession and why do you value it?

49. Do you believe in any form of censorship? Why or why not?

50. What drugs do you approve or disapprove of and why?

SUMMARY

The main idea of your thesis statement should be divided into two or three parts or supports. The most common form of the supported thesis statement is that in which you first state the main idea or subject and then proceed to state the parts or supports of it. The supports are often introduced by such words as *because, as,* or *due to* or by a punctuation mark, the colon (:). Sometimes the order of the thesis statement is reversed, the supports preceding the main idea for reasons of style or for emphasis. Another form of the thesis statement is the one that announces a comparison or contrast of two or more subjects.

You will find that all forms of the supported thesis statement require effort and practice to be mastered because they demand careful thinking and organizing. The effort and practice should prove worthwhile, however, because the skill you will acquire will aid you greatly in all your college courses.

12

Organizing the Discussion

1. EVOLVE A PLAN

When you first consider a subject and think about writing a composition about it, you may not be sure exactly what direction you will want to take with it. If you are unfamiliar with the subject, you will feel especially hesitant. You will need to do some research, study and think about it, possibly discuss it with people who know the topic well. If you are already familiar with the subject, it will probably still require some thought and imagination, some mulling over, before a plan for your composition begins to evolve in your mind and on paper. You may need to plunge into a rough draft without a plan and muddle about for a time, writing this way and that, until a light begins to dawn and something worthwhile starts to take shape. Then you might be ready to sketch out your first, tentative thesis statement.

While you are in the rough draft stage, it might be well to think of your thesis, like every other aspect of your composition, as experimental. You may change your mind, try out different ideas, shift things around, even start over with a whole new approach. You may write several rough drafts before you are satisfied. However, once your direction is clear and your ideas and their development are firm, you should be ready to write your final draft. Your thesis statement will then become a fixed plan, an exact indication of the way the discussion is to be organized.

2. FOLLOW YOUR PLAN . . .

If you are in command of the thesis statement, you should have no trouble organizing the discussion. However, an inexperienced writer sometimes fails to see that there is a direct connection between the thesis and the discussion. He or she may write a beautiful thesis but then follow it with a discussion that is totally unrelated to it. Be sure that you do not make this mistake! You need to understand that the thesis statement announces the plan of the discussion. Do not plan one thing and then do another. Follow your plan!

3. EXACTLY!

The thesis statement gives an exact plan, and the discussion must *follow* it *exactly*. The thesis is divided into two to three parts or supports. These parts are restated in the discussion, becoming the topic sentences that begin the discussion paragraphs. The *order* of the thesis must also be maintained in the discussion. That is, the first part of the thesis becomes the first topic of the discussion. The second part is discussed next, and if there is a third part, it follows. The *wording* of the thesis is also approximated in the topic sentences of the discussion. The key words are the same, or for variety, synonyms or phrases meaning the same thing are used. The thesis statement sets up the basic structure of the discussion, and the discussion must not violate the thesis plan.

Examine Figure 12–1, which gives an overview of a whole composition based on a thesis statement that has three parts *(age, race,* and *politics)*. The composition in this case is five paragraphs long, beginning with an introductory paragraph (the thesis statement may or may not constitute the entire introduction) and ending with a concluding paragraph. Notice that the topic sentences of the three discussion paragraphs (only the topic sentences are given, not the entire paragraphs) duplicate the arrangement of the thesis statement. The order is the same, and the wording, with some slight variation, is close to that of the thesis. In other words, the discussion follows the thesis plan. The two are an unmistakable match.

4. THE PLAN IS THE SAME, REGARDLESS OF LENGTH

If the composition were longer, each part of the thesis might be discussed in more than a single paragraph, but the principle of order and wording would

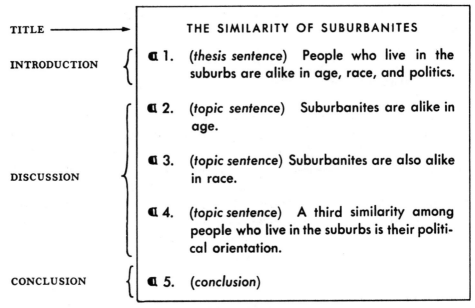

Figure 12–1

remain the same. Suppose each part of the thesis in the preceding illustration were to be discussed in two paragraphs instead of one. Then it would be necessary to break each part into two subparts. For instance, consider the first topic sentence, "Suburbanites are alike in age." This topic might be divided into two parts (and two topic sentences) as follows: "Suburban adults are alike in age." "Suburban children are also similar in age." The first of these sentences might open up the discussion of age, and the second could continue it in a second paragraph. After that, the discussion would take up the next topic given in the thesis. This, too, might be divided into two parts, and so with the third part of the thesis.

Notice the word *also* in the second of the two topic sentences, and be reminded of the need for transitional words to provide continuity (see Chapter 5) within the paragraph and between paragraphs. A well-organized discussion does not lose its reader along the way. It does everything possible to guide the reader. You need to signal your reader (see p. 137) when you are continuing in the same direction or changing direction in your discussion. Point the way so that your reader can follow you.

5. WEIGHT OR LENGTH OF EACH PART DEPENDS ON THE THESIS

Ordinarily equal weight or length of discussion is given to each part of the thesis statement. In the illustration on the subject of suburbanites, for example, the three parts of the thesis (age, race, and politics) would be discussed at the same length—a paragraph of approximately the same length for each or two or three paragraphs for each. Nothing in the thesis suggests that one part is to be given more emphasis than another, and thus the discussion must treat each of the three equally.

It is also possible for the discussion to emphasize one part of the thesis more than another *if* that is what the thesis statement indicates the discussion will do. Remember, thesis and discussion must match! Suppose the thesis in the illustration on suburbanites were changed, for example, as follows:

People who live in the suburbs are alike in age, race, and especially in politics.

Now the thesis draws special attention to the last of its three parts, and therefore that part must be discussed more fully than the other two. The thesis might be changed in still another (and perhaps more current) way as follows:

People who live in the suburbs are more alike in age and politics than they are in race.

Now the thesis suggests greater similarity in the first two parts than it does in the third, and the discussion must follow accordingly. The most important point to remember about the relationship between the thesis statement and the discussion is that they must match. One (the thesis) announces the other (the discussion).

EXERCISES

The exercises that follow are designed to give you practice in organizing a discussion. Select a number of the following thesis statements, and for each one write the topic sentences that might begin each paragraph of the discussion. Notice that some of the thesis statements are divided into two parts and some contain three parts. Write your topic sentences accordingly. Take care that your topic sentences match the order and approximate the wording of the thesis statement. The key words should be the same or, for variety, synonyms or phrases meaning the same thing may be used. Remember to use transitional words where needed. Use the following example to guide you.

EXAMPLE

(THESIS) People who live in the suburbs are alike in age, race, and politics.

(TOPIC SENTENCES) Suburbanites are alike in age.
Suburbanites are also alike in race.
A third similarity among people who live in the suburbs is their political orientation.

1. Cultivating a vegetable garden has three important benefits: it requires needed exercise, it produces fresh and nourishing food, and it saves money.
2. Jogging is good for both the body and the mind.
3. Children can be a headache when they are noisy, demanding, and destructive.
4. The Guessa is a fine automobile because the body is well designed, the motor is powerful, and the car is economical to operate.
5. The word *discrimination* has a positive as well as a negative meaning.
6. Poetry can be classified into three types: narrative, dramatic, and lyric.
7. Wilderness is needed in Alaska to preserve the polar bear and the caribou.
8. A good composition is well organized, well developed and imaginative.
9. Three of my favorite comics are "Fred Basset," "Gordo," and "Doonesbury."
10. The excitement of the auction was due to the quality of the merchandise, the talent of the auctioneer, and the competitiveness of the bidders.
11. The female praying mantis is a remarkable creature that has five eyes, turns from green to brown as leaves do, and eats her spouse after mating with him.
12. Navajo rugs from the Two Gray Hills area are very finely woven and very expensive.
13. Television performs three important services: it entertains, it instructs, and it induces sleep.
14. Women are still struggling for rights and opportunities equal to those enjoyed by men.

15. Three of the most intelligent mammals of the ocean are also the most abused: the whale, the porpoise, and the dolphin.

6. DEVELOPMENT WITHIN THE PARAGRAPH MUST STAY ON COURSE

Keep in mind that while the thesis statement plots the course of the discussion, and the topic sentence of each paragraph holds that direction, the development within the paragraphs must also stay on course! It is not enough for the structure to be trim and in perfect order. The development of the discussion paragraphs must give that frame support and stiffening. Remember that each paragraph must contain no more than one central idea and must have unity. (See pp. 23–26.) Stick to the subject! Do not be distracted by interesting but unrelated ideas. Just as the topic sentences must follow the thesis plan, so the development of the discussion paragraphs must follow the topic sentences.

SUMMARY

Organizing the discussion is a matter of following the thesis statement, which announces the plan of the discussion. The parts or supports of the thesis statement determine the content, the order, and the approximate wording of the topic sentences that begin the paragraphs of the discussion. The topic sentences, in turn, indicate the organization of the paragraphs.

13

Developing the Discussion

1. IS ANYBODY LISTENING?

Think about the meaning of the word *discussion*. When the word is applied to speaking rather than writing, it means two people or a group of people talking about or exchanging ideas about a given subject. In writing, of course, only one person does the "talking," but it is important to keep in mind that another person, your reader, is "listening." Your reader, furthermore, is an *active*, not a passive listener. In her mind she is constantly putting questions to your discussion. She asks such questions as "What do you mean by that?" and "What is your proof?" Your reader also has ideas of her own. She has been around, lived life, and been exposed to the kinds of issues or ideas you are likely to discuss. Possibly she knows quite a bit about your topic. She waits to see in your discussion how much you know and have thought about. If you disappoint her, she calls to you from the margin of your paper, "Develop!"

2. THINK ABOUT YOUR READER

Prepare your discussion with your reader in mind. Think about your reader as you write. Imagine that you are speaking to a live person who is also a friendly stranger. He wants to know what you mean, but he doesn't know you well enough to guess your meaning. You have to spell it out for him. *Say* what you mean. Your reader is also not easily convinced. He hangs back. He has doubts. He thinks of counterarguments. He waits to be impressed. He wants you to succeed, but he wants you to work at it, to make your discussion compelling, convincing, complete. Nothing is as frustrating to your reader as a promising discussion that doesn't deliver, that goes nowhere, or that dabbles where it ought to dig into a subject. Nothing is as pleasing to your reader as a discussion that fulfills its promises and realizes its potentialities. You can make your reader your adversary or your ally, depending on how well you develop your discussion.

3. WHAT DOES IT MEAN TO DEVELOP?

The word *develop* means to explain more clearly or fully, to enlarge on, to elaborate on, and to bring out the possibilities of a topic or to make it better known. In photography, the word means to make a picture visible. It is easy to apply this meaning to writing. An undeveloped discussion is like exposed but undeveloped film. Both have potentialities, but the possibilities of both lurk in the murk. Only through the process of development do they both gradually become clearer and clearer until they are finally sharp and vivid.

4. STUDY EXAMPLES

Following are examples of undeveloped discussion paragraphs and their improved, more fully developed versions. Notice that although the first paragraph in each set of two is shorter than the second, insufficient *length* is not its only or even its most important problem. Making a paragraph longer may or may not make it better, as a long paragraph may be as unclear or as unconvincing as a short one, if not more so.

The following three sets of paragraphs illustrate three different problems and their solutions. In the first paragraph that follows (A^1), the discussion does not satisfy the reader's need to know exactly what the writer means. The "picture" is murky rather than clear. As you read the paragraph, think about what is missing or what needs to be developed to satisfy the reader's question: *What do you mean by that?*

A¹ Another reason some people collect early California paintings is to satisfy their nostalgia. They want to see California as it once was or as they remember it. So much has changed that it is difficult to imagine the state as it was before it became so heavily developed and populated. However, early California paintings clarify this vision of the past and satisfy the longing of some people to return to it.

A² Another reason some people collect early California paintings is to satisfy their nostalgia. They want to see California as it once was or as they remember it. For example, they may want to visualize Yosemite when it was inhabited by Indians before it became the white man's park. They may want to see Spanish missions such as Santa Barbara or San Juan Bautista as they once were or other early settlements such as Fort Ross when it was occupied by Russian fur traders. San Francisco Bay with the old sailing ships in it or the Golden Gate before the bridge was built may hold a fascination. People may want to see San Jose when it was a sleepy little town or Berkeley when it was rolling hills and only a few farms. So much has changed that it is difficult to imagine the state as it was before it became so heavily developed and populated. However, early California paintings clarify this vision of the past and satisfy the longing of some people to return to it.

The second paragraph is clearer than the first in satisfying the reader's need to know exactly what the writer means. The examples of what some early California paintings depict help the reader understand the exact nature of the collector's nostalgia and specifically what he or she looks for and enjoys in these paintings. The subject is not so vague as it is in the first paragraph, becoming sharper and more vivid through example.

In the next paragraph the problem is not only being clear but being convincing. The first paragraph that follows makes claims but does not support them with evidence. As you read the paragraph, think about what is needed to satisfy the question: *What is your proof?*

B¹ Life—or death—looks truly absurd at times. A person may live his life very reasonably, taking few chances, yet he may be killed by an impulsive madman. On the other hand, a person may live quite dangerously, taking great risks, fighting in a war, perhaps, or simply overexposing himself to hazard or possible accident, yet he may die under the most innocuous circumstances. Life is not reasonable or rational. Living or dying often means confronting the absurd.

B² Life—or death—looks truly absurd at times. A person may live his life very reasonably, taking few chances, yet he may be killed by an impulsive madman. To illustrate, recently eight people were minding their own business, working in a Miami machine shop, when a disgruntled customer walked in and, without warning, blasted them into oblivion with a shotgun. The victims were ordinary people doing their daily work, and there was no way they could have anticipated the disaster or protected themselves. According to police, the killer "just went nuts." On the other hand, a person may live quite dangerously, taking great risks, fighting in a war, perhaps, or simply overexposing himself to hazard or possible accident, yet he may die under the most innocuous circumstances. The classic example is Albert Camus, the French writer who had also been active in the Resistance movement during World War II. He was working in the theater when he was killed in an automobile accident after he decided at the last moment not to take the train but to return to Paris in a friend's car instead. In his pocket was found his unused railway ticket. Just as unreasonable and ironic is the recent death of Calvin Simmons, the young conductor of the Oakland Symphony Orchestra. Resting from a strenuous schedule, he took a canoe out on a quiet pond in upstate New York. Although he was an experienced canoeist and had been to that pond many times before, his canoe overturned and he drowned. A young woman camping along the pond had got out her camera to record the peaceful, twilight scene of the man in his canoe; instead, she witnessed his demise. With a brilliant career already established, an international reputation on the way, Simmons must have experienced numerous close calls as he traveled the world by plane, train, and car to keep up his frantic pace. Yet he died at thirty-two in a quiet pond in the wilderness. Thus, life is not reasonable or rational. Living or dying often means confronting the absurd.

The second paragraph, unlike the first, presents evidence to support its claims. Because it supports and proves what it claims, it is more convincing and believable than the first. Keep in mind that it is not very meaningful to fill a discussion with unsupported or unsubstantiated statements. You need to prove them with evidence, example, and further explanation to make them meaningful and convincing.

In the first paragraph that follows, evidence is needed not only to support the topic but to permit the reader to *participate* in the experience the writer has had. As you may see, the writer has left the heart out of the paragraph, for there is little indication of what has *caused* the intense reaction described at the end of the paragraph. Therefore, the experience is difficult for the reader to feel and understand.

C¹ One of my most frightening experiences occurred one summer on a two-lane highway in the Sierra mountains when I was driving back from Pinecrest Lake to the Bay Area. My friend Shirley and I had met Jim, a friend of hers, and two other young men at the lake, and we all enjoyed the lake together, as well as the discovery that the cars Jim and I drove were almost identical. When it was time to go home, we all decided that our twin convertible Fords should not be separated, so we followed each other down the mountains at a rather rapid pace, Shirley riding in Jim's car ahead of mine, one of the other men riding with me. With tops down, radios blaring, we spun turns as if we were immortal, laughing and making signs to each other from car to car. There was a sharp bend in the road at one point, where I lost sight of Jim's car. Then suddenly, going much too fast to stop, I discovered his car stopped in the road ahead of me. The next thing I knew was that I had got around Jim's car and was ahead of it, stopped and shaking while the others marveled at my maneuver that may have saved our lives.

C² One of my most frightening experiences occurred one summer on a two-lane highway in the Sierra mountains when I was driving back from Pinecrest Lake to the Bay Area. My friend Shirley and I had met Jim, a friend of hers, and two other young men at the lake, and we all enjoyed the lake together as well as the discovery that the cars Jim and I drove were almost identical. When it was time to go home, we all decided that our twin convertible Fords should not be separated, so we followed each other down the mountains at a rather rapid pace, Shirley riding in Jim's car ahead of mine, one of the other men riding with me. With tops down, radios blaring, we spun turns as if we were immortal, laughing and making signs to each other from car to car. There was a sharp bend in the road at one point, when I lost sight of Jim's car. Then suddenly, going much too fast to stop, I discovered his car stopped in the road ahead of me. The three in the car ahead turned in horror at what was about to happen, but then I spotted a trail winding up an embankment and around a tree just in back and to the right of them. It looked like an impossible route, for the bank could easily flip my convertible over, or I might just as easily run into the tree, but I had to try. Up we went, my companion turning green as he hung on, my concentration divided into too many parts: alternating gas and brake; turning the wheel; returning, while dirt kicked up and flew all over us; the tree scratching my car, our faces and arms. Then we skidded past the tree and miraculously bounded our way back down to the highway again, ahead of the car we had been following. I stopped my car, but I could not stop shaking while Shirley and Jim told about the traffic tieup that had blocked them. My passenger was speechless, but the others marveled at my maneuver that may have saved our lives.

The second paragraph, unlike the first, explains the *cause* of the reaction with which the paragraph ends, supplying the details needed to permit the reader to participate in the experience the writer has had, to follow the action and feel the terror of the near catastrophe. After reading the paragraph, the reader can say, "I see what you mean."

In developing your discussion paragraphs, keep in mind the reader's questions:

1. What do you mean by that?
2. What is your proof?

To these questions, another should be added:

3. How can I participate?

Make your meaning clear to your reader through explanation and example, using synonyms when needed. Support and prove your statements with evidence that is convincing. In addition, permit your reader to participate in experiences you relate, to feel and understand them, by explaining the causes, not just the results, of your reactions.

5. DO NOT SIMPLY MAKE THE DISCUSSION LONGER

As mentioned earlier, developing a discussion is not simply a matter of making it longer. In fact, it is possible to make your discussion deadly dull by laboring it—that is, by overworking it with seemingly endless development. Closely related to this problem are those of being wordy and repetitious, also to be avoided. As you develop your discussion, check to see that you are really advancing it and making it more meaningful, not simply making it drag on and on. When you have made your point, stop!

6. KNOW YOUR SUBJECT

A weak or poorly developed discussion is usually one that is vague, too general, and/or not illustrated. It views its subject from too great a distance, with uncertainty, seeing it as a dim lump or an indefinite blur. It may be that the writer does not know enough about the subject to write about it at all, much less with the particularity that is called for in a good discussion. Be sure you *know your subject*! A good writer always writes from experience, or acquires the experience that is necessary for good writing. If you have trouble developing your discussion, make sure the problem is not that you need to make a trip to the library or wherever it would be appropriate to go to learn what you need to know before you can write about it.

EXERCISES

The exercises that follow, like the original, rather than the revised and developed examples in this chapter (see pp. 162–164)—are undernourished paragraphs that need revision and development. As you consider them, think about the reader's questions: (1) What do you mean by that? (2) What is your proof? (3) How can I participate? These questions should help to guide you to the necessary corrections or developments. You may decide that the following paragraphs need revision in one or more of these ways:

1. The exact meaning may be unclear. The paragraph may call for examples to clarify meaning and explanation and the use of synonyms to clarify certain words or terms.
2. The paragraph may be unconvincing or lack proof. It may call for evidence to support its claims. Explanation and example may be needed to make statements meaningful and believable.
3. The discussion, by presenting only the result and not the cause of something, may make it difficult or impossible for the reader to participate in, feel, or understand the subject. The paragraph may call for detailing the action or event that produced the reaction given in the discussion. Such a paragraph will call for you to make up or invent a "story" in which the reader can participate so that he or she can feel and understand what is said in the paragraph.
4. The paragraph may simply be too brief and call for further development in one or more of the ways previously suggested.

You will see that the subject matter of all the paragraphs that follow is relatively simple, so that no specialized knowledge is required to develop them. Consequently, you are called on to use your imagination as well as your reasoning ability to invent the development needed. Select a number of the following exercises and repair and develop them as you think necessary.

The dots (•) in the exercises indicate the points at which revision or development is appropriate, though you may be selective and not wish to develop every point. There is no need to change existing sentences, only to supply what is missing or needed.

1. Sometimes I feel sure that my dog is my best friend. We are perfect companions. She understands me, and I understand her.• We get along well

together, and we like a lot of the same things.• When I feel unloved by people, I am grateful for my dog, my friend who never deserts me.

2. *Star Wars* is one of the best movies I have ever seen. The action is exciting, and the special effects are fabulous.• The characters are good, too.• I liked the robots especially.• *Star Wars* lives up to its billing. It is a fantastic space-age odyssey nobody should miss.

3. English is my hardest class this semester, which doesn't surprise me. I've never been good in English, not even in high school, where it was a lot easier than it is in college.• I have trouble especially with compositions.• I just can't write. My instructor says I could be good if I tried, but I'm not interested, I guess.

4. Marijuana should be legalized because it is a benevolent drug. It makes people feel good.• It does not make them nasty the way alcohol does.• It does not have the bad aftereffects, either.• It is hard to understand why some people oppose the legalization of marijuana.

5. Teenagers are crazy about most video games, though they like some better than others.• These favorites are fascinating for reasons many older people do not understand.• Parents worry and wonder about the powerful grip video games have on their kids.

6. Barbara is a very blunt person. She is not afraid to speak her mind.• Sometimes she is so frank that I wonder how she keeps her friends.• Barbara calls her behavior being honest. I call it Barbara Blunt.

7. If disco dancing is on the way out, one may speculate about what the next rage will be. It might be something fast or slow.• It might be something complicated or very simple.• No doubt people will keep dancing!

8. My boss is difficult to get along with. She takes her job too seriously, and she treats the workers under her very badly.• Several of them have quit in the last few months because of her.• I'd like to quit and be done with her, too, but I can't afford to.

9. He was a loner, which was surprising because he had a lot of charm. When he told me what had happened to him, however, I understood his caution with people. He had been badly hurt as a teenager.• It was difficult for him to forget a hurt like that.

10. The trouble with many young people today is that they are lazy. They don't want to work.• They want money, but they don't want to earn it.• They want an easy life.• Young people used to have to work for a living. Now they play and get paid for it.

11. The divorce was a relief because the marriage had been a tragedy. They were not a perfect match to begin with.• They were very different kinds of people.• He was also unfaithful to her.• Then she became a nag.• He grew

insulting.● The children became nervous and neurotic.● The divorce made all concerned feel reborn.

12. Disneyland attracts people of all ages, not just children. There is much to see at Disneyland and many activities that can be enjoyed by everyone.● It is no wonder the place is popular.

13. Housework is a dubious challenge to every homemaker. It is an accomplishment to be proud of when he or she manages to keep an orderly and smoothly running home, but the everyday task of doing it is hardly romantic.● The job requires fortitude as much as finesse.

14. Mildred is worn and weary. She has worked hard all her life, often doing incredibly difficult and draining labor.● She deserves a rest. Mildred has more than earned her retirement benefits.

15. A sports car is a must for anyone who wants top performance in an automobile. A sports car is superior to a standard or compact car in every way.● No other type of car performs as well as a sports car.

SUMMARY

It is important to think about your reader as well as your subject as you develop your discussion. To make your discussion clear and convincing, keep in mind the reader's questions, "What do you mean by that?" and "What is your proof?" To permit your reader to follow and feel experiences you relate, remember a third question, "How can I participate?" and supply the details needed of actions or events, not simply your reactions to them, so that the reader can understand them. Be careful to clarify general statements and to support them with specific explanation and example. Know your subject, and develop your discussion of it so that it fulfills its promises and realizes its potentialities.

14

Introducing and Concluding the Short Composition

Introductory and concluding paragraphs are special and different from discussion paragraphs. First of all, they are relatively short. The introduction may consist simply of one sentence, the thesis, although stated by itself without some preparation, the thesis may strike readers somewhat like a plunge into cold water. The composition may conclude even more abruptly with the final sentence of the last discussion paragraph, but the suddenness of such an ending can be unsettling. Instead of causing readers to reflect on the composition as a whole, such an ending may prompt them to see if the ink is dry or to search for a missing page. These extremes are not the desired goals of either the introduction or the conclusion, but brevity is. Three to five sentences, approximately, should suffice for both in a short composition.

Another way introductory and concluding paragraphs differ from discussion paragraphs is in their tendency to make general rather than specific statements or to typify rather than specify, as may be the case with a sample "teaser" or anecdote leading to the thesis sentence. The introduction approaches the subject of the composition and declares what it *will be,* but the subject *is not* discussed at that point except in the most general terms. The conclusion performs a similar function, only in reverse. Standing back from the subject, the conclusion indicates what it *has been,* and although the conclusion may make a final comment on the subject, it contains no further specific discussion of it. Such specific or concrete discussion is the task of the discussion paragraphs exclusively.

Finally, as already suggested, introductory and concluding paragraphs differ from discussion paragraphs in purpose or function. The purpose of the introduction is to prepare readers for the subject, to engage their interest in it if possible, to explain it if necessary, and then to lead to the discussion of it. The purpose of the conclusion is to bring the discussion to a close, to summarize it briefly if necessary, to give its point in a culminating statement if possible, and to leave readers reflective and satisfied.

1. HOW IS THE INTRODUCTION ORGANIZED?

Organize your introduction as follows:

1. Write an opening sentence or two to attract readers' attention and to focus their interest on the thesis or subject matter of the composition.
2. If necessary, write a sentence or two, either before the thesis or after it, to give background on the subject, to set the limits of the discussion, or to clarify the meaning of the key words to be used.
3. Write your thesis sentence.

2. HOW IS THE CONCLUSION ORGANIZED?

Organize your conclusion as follows:

1. Make a general statement (a sentence or two) about the subject that will signal for readers a shift in focus from discussion to conclusion.
2. Write a sentence or two that summarizes or touches on the main points of the discussion.
3. If possible, end with a culminating sentence or one that gives special emphasis to the discussion.

3. CONSIDER SOME INTRODUCTORY TECHNIQUES

Keep in mind that the main objective of an introduction is to be clear and concise, and that the most vital part of the introduction is the thesis statement, you may find it helpful to consider some common techniques for writing introductions. These methods may lessen the problem of how to get started and give your introductions greater smoothness, variety, and interest. Of course, you must remember that your subject matter or approach to it determines which of these techniques is most valuable or appropriate. Be sure that your introductory state-ments are always *to the point of your thesis;* that is, that they are in keeping with both the content and mood of your subject. Be selective in your use of them. Among these techniques are the following:

A. Dramatize or present part of an anecdote.   A vigorous way to begin your introduction may be to present a brief, dramatic scene or part of an inter-esting or humorous story, as in the introductions on pages 175, 188, and 193. In the opening two to three sentences of your introduction, it is impossible for you to tell very much about anything, much less a complete story, but you can present a representative part of it if you plan it carefully. The part might consist of a momentary glimpse of someone or something you will discuss later in your com-position but wish to characterize beforehand, or it might be a highlight or pre-view of an incident you will present in a more complete form in your discussion.

B. Begin with a quotation.   You may find a statement in such sources as plays, novels, short stories, poems, songs, newspapers, and magazines (some-times even in textbooks) that you think captures or sums up an idea better than you can. The statement, properly acknowledged and set within quotation marks, may get your composition off to a good start. Be careful that the quotation is not too long, however. If it seems to be, consider using only part of it. A long quo-tation tends to drag down a composition, especially in an introduction, which should be as lively as possible. Moreover, your readers want to hear from you early in your introduction. Hence, you should follow the quotation with your own words, making your use of it obvious. For examples of introductions using quotations, turn to pages 183 and 190.

C. Surprise with an unexpected point of view.   One way to grab readers' attention is to begin your introduction with a point of view they do not expect or to contradict what you think they assume as true or right. Such an approach may catch your readers off guard and make them sit up and take notice. Be sure you startle your readers with cause, however, and know what you are about, because you are obliged to make your unusual point of view meaningful, not just surprising. For examples of such introductions, turn to page 177.

D. Begin with a question.   A rhetorical question is one to which no answer is expected or to which only one answer may be made—in this case, the answer presented in the thesis statement. The rhetorical question is a device to attract reader participation; that is, to engage readers in thinking actively about the question asked before they are led to the writer's conclusion stated in the thesis statement. It is a somewhat worn technique that should be used with discretion. In other words, if you decide to begin your introduction with a question, make it a good one. You will find an example of this device in the introduction on page 196.

E. Build background.   Sometimes the most forceful way to lead to the the-sis sentence is to present background information in a series of statements that steadily build toward and strengthen the thesis. This method is particularly effective because it involves readers in the subject right from the beginning and continues to develop their interest until the climactic presentation of the thesis at the end of the introductory paragraph. This is perhaps one of the more difficult techniques because it calls for considerable knowledge of or experience with the subject, as well as sensitivity and skill in building the paragraph with increasing intensity. It is quite a rewarding challenge, however. For an example, see pages 179 and 181.

F. Combine these techniques or simplify them.   These introductory techniques are sometimes combined and can also be simplified. For instance, an anecdote can include a quotation (to be distinguished from dialogue, also set within quotation marks), or a rhetorical question may precede a surprise point of view. A dramatic scene can be simplified (not without losing some luster, however) by summing it up in a sentence rather than showing it acted out. Background information can also be shortened. As you practice writing introductions, experiment to see what works best for you.

4. MAKE THE CONCLUSION SHORT AND SIMPLE

You are essentially finished by the time you reach your conclusion, but if your discussion has been successful, it has gathered a momentum that needs to be slowed down before it is stopped. Your readers, who have been propelled along by your discussion, need a chance to shift gears, take a backward glance, and then come to a rest. This process is not complicated, however, and should not be dragged out. Therefore, make your conclusion short and simple.

Study the conclusions in the model composition in Chapter 15 and notice how they are constructed. First, a general statement about the subject is made, to signal readers to shift their perspective from the specifics of the preceding discussion to the subject or discussion as a whole. This statement is usually followed by a sentence that touches on the main points of the discussion (which are taken from the thesis) or that summarizes them. Finally, there may be a closing statement for special emphasis. The composition should not end abruptly or fade away. The end should come naturally, the main purpose completed, the final statement made.

ABOUT EXERCISES

There are no exercises as such in this chapter, although you are free to practice the structure and techniques suggested here. You should realize, however, that whereas the organization remains about the same in the introductions and conclusions you are likely to write, the techniques that govern content will vary considerably and will be determined by your *subject* and your *approach* to it.

Therefore, you should think about and practice these beginnings and endings in relation to the composition as a whole. As you proceed through Chapter 15, you may want to turn back to this one from time to time for guidance.

SUMMARY

Introductory and concluding paragraphs differ from discussion paragraphs in their brevity, in their need to typify or generalize, and in their purpose. They should be carefully organized to serve their purpose. There are a number of introductory techniques that can be used, depending on subject and approach, and they must always be to the point of the thesis. Conclusions also vary but should be kept short and simple.

15

Practicing the Short Composition

The main purpose of the model compositions that follow is to guide the structure, or organization, of your own compositions. However, the following examples may be helpful in other ways as well. They may irritate or soothe you with their subject matter. They may stimulate you to think. They may suggest ways in which you can develop as well as structure your own ideas. If the models are successful, you should do quite well without them before long.

EXERCISE 31. WRITE A PORTRAIT OF A RELATIVE

Write a composition in which you present a verbal picture of one of your relatives. (You might repeat this exercise using a friend or a fictional character as the subject.) Your portrait might concentrate on aspects of your relative's personality or on his or her physical appearance, or on both. Because this composition, your first, is not expected to be very long or complex, you will need to be selective, limiting yourself to only the most outstanding aspects of your relative.

Make your composition about the length of the following example, which is four paragraphs long. The first paragraph is a brief introduction that terminates with the thesis statement. Divide your thesis into *two* parts or supports. Discuss the first part in the second paragraph of your composition; discuss the second part in the third paragraph. The final paragraph is a brief conclusion.

Be careful to use the verb tenses that are appropriate to your subject. If your relative is living, use present tenses. If your relative is deceased, as in the following example, past tenses are called for.

EXAMPLE

MY FATHER

"I hate the bloody stuff," my father used to say, tossing down straight shots of whiskey. "Ah . . ." Once he had conquered the agony of getting it down, he glowed with the pleasure of it. His response to life was a little like his reaction to whiskey, which he hated and loved. (THESIS STATEMENT) My father had a mercurial Irish personality, and his facial features could be just as changeable.

My father was Irish in the extreme and abrupt changeability of his moods. In the middle of intense anger, he could break himself up laughing. Once when I had driven a seven-inch spike, on which I had planned to hang my saddle, completely through the side of our garage, through the wall, the outside stucco and all, with the point of the nail glaring at my father from the outside, he flew into one of his rages. ". . . ! . . .!" he screamed, "don't you know you should hammer a nail into the studs, not into the siding? And why in hell did you use such a big nail?" I stood there, sheepishly, taking my "what-for" from my father, when suddenly he burst into laughter, covering his mouth with his hands as he always did with a big laugh. He finally said, "How in hell did you do it?" True, I was only nine years old at the time, and I had worked very hard banging at that big nail before I got it through the wall. Though what I had done had made him mad, my father could also appreciate my effort.

Besides being quick in altering his moods, my father could also make dynamic changes in his facial expression. He had very thick and very long eyebrows that, together with his dark eyes, probably said as much or more than any other part of his bony face and body. When he was mad, his eyebrows whipped about and then lowered so that his eyes almost disappeared except for the fire that I could see or feel was in them. That was the look that sent dogs under chairs and children running for cover. Even adults backed off, giving my father the widest possible berth. When he was joyous or sentimental in song (he could not sing; he knew it, but he tried anyway), his eyebrows would lift into an arch above his nose. At the top of the arch, they pointed heavenward, like a steeple, and under the steeple, his eyes glowed multicolored, like the windows of a fine old church.

These memories of my father go back many years, but time has sharpened rather than dimmed the most outstanding aspects of his personality and face that I remember. If he were alive today, I'm sure my father would look at this portrait and say, "I'm damned if that isn't me!"

Suggested topics: father; mother; brother; sister; uncle; aunt; grandfather or grandmother; cousin; husband; wife; son; daughter; in-law. (Remember to limit your portrait to only a few or the most outstanding aspects of your relative's personality and/or physical features.)

EXERCISE 32. EXPLAIN WHAT YOU ADMIRE ABOUT A FRIEND

Write a composition in which you explain two or three of the qualities you admire in a close friend. Although it is somewhat like Exercise 31, this one differs in its focus. Here you are asked not only to describe your friend, but to make clear that you are praising him or her for the characteristics that you describe. This process is called a *eulogy*, which is a tribute to someone's virtues or achievements.

Present the qualities or characteristics of your friend in a thesis divided into *two* or *three* parts or supports. Each of the parts of the thesis should be developed into a paragraph of the discussion. In addition, write a brief introduction and conclusion. Use the following example as a guide.

EXAMPLE

MY FRIEND ANNE

She doesn't go out of her way for most people: she almost never gives a party, she rarely invites people to dinner, she seldom calls anyone on the telephone. Most people tend to bore her. Is she an unhappy, maladjusted recluse? Quite on the contrary; people are attracted to her because she is so well adjusted. (Thesis Statement) I admire my friend Anne Perry because she is self-assured and discriminating.

Unlike some people I know, Anne has confidence in herself. She is not plagued with insecurity and self-doubt. Some people carry little monsters in their heads that tell them, "You're no good. Don't try to dress well; you have no taste. Don't go to that elegant restaurant, the waiter will snub you. Don't try to meet that important person; you're not interesting. Stay in your hole and hang your head." Not so with Anne. A happy little troll lives in her head, and it says, "Hi, sweetie, glad you're here. What can I offer you? Make yourself at home!" On the other hand, Anne is not so self-assured that she is arrogant, but she likes herself. As a result, it is a pleasure to be with her. She relaxes people because she does not lean on them neurotically for support. Her faith in herself is contagious. Her self-possession inspires others to be like her, and her appreciation of her life spills over to her friends.

Being confident probably helps Anne to be discriminating. She sees no reason to settle for second best, and she hardly ever does. Why spend an evening with boring people just to be with people? Why not spend an interesting evening at home alone? Why go to a bad play or sit in a bad seat to see a good one? Instead, wait for a good play and save money, if need be, to sit in a good seat. These are the choices Anne makes. She prefers old friends to strangers or mere acquaintances, and she will do just about anything for her friends—short of making dinner for them, which she does rarely because she wants to do it well or not at all. As infrequent as her invitations are, they are highly prized because she is a gourmet cook. Few people I know are as discriminating as Anne is, and I admire her for her insight and her taste. She knows that life is precious, and because she is selective, she makes the most of it.

Anne is aware that some people call her a snob, but those who know her well respect her for her confident and discriminating personality. As a result, the few who are chosen are honored to be her friends.

Suggested topics: virtues such as being thoughtful or considerate, fun or funny, wise or witty, clever, creative, conscientious, honest, a good listener, talented or entertaining, helpful, loyal, a good critic, supportive, patient, understanding, a hard worker, a good sport, fair; achievements such as being a good athlete, student, salesperson, teacher, painter or sculptor, driver, musician, writer, cook, model, dresser, housekeeper, parent, gardener, dancer.

EXERCISE 33. DISCUSS SOMETHING YOU DISLIKE

Write a composition in which you present two or three reasons you dislike something *or* in which you present two or three things you dislike, as in the example that follows. If you choose to do the latter, be sure the things you write about are closely related; for instance, two sounds or noises, as in the example. This exercise contrasts with the preceding one; however, you may or may not write about a person here. Your objective is to focus on something, an object or experience, that irritates, offends, embarrasses, or angers you. Think about what is generally true for you rather than a single event you have experienced. Be sure to note the list of suggested topics following the example.

Divide your thesis into *two* or *three* parts or supports. Develop each part into a paragraph of discussion in which you explain and illustrate your meaning in some detail. Also write a brief introduction and conclusion. Use the following example as a guide.

EXAMPLE

TWO HATEFUL NOISEMAKERS

The world is becoming a painfully noisy place. Lately even my relatively peaceful neighborhood has turned to bedlam with the sounds of construction. Houses being built require the work of bulldozers and other heavy equipment, huge trucks to haul dirt downhill, others to struggle slowly uphill with concrete. Some trucks spend much of the day in reverse, it seems, repeating a high, piercing, electronic signal. These and other harsh sounds that have lessened the quality of life in the vicinity make me think about the noisemakers I like least in all the world. (THESIS STATEMENT) Among them, two of the most hateful are the chain saw and the leaf blower.

The chain saw makes an ugly sound, partly because of what it does. When I hear one at work, I have a horrible fantasy of the parched earth being covered over with astroturf as yet another tree is denuded and then cut down. "The damned thing blocks my view," I can hear a neighbor say to the man who will spike his way up the pine. The tree man whines away to the top, and great limbs fall, while another man below drags them off to the grinder where they are processed into little bits. The trunk is bare after a few hours and looks pathetic with its short stumps where the branches had been, and then the trunk is dropped, slab by slab. Throughout this transformation, the chain saw works in furious spurts, sometimes wailing to a high pitch, sometimes choking up, getting snagged, stopping abruptly. For a moment my ears almost ring with the quiet, but the relief is brief, the racket resumes, the saw snarling and spitting the poor pine into oblivion. I wait for the chain saw to go away, eventually, but it never does. It simply moves around, sometimes off in the distance, sometimes nearer, always somewhere, like an insistent, buzzing insect I cannot wave away.

Cacophonous mate to the chain saw, the leaf blower may be even more offensive. An almost unbearable sound, the leaf blower (illegal in some areas) goes into a high-pitched roar and stays there, without relief, until the job is done. A misbegotten "cure" where there was no disease, the leaf blower replaces the simple rake, and its only justification is that it saves a little time and effort, effort that used to keep gardeners trim and time that permitted them to stay in touch with nature and their own souls. Now gardeners come upon the scene like pneumatic tyrants, like enemies at war with the garden, and they huff and puff them into submission, using nonrenewable fossil fuel to do the work. The shrill blasts send the leaves flying into the street or into the yards of neighbors as gardeners work at a steady pace, their ears plugged or tuned to a favorite channel of their stereo headset radios. They appear to be unconnected to what they do and unaware of how they disturb the neighborhood with that jarring noise. Relief comes only when they leave, though they are never fully gone. The leaf blower, like the chain saw, is always somewhere in the area.

The chain saw and the leaf blower are conveniences that are not likely to disappear from the workaday world. However, if these two hateful sounds are not soon muffled, the day will come, as in the movie *Network*, when I will open my window and cry out to all the world, "I'm mad as hell, and I'm not going to take it anymore!"

Suggested topics: sounds such as barking dogs, honking horns, house or auto security alarms, dental drills, nails on a chalkboard, snoring, construction noises, airplanes flying too low or fast; odors such as strong cheese, sour milk, an outgoing tide, strong perfume, body odor; sights such as garbage or litter in the streets, dying flowers, billboards, ashtrays full of cigarettes, air pollution, too much makeup; experiences with other people such as guests arriving late or early, someone forgetting a date with you, someone standing too close, lecturing, or otherwise boring you; independent experiences such as forgetting someone's name or birthday, breaking a shoe lace, getting junk mail, missing a bus, losing track of time.

EXERCISE 34. DISCUSS A GOOD OR BAD JOB

Think of the various part-time or full-time jobs you have held, and write about one you have either liked or disliked. Consider what has made the job a good one for you or a bad one, and present your case for or against the job in a thesis divided into *three* parts or supports. Each of the three parts of the thesis should be discussed in a paragraph of the discussion, making the composition, together with an introductory and concluding paragraph, a total of five paragraphs in length. Use the example that follows to guide you.

EXAMPLE

MY JOB AS A WAITRESS

While working my way through college, I have held some dull and difficult jobs. I have spent a summer picking tomatoes in hot and seemingly endless fields. I have sold toys during the Christmas rush to screaming children and harassed parents in the crowded basement of a large department store. I have worked through the night sorting mail in a cold and dreary post office. However, none of these jobs was as bad as my work as a waitress in a combination restaurant and ice cream parlor. (THESIS STATEMENT) The work there was physically hard; the pay was poor; and most of all, the working conditions were deplorable.

First of all, the job made great demands on my energy and endurance. From 4:30 in the afternoon until 1:00 or 2:00 in the morning, I spent most of my time on my feet waiting on customers; walking from counter to kitchen to table; carrying trays heavy with plates of food and giant ice cream sundaes, sodas, and shakes. The restaurant was a popular hangout for teenagers, whose needs for another straw, another spoon, another glass of water kept me in almost constant motion. Families were also drawn to the place and overflowed the booths, their little ones spewing malted magic down the seats, often followed by broken glass—targets for the broom and mop that I wielded in my "spare" time. In fact, in the rare moments when business slowed down, I was expected to mop the entire floor and to clean down walls as well as to polish the extensive fountain area. In addition to waiting tables, I was required to work in the kitchen some of the time and to make the ice cream orders for all of my customers. My hands and arms ached by the end of the night from scooping hard ice cream. When I went home, I had to soak my sore body in a tub for at least a half hour before I could sleep.

The physical hardship might not have been so hard to bear if the pay had not been so poor. I was paid the minimum wage at that time, which was

$1.75 an hour, and on a good night, I made another three or four dollars in tips. Because of the low pay, I often worked overtime on weekends to increase my paycheck. I was naive and didn't at first realize that weekends attracted the "big spenders," who promised substantial tips that rarely materialized in return for extra attention and faster service. Although I catered to them and flew as fast as I could, when I cleared their tables I might find a quarter or sometimes nothing at all as tip for a table of four and a bill of $20 or more. Of course, in addition to longer hours, weekends meant heavier traffic in the restaurant, but as a rule I made little more money on weekends than I did on my regular shifts. My take-home pay was usually under $200 a week, including tips. I was promised a Christmas bonus of a two-pound box of candy, but I forfeited that reward by leaving the job the week before.

Even worse than the physical strain and the low pay, what upset me about the job were the working conditions. My boss was a slave driver and a dirty old man who liked to pinch pennies as well as various parts of my anatomy. On the cook's days off, he did the cooking himself but expected me to help him out in the kitchen in addition to my regular work. While I cleaned vegetables, prepared salads, and made desserts, I also had to listen to his obscene jokes and fight off his amorous advances. Rejecting him put him in an ugly mood, and then he would find special jobs for me, such as cleaning the ovens and scraping down the grills. He would demand that I work harder, and he would criticize me when I sat down for the brief rest breaks that were due me. During rush hours his wife sometimes worked as cashier, and her raised eyebrows and insinuating remarks about my relationship with her husband made me furious. Finally, when she came right out and accused me of trying to seduce him, I told her what I really thought of him as well as the job. There was a terrible scene, and it wasn't clear at that point whether I quit or was fired. It was enough to know I would never work there again.

I had worked at that job for seven months, barely able to endure the work load, the poor pay, and the degrading working conditions. When the moment of my liberation came, I was too enraged to worry about how I would continue to support myself and pay for my education, but that miserable job made me even more determined to do so.

Suggested topics: any part-time or full-time job such as clerk, cashier, salesperson, gardener, bank teller, waiter, bus boy/girl, dish washer, custodian, cleaning person, gas station attendant, hospital worker, field hand, laundry worker, medical assistant, office worker, baby-sitter, handyperson.

EXERCISE 35. EXPLAIN A RULE BY WHICH YOU LIVE

Write a composition in which you discuss *one* of the rules by which you live. Explain why you believe in this rule or why and how it works for you. Your thesis statement should present your rule or belief with *three* divisions of the subject or supports for your position. Each of the three parts of the thesis should be discussed in a paragraph of the discussion, making the composition, together with an introductory and concluding paragraph, a total of five paragraphs long. Use the following example to guide you.

EXAMPLE

LIVING IN THE PRESENT

About one of man's frailties Thomas Wolfe wrote, "he talks of the future and he wastes it as it comes." This observation is related to a principle by which I try (without always succeeding) to live. (THESIS STATEMENT) I believe in living in the present because it is futile to dwell on the past, to worry about the future, or to miss anything in the only reality I know.

It is futile to dwell on the past. What existed or happened in the past may have been beautiful or exciting and may now bring profound and precious memories; but the past is dead, and it is not healthy for living spirits to linger over a world inhabited by ghosts. The past may also be a place of horror, of regret, of spilled milk, of unfortunate deeds that "cannot be undone," of sad words like "might have been." However, it is painful and pointless to fixate on a period that cannot be relived or repaired. It is unproductive self-punishment. The past must be kept in its place, outlived and outgrown.

It is also useless to worry about the future. Why fly to heaven before it's time? What anxious visions haunt a person who thinks too much about the future? He may envision the horrible mushroom cloud; the earth shriveling from radiation; the overpopulated, abused earth gone dead. He may imagine his own life going awry, appointments missed; advancements given to someone else; his house burned to the ground; his love lost; everything in his life, as in a nightmare, slipping away. There is no end to the disasters a person can worry about when focusing anxiously on the future. There are events in his future, including his own demise, over which he has little or no control, but which can ruin his life by worrying about them. There are some disasters he may be able to prevent, but he must do that by living well in the present, not simply by worrying about the future.

The present moment, which is even now moving into the past, is the only reality I know, and I don't want to miss it. The wild-cherry cough drop dissolving in my mouth is sweet and soothing. Even my sore throat and back-ache have meaning. The cool night air, the crackling noises of my furnace, my cat yawning and stretching—these are the tangible realities I can recognize. They exist in this moment, together with my own breathing, the warm lamp overhead, the jerking of my typewriter. Along with these are the realities of other people and of all life on this earth, which matters to me now, not at some past or future time.

Everyone needs a sense of history, I think, particularly a feeling for his or her own roots, but history needs to keep its distance to be appreciated. It is also vital to have some sense of direction, which means making plans for the future but not becoming preoccupied with them. What is most important, I believe, is living in the present, that is, being alive *now*.

Suggested topics: being friendly; being helpful; trusting people; turning the other cheek; expecting the best or worst in people; being honest; looking out for number one; winning, losing, playing the game; being competitive; being loyal or faithful; being aggressive; doing all things in moderation; living dangerously; taking chances; playing it safe; being selfish or unselfish; being rich or poor; getting exercise; being a vegetarian; eating healthful foods, dieting, or fasting; getting close to nature; being outgoing; being defensive; working hard; being independent; being loving; traveling in the fast lane.

EXERCISE 36. PRESENT TWO SIDES OF AN ISSUE

Write a composition in which you present the advantages and disadvantages of something or in which you argue both for and against something. Present the two sides in your thesis statement, and in your discussion devote two or three paragraphs to each side. Try to be objective and fair in discussing each side, giving about equal time or space to each. In your conclusion you may or may not show that you favor one side over the other.

Be careful in your thesis statement to present two sides of *one* issue. Don't be confused into thinking that your objective is to give first the advantages of one thing and then the disadvantages of something else. On the other hand, some topics suggest or imply others. For example, if you discuss the advantages and disadvantages of owning a home, you will naturally think of the subject in terms of its alternatives, such as renting a home or renting an apartment. Keep your focus, nonetheless, on home ownership. Don't shift it to the alternatives. Don't even discuss the alternatives, except as they clarify your arguments for and against owning a home.

Notice also that your thesis statement may give categories, as in the example that follows, rather than the specifics within those categories that can be dealt with later in the discussion. For instance, note that one of the advantages given in the following thesis is "general well-being." This category is later presented more specifically in terms of improved prosperity, savings in wear and tear and cleaning of clothes, improved personal hygiene, and a calmer disposition. You may wish to use this scheme or you may want to employ specifics immediately in your thesis statement.

EXAMPLE

THE ADVANTAGES AND DISADVANTAGES OF BEING
A RECOVERING SMOKER

Reforming can be a risky business. Prime examples are recovering smokers who exhibit holier-than-thou self-satisfaction that alienates and antagonizes everyone around them, including people who have never smoked as well as those who still do. Of course, research indicates that former smokers are wise to have stopped, but they do not automatically fall into paradise for having done so. There are not only advantages but also some disadvantages in giving up cigarettes. (THESIS STATEMENT) Among the advantages to recovering smokers are better prospects for good health and general well-being, but the disadvantages include some interpersonal as well as personal problems.

The prime advantage in giving up cigarettes is that it gives recovering smokers a better chance of having good health. For example, it comes as a pleasant surprise to former smokers that coughing is not the most natural way of coming to consciousness every morning. They may wake, as usual, with their feet on an icy floor, but they go about the morning with a difference, ever so quietly, without hack, sneeze, or wheeze. They discover the joy of breathing deeply in the morning air, of tasting their food, of feeling energy they thought they had lost in the smoky passing of the years. Their dentists praise them for their bright new gums. Their doctors note the clearing of their lungs. Their blood pressure goes down. They have fewer colds. Indeed, there is no guarantee for long life, but they are healthier, and indications are that they may stay that way for a reasonable stretch of time, thanks in part, at least, to conquering their addiction to cigarettes.

Besides better health, recovering smokers enjoy an improved sense of general well-being. For one thing, they are a bit more prosperous for having given up an increasingly expensive habit, which formerly included not only cigarettes but also such equipment as cigarette holders, lighters, cases, and so forth. In addition, they no longer need to worry about burn holes in their clothing that required expensive "invisible" mending, and their clothes do not need to be cleaned as often, nor do they any longer grow rank and reek with smoke. Their personal hygiene has improved immeasurably, since neither their bodies nor their hair is contaminated by cigarettes. Finally, they are calmer and more contained persons who no longer need to wonder about their next cigarette break or to feel the desperate agitation that comes from needing nicotine. They can enjoy a leisurely dinner without interruption and the theater without a mad dash to the lobby. These are now pleasures in themselves, not impediments to the next cigarette.

Not at first as apparent as the advantages, perhaps, the disadvantages of being a recovering smoker include some knotty interpersonal problems. Partly to reinforce the effort to break their smoking addiction, former smokers may adopt an attitude of new "purity" and clean up their immediate environment, ridding themselves of any positive associations with smoking. Ashtrays have to go, some handsome pieces removed reluctantly, and then the cigarette containers offered guests, and all cigarettes, lighters, and matches. After that, suppose the new nonsmokers give their first dinner party. Old friends arrive, and many of them still smoke. So much for purity, as the house disappears in clouds of smoke, and cigarette butts develop longer and longer ashes. "Where are all the ashtrays?" someone asks, and the hosts unhappily find a very small one for everyone to share. The hosts resent their guests smoking and want to ask them to do it outside, but haven't the courage to say so. However, very gradually, especially as more and more people stop smoking and the general attitude begins to change, some disgruntled smokers do learn to step outside, though it is hard to insist on that consideration when the weather is harsh. But there is always the clod who will light up at the dinner table, even while others are eating, and create a scene if asked to smoke elsewhere. Similarly, in planes, restaurants, and elsewhere, it can be difficult for smokers and nonsmokers to relate.

Another disadvantage of being a recovering smoker is that the new reform poses a number of personal problems. One of the worst is fat. Few people quit smoking without gaining weight. Besides the natural weight-gaining changes they experience in response to cigarette withdrawal, former smokers overcompensate for lost oral pleasures by munching. After all, meals no longer end when there is no cigarette with which to conclude them. Instead, they spill into each other. In the first few months, the most difficult period in the smoke-ending process, it is not unusual for former smokers to gain twenty pounds or more, tough to carry around and hard on their self-esteem. Recovering smokers also tend to become grouchy. The more mean and hateful they become, the less they like themselves, and only their best friends can tolerate them. Their outlook on the world grows worse, in addition, as their sense of smell returns. While smokers, they had been deprived of the things they liked to smell as well as those they didn't. Now, besides the smell of bread baking and other lovely cooking aromas, they can smell the exhaust from cars and buses, the stench of sewers, the leaden scent of heavy perfume, the pollution of the world. It is a grim life without cigarettes, at least at first. Personal problems may linger for months or years before recovering smokers finally adjust.

To stop smoking requires all kinds of grit and will power and is not nearly as romantic as smoking promised to be, when it was sold through song and sexy sales pitches. Smokers who want to recover from the addiction may need to weigh the advantages of quitting to health and general well-being against the personal and interpersonal disadvantages. However, they might enjoy life more fully, in this case, if they leaped to their conclusion.

Suggested topics: getting married; staying single; having a large (small) family; being a child in a large (small) family; being an only child; getting a divorce; being a child of divorced parents; owning a car; owning a compact car; making a career in the army or navy; going to college; working for a large (small) company; being self-employed; being an older student returning to college; being a working wife or mother; marrying someone of another race or religion; living in a big city; living in a small town; living in suburbia; living in the country; having a job that requires a lot of traveling; owning a home; renting an apartment; being a man; being a woman; being in love.

EXERCISE 37. DESCRIBE AN EVENT IN YOUR LIFE

Write a composition of four to five paragraphs in which you narrate an event in your life or tell a story about an experience you have had. Your thesis statement should indicate the nature, scope, and chronology of the event so that the reader can anticipate what is coming in the composition and how it will be presented. Use the example that follows to guide you.

EXAMPLE

RIDING AN OUTRIGGER

At the precise moment when the big wave began to swell and roll shoreward, the beach boy sitting in the stern of the outrigger shouted to us, "Now paddle! Wikiwiki!" A tourist in Hawaii, I was sitting in the middle of the boat with other tourists as we all began to paddle furiously to catch the big wave. Catching it just right, we lifted our paddles up and felt it hurl us toward the beach. (THESIS SENTENCE) This moment was the greatest thrill of riding an outrigger canoe, an experience I found exciting from beginning to end.

The adventure began with amusing contrast. Against the beautifully tanned and muscular bodies of the beach boys, we pale or sunburned tourists, who ranged in age from six to sixty, appeared especially knobby-kneed and pot-bellied. The laughing faces of the beach boys exposed incredibly white and perfect teeth as they welcomed us to make our way awkwardly into the hollowed-out boat. We tourists, like ducks, sat in a line in the boat, each of us grasping a short-necked, fat paddle with two hands. The beach boys pushed the canoe out into the surf, jumped into it, and with the help of their inexperienced crew, conveyed the craft seaward.

The way out was fairly effortless for us tourists. The beach boys did most of the work while at the same time explaining to us the method and objective of the experience that was to come. Once we reached the desired point in the water, a waiting period followed. It was a delightful period in which we appreciated the balmy air of the semitropics, the magnificent view of the island paradise, and the blue-green water which, because it was shallow, revealed a myriad of coral formations beneath it. The luxury of relaxing in the sunkissed canoe was heightened with the expectancy we crew members felt as the beach boys awaited the right wave and prepared to give the signal for all of us to paddle. Then the wave came.

"Now paddle! Wikiwiki! Fast! Everybody go!" Suddenly and furiously, we obeyed the command. All paddles slashed into the water. Again and again, faster and faster—dip, out, dip, out—our paddles moved. We knew the boat must be just slightly ahead of the big wave to catch the swell. "Paddles up." Now the wave did the work. Swiftly, still more swiftly, our canoe raced toward the shore. The spray of the foam, the power of the wave, the speed of the craft, the soft breeze all combined into the excitement unique to riding an outrigger. The trip beachward was really some distance but seemed short and needed repeating. By the second and third time we had repeated the experience, we tourists were completely exhilarated by the skill as well as the romance of it.

There is the belief in Hawaii that anyone who visits the islands must return again someday. It must follow that anyone who once enjoys the sport of riding an outrigger canoe, as I did, cannot resist trying it again when he or she returns.

Suggested topics: visiting the Empire State Building; touring through a museum; skiing in the mountains or on the water; meeting a famous person; meeting a bear or a rattlesnake; flying somewhere in an airplane; visiting a strange city; seeing a bullfight; learning a new dance; learning a new custom in a foreign country; trying to speak a foreign language; going deep-sea fishing; learning to ride a horse; seeing a circus; attending a concert; attending your first day of college; running for office; campaigning for a political candidate; collecting funds for a charitable organization; earning your first paycheck; shopping for a new car; meeting the man or woman you plan to marry; traveling on a train; fighting a forest fire; having an automobile accident or seeing one; winning or losing a race; learning a lesson; achieving a goal. (Bear in mind that your composition is to be relatively short. You may not be able to tell everything about a camping trip in the mountains, for example, but you can describe an episode or some event that took place during it.)

EXERCISE 38. DESCRIBE A PLACE OR SCENE

Write a composition of about six to eight paragraphs in which you describe a place or scene. Your thesis statement should indicate not only the nature and scope of your subject, but also that you intend to organize your composition geographically. Use the example that follows as a guide.

EXAMPLE

THE GRANDEST STATE OF ALL

"I love you, California. You're the grandest state of all." These words from a sentimental old song sum up the feelings of most Californians about their home state. (THESIS SENTENCE) Other states make many claims about their beautiful mountains, deserts, lakes, cities, and people, but California, from the top to the bottom of the state, has all these attributes and many of them in greater abundance than any other state in the country. In fact, California has just about everything.

Northern California offers the cool climate and scenic beauty that is claimed by Oregon and Washington. On the coast, near the Oregon line, is the Del Norte Coast Redwoods State Park with its fern-carpeted forest of rugged redwood trees. Tourists can drive or go by foot through the dense forest to the ocean where the giant redwoods, found only on the Pacific coast, grow almost to the shore. Also to be enjoyed from April to July are outstanding displays of rhododendrons and azaleas. Inland in the north are many other beautiful parks, including Mount Shasta. Besides an abundance of skiing terrain, this park contains white water in deep canyons, exquisite lakes, thick forests, and open valleys. Not far from Mount Shasta is Lassen Volcanic National Park with over one hundred and fifty miles of trails with access to a remarkable variety of natural wonders: glacial lakes, permanent snowpacks, boiling hot springs, striking waterfalls, and lush meadows. California also owns the greater portion of the beautiful Lake Tahoe, the largest body of water on the continent at its elevation, a small part of which it shares with Nevada.

Traveling down the state toward San Francisco, tourists can experience natural wonders that equal or exceed most of those in all the northern states in the country. They may choose the inland route through the Sierras, the largest single mountain range in the country, with peaks of 14,000 feet, and then across the fertile Sacramento Valley. The city of Sacramento, once a boom town with its roots in the gold rush of 1849, is now the state capital with a beautifully restored capitol building surrounded by a park, an oasis on hot valley days, with forty acres of plants and trees from all over the world. Instead of going inland, travelers may decide to journey down the virtually unspoiled coast that stretches almost four hundred miles from the southern border of Oregon to the San Francisco Bay. The oceanside highway offers magnificent views of the dramatic coast with its precipitous cliffs and rocky, windswept shore. The highway passes numerous beaches, many that are spacious and uncrowded, and interesting sites such as Mendocino, a nineteenth-century town of weathered wood houses, now an artists' mecca; Gualala, an old lumber port; and Fort Ross, once a Russian outpost. Finally, visitors come to one of the engineering wonders of the world, the Golden Gate Bridge, the northern entrance to San Francisco.

San Francisco, though not the largest city in the country, is probably the most cosmopolitan, with a unique blend of races, customs, and nationalities, including the largest Asian community outside the Orient centered in its colorful if overcrowded Chinatown. The city's many fine restaurants reflect its international character and offer the gourmet numerous choices, including Chinese, Japanese, Vietnamese, Korean, Indian, Italian, Spanish, Greek, and an almost infinite variety of other menus. The city also offers cultural opportunities with its excellent museums, its civic center with one of the country's finest opera houses, symphony hall, theater, library, subterranean exhibit hall, and civic auditorium. The city is also a delight to shoppers in its downtown and other areas. Surrounded on three sides by water, San Francisco is a compact city of hills. From one of its hill-climbing cable cars or from the tops of its many excellent hotels, the view of the bay area with its great bridges, the neighboring cities in the distance, including Berkeley, headquarters of the world's largest university, is an unforgettable vista.

Leaving San Francisco, travelers can journey inland again and enjoy some of the nation's greatest parks—Yosemite, King's Canyon, or Sequoia—for either summer or winter sports, including a hike up Mount Whitney, the highest peak in the continental United States. Visitors can also head south along the scenic coast highway or along the San Francisco Peninsula through an area called Silicon Valley for its large electronics industry, and then past another great university, Stanford, to the Santa Cruz region with its excellent beach parks. Before long they will come to the beautiful Monterey Peninsula. Characterized by white beaches, craggy rocks, pounding surf, and twisted cypresses, the peninsula contains an exceptionally scenic route known as 17 Mile Drive, permitting tourists to drive through thick woods, past elegant homes and clubs, and along a spectacular shoreline. Monterey, Carmel, and their neighbor to the south, Santa Barbara, all attractive because of their setting and intriguing shopping, are also interesting historically, vestiges of early settlements still evident, among them the Franciscan missions. Parallel to these early Spanish and Mexican mission sites are inland valleys that are among the richest agricultural areas in the country. From Salinas, famous for lettuce as well as John Steinbeck, through Merced, Fresno, and Bakersfield, the soil is as productive as any found in such midwestern states as Kansas, Iowa, or Minnesota. Citrus groves, which appear in the lower valleys, tell travelers that they are in Southern California and nearing Los Angeles.

Los Angeles, California's largest city, is a vast sprawl of intermingling communities held together by the most extensive freeway system in the world. The best way to get around the city is by car, and though the freeways are constantly crowded, the system works quite well when understood and carefully followed. Seeing the immense expanse the city has become, it is difficult to imagine the small Mexican community, founded in 1781, that it once was, though a tiny sample of that beginning remains on Olivera Street, closed to traffic and preserved as a Mexican street of over a century ago. Los Angeles was greatly expanded during World War II and is now noted for its large aircraft and missile industry, for such places as Beverly Hills with its elegant Rodeo Drive, as well as for movie stars, and is one of the most populated cities in the country. In the summertime, much of this population can be seen along the many fine beaches that stretch between Los Angeles and San Diego. In fact, Southern California is a paradise for sunlovers, from its coast to its inland desert areas, including the famous Death Valley National Monument. Southern California offers just about everything that states such as Arizona, Colorado, and New Mexico boast of. It also competes with the pleasures of Florida.

California has just about everything, from cowboys to Indians and from urbia to suburbia. It has Texas oil. It has Minnesota lakes. It has Arizona deserts, Vermont snow, and Wyoming mountains. It has more people than New York. The sentimental old song was never truer of California than it is today. It is the grandest state of all.

Suggested topics: your block; your neighborhood; your hometown; your part of a state or your whole state; your school; a nearby park; the place where you work; a place where you used to live; a place you have visited many times; your house or yard; a scene from your window; your room; a building or place in your town you particularly like or dislike; a painting you enjoy. (Be sure you write about an area you really know, and limit your area; the model composition covers more ground than you may want to try to cope with.)

EXERCISE 39. DISCUSS YOUR EXPERIENCE WITH MECHANIZATION AND/OR DEPERSONALIZATION

Write a composition in which you discuss an experience you have had, preferably negative or adverse, with mechanization and/or depersonalization. The word *mechanization* refers to operations or labor done by machine, making a task automatic, unspontaneous, routine, or monotonous. *Depersonalization* means the state or condition in which a person is deprived of his or her individual character or personality; that is, made impersonal.

The advantages of the machine age are numerous, and few people want to give up their multicycled washing machines to return to scrubbing boards, for example. However, so-called progress has brought about losses as well as gains. Many people who used to keep healthy through vigorous labor now have to compensate for the machines that have made life easy for them by taking exercise classes or jogging. In addition, mechanization can make life humdrum or monotonous, turning out products that are uniform or that lack individuality and organizing or translating people into numbers, codes, or other systems that tend to deprive them of their uniqueness and personality. Thus, mechanization and depersonalization can be closely related.

Think about your experience with mechanization and/or depersonalization and decide on the influence of one or both on your life, your attitudes, or values. Present these influences in a thesis statement divided into *two* or *three* parts or supports. Develop each part into a paragraph of discussion in which you explain and illustrate your view. In addition, write a brief introduction and conclusion. Use the following example as a guide.

EXAMPLE

HELLO. THIS IS A RECORDING. . . .

Faint memory returns of a time, light-years ago, or so it seems, when there were no dials on the telephone. To make a call, I first took the receiver off the "hook" and then waited for the dulcet tones of the telephone operator, "Number, please." That was a live voice, not a recording, and for an instant there was a real transaction, a dynamic relationship between us, and we spoke to each other. That page of my tattered memory book has almost disintegrated with the passage of time, and I have long since become so conditioned by mechanization and depersonalization that I am startled and disoriented by such things as live voices. (Thesis Statement) Sometimes I am convinced that machines and the impersonal people who work for them are making me an automaton.

Mechanization may systematize and speed up the process of the working world, but it is also making me feel like a zombie. If I discover I am bleeding at the hip, for instance, do I hurry to the nearest doctor? Of course not. Instead, I prepare myself for being processed at the emergency hospital, medical card in hand, slowly sinking while I am coded and properly entered into the computer system, which may, at last, permit me to receive aid. If I want to dispute a bill with a large department store, I gear myself for the experience as I pick up the telephone. There will be the first recording, and then the music, for it is clear that I must never be left alone with my thoughts while I await the accounts person. After ten minutes of that soporific music, I am reduced to such a trancelike state that I must make notes to myself to remember why I placed the call. One time when I went to Europe for the summer, I paid a large credit system twice the normal amount, attaching a note of explanation. When I returned, however, I was in trouble, for the system could not read my note, could not be paid ahead of time, could not but fault me for being away when it was time to pay. Now when I travel abroad, picking my way through the glorious ruins of the Acropolis, admiring Paris from atop the Eiffel Tower, or being spirited by gondola through fascinating Venice, I know the moment when it comes, and I drop everything else so that I can sit down and write out my check to the Big System. Such is the hold the mechanized world has on me.

Strongly resembling the machines for which they work, the people who staff the mechanized world also have a deadening effect on my spirit. Most often we connect by telephone, for I have learned that it does not pay to appear in "person" if I want fast action. Clerks and other servicepersons always give the telephone top priority, letting other customers wait. I get the most attention when I am an anonymous voice. "Hello, this is . . ." I start to say, when I am interrupted by the other voice, with even, steel courtesy, totally devoid of human imperfection or identity. "Your account number, please?" it says, and then I quickly survey my statement for the correct series of numbers, and I note that one goes clear across the page. The time that I got in trouble with the Big System, the other voice grew rigid with authority. "That is against company policy," the other voice said, with a sober sense of righteousness, in complete support of the machine that couldn't read and couldn't make exceptions. "Is there someone else that I can speak to?" I asked. "Just a moment, please," it measured out, like toothpaste. The next voice, more velvety but just as rigid in supporting policy, said, "The computer is programmed to expect payment every month." At last I reached an officer with some authority, and a "lifetime exception" was made for me to clear my credit. "Do you mean that literally?" I asked. "Yes, this is the one exception we can ever make for you." "Ever in my life?" I suppressed my anguished giggles, but there was no humor in the affirmative reply. As I put down the telephone I felt as if I had been doomed to spend a lifetime on probation, with detached and heartless voices ready to seal my fate if I should ever slip again.

It is a long time since I used to take the receiver off the hook of an upright telephone and wait for the human warmth and lively interaction that could ensue. Now when my telephone rings, I cope automatically with the world of machines and impersonal people. "Hello," my message begins. "This is a recording. . . ."

Suggested topics: experiences you have had with machines and/or impersonal people and your reactions to either or both in the following situations: on the job or applying for a job; drawing unemployment benefits or medical or other insurance; at your college during registration or another procedure; at home when you are approached in person by a representative of a company or reached by telephone or when you try to approach or reach the same; when you try to make travel arrangements or obtain tickets to the theater, a concert, or a sports event; when you want to make a complaint about a product or dispute a bill; when you use the automatic teller at your bank; any other such situations.

EXERCISE 40. DISCUSS LOVE

Write a composition in which you discuss love. You may write about romantic love or some other kind of love, such as brotherly love or parental love. The
important objective in this exercise is to find a fresh or unusual approach to the
subject. That is, you should not labor to say what has already been worn out
about the subject. Ponder the subject (or perhaps your particular love object) for
a while until you come up with a thesis that is fresh and meaningful. You may
put a question to yourself about love, as in the following example, and then
proceed to answer it.

EXAMPLE

STACCATO OR LEGATO?

Among the more curious questions that can be asked about love is this:
is it staccato or legato? That is, when one feels romantic love, does he or she
feel it in breaks, with interruptions or changes, or does one feel it continuously, without interruption or change? (THESIS SENTENCE) Although the legato
position about love is appealing, the staccato argument is probably more
realistic.

Poetry and song seduce one into thinking love legato. "Love is not love
which alters when it alteration finds," wrote Shakespeare in one of his
famous sonnets. Love is "an ever-fixed mark that looks on tempests and is
never shaken," he continued. And Elizabeth Barrett Browning wrote of her
constancy to her husband Robert in such lines as this: "What I do and what I
dream include thee." Some of the greatest arias of opera are gloriously
legato about love. Tosca, Tristan and Isolde, and Madame Butterfly are only a
few of the operatic lovers whose steadfast devotion is proved by their dying
for it. "True Love" and "I Love You Truly" are two of the best-known popular
songs that go on and on about how love goes on.

In reality, love is probably staccato. First, it is difficult to suppose that
one can experience anything continuously. Sleep interrupts wakefulness, and
sleep itself is interrupted by dreams and nightmares. The feeling one has for
his lover during wakefulness may be blotted out or intensified by sleep. In
either case, the feeling changes.

When one is awake, attention cannot be fixed constantly on a single
object. He must blink, if nothing else. More likely he will look to something
else for variety or from necessity. His mind may turn to the stock market or
he may become fascinated by the operation of a pile driver on the way to
work. His focus for much of the day is on work. As he closes the door to the

office, his thoughts may turn to his love, but sitting at the desk, his eyes fix on the print and figures there. He may fall out of love and into work, or he may catch the faint perfume of his secretary.

Pain and pleasure, either one, can distract a lover from concentrating on love. Pain calls everything to itself. One can forget one's love for a period even over a stubbed toe. The pleasure of too much food or drink can be totally absorbing. The pleasure even of one's lover may pall periodically. Often the greatest distraction is oneself. At times the preoccupation with self, the worry over self, the development of self, the delight in self admit no other thought.

As lovely as legato is, one can neither live nor love continuously. At best, a lover can only echo the words of the poet Ernest Dowson, and say, "I have been faithful to thee, Cynara! in my fashion."

Suggested topics: the eternal triangle; monogamy; bigamy; polygamy; consecutive or sequential monogamy; long separation; dependence, independence, interdependence; marriage contracts; open marriages; sexual relations with or without love; the effect of the first (or other) child on love between husband and wife; teenage love; puppy love; infatuation distinguished from love; falling in or out of love; love for parents; love for children; love for sister or brother; love for one's people.

Appendixes

Appearance and Form of the Submitted Paper

To make a good first impression of your work, you should submit a paper that is neat and easy to read. Such a paper invites readers, in a pleasant manner, to begin their work. If the paper is a mess, it obviously is not very inviting. In fact, your instructor may return your paper without reading it if it is too difficult to read. Be considerate of your readers. Turn in a paper that not only reads well but looks good.

Directions for the form of the paper are as follows:

1. Write on every other line and on one side of the page only.
2. Leave generous margins for your instructor's comments or corrections.
3. Fold your paper lengthwise. If your paper contains two or more pages, arrange the pages so that when the paper is opened to be read, it can be read in its *proper order,* beginning with page one.
4. When your paper is properly folded, it looks like a little book. On the front cover write your name, your class, your instructor's name, and the date, as indicated in Figure A–1. (Your instructor may also require the number of the exercise.)

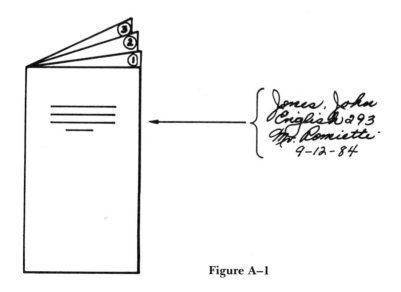

Figure A–1

APPENDIX B

Correction Symbols

agr **Agreement**

The verb must agree with the subject. If the subject is singular, the verb must be singular; if the subject is plural, the verb must be plural.

Neither John nor Mary are to be blamed for the accident. (Neither John nor Mary *is* to be blamed for the accident.)*

A pronoun must agree in number and in gender with its antecedent, that is, the noun to which the pronoun refers.

Each of the men must buy *their* (his) own uniforms. Neither Anne nor Joan brought *their* (her) lunch.

ambig **Ambiguous**

The meaning is not clear because of the possibility of two or more interpretations of the idea.

San Francisco is farther from Los Angeles than Elko, Nevada. (Which city's distance from which city is being compared?)

ap **Apostrophe Needed**

Her movements were as calculating as a cobra. (. . . as a cobra's. The idea refers to a *cobra's* movements.)

awk **Awkward or Confused Phrasing**

Muskrats work on the dikes before we get to them by burrowing through between two ponds and thus connect them

---

*All words, phrases, and sentences within parentheses are either the correction of the errors in the preceding sentence or observations leading to the correction of the preceding sentence.

when their contents are supposed to be kept separate. (Musk-rats burrow tunnels through the dikes between the ponds. Through these openings the water flows from one pond to another.)

Bpr Broad Pronoun Reference

A pronoun must have a specific noun antecedent. A pronoun's antecedent cannot be implied, nor can it refer to an entire pre-ceding action or statement.

On the first floor we were shown where the fiction books were kept; this completed the tour. (The tour was completed when we were shown where the fiction books were kept.)

Ca Wrong Case Used

The boy will give the book to whomever (whoever) comes into the room first. The secretary notified Maria and I (me) to come to the office.

Cap Capital Letter Needed

Paul Guildford, a Jefferson high school graduate, won the Thomas Paine citizen award. (Jefferson High School, Thomas Paine Citizen Award)

Coh Faulty Coherence

The sentences in the paragraph are not arranged and tied to-gether in such a way that the reader can easily and readily follow the train of thought of the development. The relationship of ideas between sentences is not clear. The reader loses the sense of focus and/or direction.

cst Faulty Sentence Construction

Sentence sense is confused, illogical, or obscure because of faulty construction of the sentence.

Privacy hindered my studying while in high school because living in a house where there are many children it is very hard to secure privacy. (A lack of privacy hindered my studying while I was in high school because I lived in a house where there were many children who distracted me.)

d   **Faulty Diction (Word) Selection**

Colloquialisms; slang; jargon; and obsolete, archaic, and dialectal words should be avoided in formal types of writing.

He calculated that the gent could be banked on. (He determined that the man was reliable.)

Frequently, the only food they had was what the mother could tote (carry) home after work.

DM   **Dangling Modifier**

Revise the sentence so that the modifier is coherently related to the word it is meant to modify.

Running across campus, the bell tower struck five. (While I was running across the campus, I heard the bell tower strike five.)

If cold, an overcoat should be worn. (Is the overcoat cold or is the weather cold?)

DR   **Divided Reverence of the Pronoun**

John told William that he had made the mistake. (Can you tell who made the mistake?)

fact   **Authenticity Questionable**

Gold was discovered in California in 1860. (It was discovered in 1849.)

focus   **Lack of Focus or Lack of Sense of Direction**

The reader is confused with respect to what you are aiming at or exactly what point you are trying to make.

frag   **Fragment Rather than a Sentence**

He came to the office Monday afternoon. Immediately after he arrived from New York. (After having arrived in New York Monday afternoon, he immediately came to the office.)

The winters are cold. Although the autumns are pleasant. (Although the autumns are pleasant, the winters are cold.)

F/Sub **Faulty Subordination**

In general, in sentences that contain a main clause and one or more subordinate clauses, the main focus—the central idea—must be placed in the main clause, not the subordinate clause.

I was looking in the store window <u>when the thief ran off with my briefcase</u>.

Probably, the more important idea is the thief running off with your briefcase, not your looking in the store window.

The thief ran off with my briefcase as I was looking in the store window.

gob **Unintelligibility of Concept**

In essence, this symbol indicates that the reader is unable to make sense out of what you are saying. You seem to be putting words together in such a way that they make no discernible sense. Some English handbooks identify this type of writing as *gobbledygook.*

As a child my grandmother perambulated hyperbolically to imbibe multitudinous prevarications.

gr **Grammar Error**

This symbol identifies all grammar errors not specifically discussed under other headings.

He walked <u>slow</u> and <u>careful</u>. (He walked *slowly* and *carefully.*)

John should have <u>spoke</u> about this accident before. (John should have *spoken* about this accident before.)

He is the <u>most tallest</u> boy in the class. (He is the *tallest* boy in the class.)

Id **Unidiomatic Phrasing**

This symbol indicates your use of an unidiomatic expression. He has agreed <u>on</u> the plans. (He has agreed to the plans.)

illeg **Illegible Word**

It **Italics**

Underline words to signify that they are to be italicized.

His favorite book is Thomas Hardy's <u>Return of the Native</u>; his favorite magazine is the London <u>Literary Times</u>.

logic **Invalid Inference, Faulty Reasoning**

? **Meaning is Unclear**

n/a **No Abbreviation**

Do not use abbreviations.

<u>J.</u> Smith went to <u>Cal.</u> in <u>Berk., Cal.</u>, in <u>Aug. '74</u> & took a course in <u>chem. tech. w/Prof.</u> Jones. (James Smith went to the University of California in Berkeley, California, in August 1974, and took a course in chemical technology with Professor Jones.)

n/ap **No Apostrophe Needed**

John returned the book to it's *(its)* owner.

There are several kind's *(kinds)* of flowers in that garden.

n/cap **No Capital Letter Needed**

Six <u>H</u>igh <u>S</u>chool students won <u>M</u>edals for <u>G</u>ood <u>C</u>itizenship. (Six high school students won medals for good citizenship.)

n/pgr
or *n/¶* **No New Paragraph Needed**

The material in this paragraph should be part of the development of the preceding paragraph. It is further support for the topic sentence of the preceding paragraph.

nwo
or *∧* **Necessary Word or Words Omitted**

The problem has and will be carefully studied. (The omission is *been*.)

O **Superfluous Punctuation**

You have used unnecessary marks of punctuation.

The cat*()*sitting on the roof*()*is mine.

Well *,* just what kind of a girl do you think I am?*(?)(?)*

=*S* **Faulty Parallel Structure**

Elements placed in a series must be of the same grammatical structure.

The duties of the vice president were to call the meeting to order, <u>collecting</u> the dues, and he <u>appointed</u> the chairmen of the various committees. (The duties of the vice president were to call the meeting to order, to *collect* the dues, and to *appoint* the chairmen of the various committees.)

p **Punctuation Error**

This symbol identifies all errors in punctuation (comma, semi-colon, colon, period, dash, parentheses, quotation marks, question mark, and exclamation point) other than those errors listed as RTS (run-together sentences). Needless or superfluous punctuation is listed under *O* .

There are three colors in the flag*;* red, white, and blue.
(There are three colors in the flag: red, white, and blue.)

pgr or ¶ **New Paragraph Needed**

When you have finished developing one idea and shift to a new direction, you need also to start a new paragraph.

pgr D **Inadequate Paragraph Development**

You have not given sufficient concrete and specific details to es-tablish or prove the topic sentence or the central idea of the paragraph.

pgr O **Weak Paragraph Organization**

The factors within the development of your paragraph are not well organized or structured. The material should be revised so that the progression of your thought from the beginning to the end has a better sense of coherence and continuity.

pgr U ## Lack of Paragraph Unity

You have material in the paragraph that is not to the point of the topic sentence or central idea and that also distracts from it.

Red ## Redundancies

Redundant terms, expressions, and ideas are to be avoided. Do not say the same thing twice. "Repeat again," "combined together," "important essentials," "two A.M. in the morning" are examples of saying the same thing twice.

Rep ## Repetitious

Avoid being repetitious. Do not say the same thing over again. (The preceding are repetitious statements.) Because you change the wording does not mean you have changed the content of the thought; you have merely trodden over the same ground in a different dress.

Good students turn their compositions in on time. They always have their work ready on the day it is due. They do not turn it in on the day after or the week after the instructor asks that it be submitted. They are never late.

The preceding statements convey the same idea four times.

R T S ## Run-together Sentences

You have linked independent clauses within the sentence without the proper punctuation. Independent clauses must be joined with either a semicolon or with a comma, provided you are using a coordinating conjunction (*and, but, for,* or *nor*) when you use the comma. Examples of the error:

The story was not true however it was interesting. (The story was not true; however, it was interesting.)

The jaws of the scoop swung open, out tumbled the dirt and debris. (A comma has been used instead of the required semicolon.)

John collected over thirty dollars but Tom collected only twenty. (A comma must be placed before the *but*.)

Sc   Split Construction

Do not shift from the active voice to the passive voice in the same sentence.

We <u>flew</u> over Chicago at noon, and the Golden Gate <u>was seen</u> by sunset. (We flew over Chicago at noon and *saw* the Golden Gate by sunset.)

Sn   Shift in Number

Do not shift the number of nouns, particularly of persons.

Be sure to take your <u>passport</u>; the customs officials always look at <u>them</u> (*it*).

Every boy in the room took off <u>their hats</u> (*his hat*).

sp   Spelling Error

Check the dictionary.

He was <u>disatisfied</u> with the grade that he had <u>recieved</u> from the <u>profesor</u>. (*dissatisfied, received, professor*)

S/p   Shift in Person

Don't shift from <u>I</u> to <u>you</u> to <u>one</u> to <u>he</u>, and so on.

I first will buy some seeds. Then <u>you</u> place them in some water. In a few days <u>a person</u> will begin to see them sprout. (After the seeds have been bought, they should be placed in some water. After a few days the seeds will begin to sprout.)

To the <u>student</u>, going to summer school is worse than having no vacation at all, for when <u>you</u> have no vacation, you do not think about all the things <u>a person</u> could do if <u>he</u> had one. (To the student, going to summer school is worse than having no vacation at all, for when he has no vacation, he does not think about all the things he could be doing if he had one.)

spec   Specific

Be more specific in the detailing; avoid the abstract.

In high school I studied Shakespeare and a Victorian novelist. (In high school I studied Shakespeare's play <u>Hamlet</u> and Charles Dickens' novel <u>Oliver Twist</u>.)

Because the weather was unpleasant outside, we didn't do much of anything. (As it was exceedingly hot and muggy outside, we sat inside sipping iced tea and occasionally playing a game of canasta.)

ℒ𝒯 Shift in Tense

You must keep the same tense of the verb throughout the discussion of the subject.

For months I had admired Susan from afar, but I haven't the courage to ask her for a date. (Use either "had admired" and "hadn't the courage" or "have admired" and "haven't the courage," but be consistent.)

Sub Subordination of Ideas

Effective writing sets up relationships between ideas by subordinating secondary ideas to primary ideas. Subordinate the underlined sentence or sentences.

The Victoria River Project was approved by the president in 1970. The plans were ready the following year. However, the actual construction did not begin until 1974. (Although plans for the Victoria River Project were ready in 1970, one year after the president approved the project, actual construction did not begin until 1974.)

Subj Subjunctive Mood of the Verb Required

If I was (were) the chairperson, I would veto the measure.

It is necessary that each student keeps (keep) his or her own notes.

Trans Transitional Link Necessary

The change of thought or direction is too abrupt between the two sentences or paragraphs. You need to provide a link between the two so that the reader can follow the progression of your thought. Build a bridge to serve as the transitional device.

Modern machinery often makes people its slaves. Last summer I worked for the Great Lakes Motor Company. (That modern machinery often makes people its slaves is a conclusion that I came to after having worked for the Great Lakes Motor Company last summer.)

trite Clichés, Hackneyed Expressions, Overused Phrases, Trite Observations

"A budding genius," "at one fell swoop," "nipped in the bud," "seething mass of humanity," "launched into eternity," "good as gold," and so on.

Vague Need More Specific Details

Your development is lacking in a sufficient number of concrete details to make the meaning of your generalization clear to the reader. The generalization may be a valid one, but the reader is not aware of what you mean by it. A generalization can always be made exact and clear if you will follow it with one or more specific examples. It is always advisable to follow an abstract idea with a specific for purposes of clarification.

The food in the cafeteria is dull.

What does *dull* mean—that there are no spices used, that the food is unimaginatively prepared or served, that there is little selection? The reader would know exactly what you meant by that generalization if you were to follow it with:

Day after day the only two courses offered on the menu are spaghetti and meatloaf.

wd Wordiness

You are using too many words. Say the same thing in fewer words. Strike out all that is superfluous.

The boy had a temperature that would be regarded under all circumstances as a dangerously high one. (The boy had a critical temperature.)

WR Weak Reference of Pronoun

You need to establish more exactly the antecedent of the pronoun.

When the baby is through drinking the milk, it should be sterilized in boiling water. (Should the bottle or the baby be sterilized?)

WT **Wrong Tense**

The wrong tense of the verb has been used.

In the drama the hero <u>was slain</u>. (In the drama the hero *is* slain.)

This scientific article, written two months ago, <u>said</u> *(says)* that the use of Drug X is dangerous.

WW **Wrong Word**

You've used an inappropriate or wrong word.

The <u>principle</u> (*principal*) speaker was James Thorne.

He <u>excepted</u> (*accepted*) the money.

I do not believe that teachers should be allowed to administer <u>capital punishment</u> (*corporal punishment*) to students.

The darling girl is a child <u>progeny</u> (*prodigy*).

APPENDIX C

Paragraph Evaluation

	A	B	C	D	F
1. Is the topic sentence clearly stated?					
2. Is the paragraph well developed and organized?					
a. Does the paragraph contain one idea only?					
b. Is the topic adequately developed or supported?					
c. Is the paragraph unified and coherent?					
d. Does the paragraph have continuity or smooth transitions?					
3. Does the paragraph contain good sentence structure?					
4. Is the word choice effective?					
5. Is the paragraph free of errors in grammar, punctuation, and spelling?					
6. Is the treatment of the subject matter imaginative and thought provoking?					

Paragraph Grade _____

Additional Comments:

Composition Evaluation

	A	B	C	D	F
1. Is the thesis sentence clear and well supported?					
2. Is the composition well organized and developed?					
a. Is the order or arrangement of the material in the composition as a whole correct, clear, and easy to follow?					
b. Does the discussion part of the composition keep a balance and support the purpose of the composition?					
c. Is there sufficient use of specific, concrete details to support any generalizations made in the composition?					
d. Is each of the paragraphs well organized and developed and is there continuity between them?					
3. Is the word choice effective and does the composition avoid wordiness?					
4. Is the composition free of errors in grammar, punctuation, spelling, sentence construction, and so forth?					
5. Is the title appropriate and effective?					
6. Does the composition as a whole reflect thought? Is it both logical and imaginative?					

Composition Grade _____

Additional Comments:

300 Words Most Frequently Misspelled

1. accelerate
   accidentally
   accommodate
   accompanied
   accumulate
   achievement
   acquainted
   across
   address
10. advice
   aggravate
   all right
   altogether
   always
   amateur
   among
   amount
   apparent
   appearance
20. appetite
   approaching
   appropriate
   approximately
   arctic
   argument
   around
   arrangement
   article
   athletic
30. awkward
   barbarous
   before
   beginning

believed
benefited
breathe
brilliant
bulletin
buried
40. business
carrying
cemetery
changeable
chosen
clothes
coming
committee
comparative
competition
50. conceive
conquer
conscientious
consider
continually
control
convenience
cooly
copies
corner
60. course
courteous
criticism
curiosity
dealt
decided
decision

definite
definition
dependent
70. description
desirable
despair
desperate
destroy
develop
different
dining
disappeared
disappointed
80. disastrous
discipline
diseases
dissatisfied
dissipation
divided
division
doesn't
eighth
efficiency
90. eliminated
embarrassed
emphasize
environment
equipped
especially
exaggerated
excellent
excitement
exhausted

100. exhilaration
   existence
   experience
   explanation
   familiar
   fascinating
   finally
   foreign
   formally
   formerly
110. forty
   fourth
   friend
   gardener
   generally
   genius
   government
   grammar
   grievance
   guard
120. handle
   height
   hindrance
   hurriedly
   imagination
   immediately
   incidentally
   independent
   indispensable
   intelligence
130. interesting
   interfere
   interpreted
   interrupted
   irresistible
   its
   itself
   knowledge
   laboratory
   laid
140. led
   leisure

   lightning
   livelihood
   loneliness
   lose
   losing
   maintenance
   mathematics
   meant
150. medicine
   miniature
   minute
   mischievous
   mysterious
   naturally
   necessary
   nevertheless
   nickel
   niece
160. ninety
   ninth
   noisily
   noticeable
   nowadays
   obstacle
   occasion
   occasionally
   occurred
   occurrence
170. off
   omission
   omitted
   operate
   opinion
   optimistic
   opportunity
   original
   outrageous
   paid
180. parallel
   paralyzed
   parliament
   particularly

   partner
   pastime
   perform
   perhaps
   permissible
   perseverance
190. persistent
   persuade
   phenomenon
   physically
   piece
   pleasant
   portrayed
   possess
   practically
   preceding
200. preference
   preferred
   prejudice
   preparations
   principal
   principles
   privilege
   probably
   procedure
   proceeded
210. professional
   professor
   prominent
   propeller
   psychology
   pursue
   quantity
   quiet
   quite
   quitting
220. quizzes
   realize
   really
   received
   recognize
   recommend

	referred		specimen		truly
	relieve		speech		twelfth
	religious		stopped		undoubtedly
	remembrance		strength		unnecessary
230.	repetition		strenuously	280.	until
	resource		stretched		usually
	restaurant		studying		valleys
	rhythm		succeed		valuable
	ridiculous		successful		varieties
	sacrifice	260.	superintendent		vegetable
	safety		supersede		vengeance
	satisfactorily		suppress		view
	scarcely		surely		vigorous
	schedule		surprise		village
240.	secretary		synonym	290.	villain
	seize		temperament		weather
	sense		their		whether
	separate		there		whole
	sergeant		together		wholly
	severely	270.	too		who's
	shining		toward		whose
	similar		tragedy		women
	sincerely		transferring		worrying
	sophomore		tremendous		writing
250.	source		tries	300.	written

Second Grade Writers

Stephanie Parsons

Second Grade Writers

Units of Study to Help Children Focus
on Audience and Purpose

HEINEMANN
Portsmouth, NH

Heinemann

A division of Reed Elsevier Inc.

361 Hanover Street

Portsmouth, NH 03801–3912

www.heinemann.com

Offices and agents throughout the world

Library of Congress Cataloging-in-Publication Data

Parsons, Stephanie.

    Second grade writers : units of study to help children focus on audience and purpose / Stephanie Parsons.

       p. cm.

    Includes bibliographical references.

    ISBN-13: 978-0-325-01031-1

    ISBN-10: 0-325-01031-5

    1. English language—Composition and exercises—Study and teaching (Primary).

    2. Second grade (Education).   I. Title.

    LB1528.P275 2007

    372.62′3—dc22
                                     2007023719

Editor: Kate Montgomery

Production: Lynne Costa

Cover design: Night & Day Design

Cover and interior photographs: Angela Jimenez

Typesetter: House of Equations, Inc.

Manufacturing: Steve Bernier

Printed in the United States of America on acid-free paper

11 10 09 08 07   EB   1 2 3 4 5

For Christina, Stuart, Stapleton, and the Peanut

Contents

Acknowledgments

I am most grateful to the teachers and writers in whose company I have been lucky enough to spend time, absorbing and learning.

I will always be thankful for my time at the Teachers College Reading and Writing Project. Working for Lucy Calkins was an extraordinary gift, whose benefits will always be with me. My colleagues at the project made up one of the most rigorous and inspiring learning communities I have known. More than that, they are true friends.

I thank Pam Allyn and Patricia Vitale-Reilly of LitLife for valuable feedback on my first book. It made writing this one much more comfortable.

From Tom Romano, Katie Ray, and Katherine Bomer I learned so much about writing purposefully, writing to learn, writing to discover, and then writing about all that writing. I so admire their clarity on the topic of writing, infused with a deep respect and understanding of children.

Virginia Lockwood Zisa taught me more about the gifts of building a strong community than I could ever say.

Elizabeth Schmidt, Emily Jenkins, and Aoibheann Sweeney gave me valuable advice about book reviews. Janet Angelillo helped me think more deeply about writing about reading.

I want to thank everyone at Heinemann for all they did to help me write my book, make it look good, and market it well. Alan Huisman combed through this book, fixing, tweaking, rewording, and rearranging so that my ideas could be as clear and elegant as possible. He even made one of my jokes funnier. Kate Montgomery, my friend and editor (frienditor?), gracefully changed roles as the book progressed. First she helped shape my proposal, then she coached me to set benchmarks. She encouraged me to keep up my pace. Most importantly, she stood at the finish line, cheering me to the end, lest I pass out before reaching it.

Special thanks are due to P.S. 8 in Brooklyn Heights. Principal Seth Phillips gave me a place in his school and trusted me to explore these units of study. Noelle Gentile, Jonathan Garbar, Melissa Browning, Julie Ross, Kristen Jennings, and Jeremy Manger graciously opened their classrooms to me, working tirelessly with their students to troubleshoot and fine-tune these units. Precious Jones-Walker and all of the parents were a great support to this work. Of course, the true stars are the children whose work you will see in these pages. My affection for them has grown exponentially as I have watched them jump into every unit, some more enthusiastically than others, of course, but always with conviction.

Introduction

My early experiences with writing, particularly in school, were a mixture of happiness and frustration, purpose and boredom, self-worth and discouragement. When I look at the common denominator of the good times, it comes down to *purpose*. I was never one to enjoy a task or assignment without knowing why I was doing it. A few years ago, while helping my mother move, I found a big box in her garage that contained all my old school photographs and report cards. As a teacher, I am very good at reading report card comments and knowing exactly what they mean. Was it a coincidence that the teachers who complained of my "inability to work to potential" were the same ones whose assignments seemed to have no purpose? And that the ones who raved about me are the ones I so fondly remember giving me work I could sink my teeth into? I don't think so. In a way I wrote this book for the younger me and for those teachers who gave purposeless assignments and whom I must have frustrated to no end. Work has to be done in second grade, certainly. But we can invite all children to participate in it joyfully and purposefully.

The five units in this book develop children's abilities to identify and connect with a purpose for writing comprehensible, complete pieces. The first unit, on setting up a strong community, supports the work in the remaining units—writing for change, writing a book review, exploring humor, and writing about research. Each unit requires students to consider their audience and write to achieve a specific purpose with that audience. Naturally, a writing workshop includes other units that develop other writing skills. Many of these units are contained in the Units of Study in the Primary Writing Workshop series, by

Lucy Calkins and the Teachers College Reading and Writing Project. Figure 1 is a calendar showing one possible way that all these units can work together.

The units in this book deal with the writing skills I most want to share with you, but they are not the only choices! You may want to create a unit of study of your own based on your needs and those of your students. If you do, I highly recommend Katie Wood Ray's amazing book *Study Driven* (2006). With great clarity, Katie will inspire you to lead your children to exciting places in their writing.

In choosing which units of study to teach, we must consider balance, standards, our favorite literature, and the life of our classroom. A curriculum needs balance. Some units will be genre based (poetry, for example), while others will focus on a skill (perhaps revision). We may also want to vary the pace, following long units with short ones and vice versa. Of course our curriculum must also address the requirements set forth by our school, district, or state. Then, too, we should all be allowed to teach what we love, if for no other reason than to model for children how loving something makes it more fun to learn about. Finally, the life of the classroom should be a factor in some curriculum decisions.

Of necessity, much of our year is mapped out before we really know our students, but flexibility is essential. Here's a case in point. A friend of mine was going to help me do research for this book by teaching the humor unit to her class. A week before she was going to begin, one of her students lost a parent.

MONTH	UNIT OF STUDY
September	Becoming a Community of Writers
October	Personal Narrative
November	Writing for Readers or Revision
December	Writing for Change
January	Nonfiction: Topics of Personal Interest or Experience
February	Exploring Humor
March	Author Study or Personal Narrative Again
April	Poetry
May	Writing About Research
June	Realistic Fiction

Figure I–1 Possible Calendar for Writing Workshop

Humor at this time would have been totally inappropriate. She chose instead to create a unit on writing to heal and come together. It was a worthwhile unit and one the class could fully embrace. It will probably never be part of any standard curriculum, but it belonged completely in my friend's class.

■ How the Units Are Set Up

Every unit of study in this book is presented in a similar way: a brief overview followed by a more detailed description of the steps in planning and teaching it. These steps are discussed below.

Goals/Outcomes

The goals for each unit are divided into four categories: *writing quality, writing conventions, writing habits,* and *community*. These goals take into account not only children's ability to write with a conscious purpose but also some other beliefs about young writers, namely that our classes must be communities and our children must become independent if they are going to write authentically and from the heart. Deciding the goals of any given unit of study can be difficult. As teachers, we want to teach it all at the same time. It's hard to wait to teach something that we wish our kids could do now. That's why this step is so important. We *can't* teach it all at once! We have to set goals for each unit that are realistic and that build on the work of prior units so that we are able to teach it all by the end of the year.

Getting Ready to Teach

Before we begin a new unit of study, we need to prepare physically and mentally for the demands posed by the curriculum. We must identify the materials we will need and think about what lessons will be best for these particular children. This preparation requires reflecting on the unit that came before, looking at how we guided our students toward the goals we set there, and planning how we will continue to guide them toward the goals of the next unit. Understanding our students' needs and the kind of literature we are studying will help us design writing paper for children to use.

Gathering Materials

We then gather and study *mentor texts*—literature that can serve as models of good writing in a particular genre or with a particular structure, both for our students and for us. We may of course refer to other books during the unit, but we must have these core books to which we can return again and again as we teach skills and qualities of good writing. We should see strong and clear qualities of good writing in the books we choose, as these will become the examples we use to teach children how to develop those same qualities in their own writing. A book makes a great mentor text when we see lots of teaching possibilities in it.

After we gather these books, we must read them all carefully, looking for possible teaching points. Thoroughly understanding what our mentor texts have to offer gives us a greater vision of what our students can do. We need no longer be bogged down with that old standby admonition to "add details." From a single book we might want to show examples of how a writer chooses words to create mental images, uses punctuation to build tension, or includes dialogue to help the reader feel part of the story. We decide which of these many qualities to teach based on the needs of the current unit of study and the readiness of these particular children to learn them. For example, we needn't teach children about using dialogue early in the year, when they may be using only a few simple sentences to tell a story, or in a nonfiction unit.

A helpful technique is to keep sticky notes inside each book on which we have written the page numbers of good examples of quality writing that will help us as we do the following:

● *Plan lessons.* Since we have some ideas about what we want to teach based both on the needs of the class and the unit of study, we can look in the books for lesson ideas and possible examples. Knowing the books at our disposal is essential to being able to plan lessons that will meet the children's needs as closely as possible.

● *Prepare for conferences.* There are going to be as many needs in a primary class as there are children. One student may need to see an example of a certain way to organize ideas, another may need a book from which to do some research, while a third may need to see a variety of ways to break away from a format that has become habitual. Knowing a wide variety of books helps us meet all these needs better and more quickly.

● *Prepare for small-group work.* Often, a conference that benefits one child will also benefit a few others. We can assemble multiple copies of a book, get an enlarged copy of it, or photocopy a given page or passage and then gather a small group of children and use the selected material to teach them the strategy or technique.

We can then use the sticky notes to find clear examples of each writing skill or strategy we teach. We may not use every single example we find, but if something comes up and we need to change direction a bit, we'll be prepared.

Considering the Students

Next we look at the students' work not just as an assessment of the unit they are finishing but as an assessment of their needs in the unit to come. Both their published work and the daily writing that accumulates in their folders give us information about what they will need in lessons and conferences to facilitate their progress.

Published work tells us how students shape a piece of writing. We can learn how much ownership they take of their writing and how they use writing and revision strategies:

- Did this child love this piece of writing or did she choose it for publication because it was getting close to our celebration date?
- Is her voice apparent in this writing? Does it seem as though she developed the work according to her own ideas?
- Is there evidence that she made changes—carets, cross-outs, additions? What kinds of changes—single words, whole sentences, entire pages added or removed, spelling changes, wording changes?
- Did her revisions make the piece more focused, clear, and complete or less so?
- Has she corrected spelling and punctuation she has learned since the piece was first written?

It is important to consider the daily writing that builds up in children's folders as thoughtfully as we consider their published work. This is how we learn about their writing habits, their willingness to take risks, and their comfort with new skills and strategies.

- Does he try new kinds of writing or new topics? Does he have a favorite topic to which he returns often? If so, does he write about it in the same way, or does he try to approach it differently in new pieces of writing?
- Does he make changes to the writing as he goes?
- Does he return to writing? Does he have any ongoing projects, such as a book or a long story?
- Does he seem to have fun? Does he seem to want perfection? Does this help or hurt him?
- Does he use new skills or spelling words I have taught? Can I read the writing better than I could last time I looked?
- Does the use of conventions improve over time?

Preparing Demonstration Materials

Demonstrating makes all the difference. In fact, according to Brian Cambourne (1988), it is a condition of learning. When teaching skills or strategies, we need to keep in mind that we are not modeling but demonstrating. Demonstrating is more deliberate and focused and has certain qualities that make it an effective method for teaching strategies. Following are the important principles of a demonstration:

- *One thing is being demonstrated or highlighted.* A demonstration is most clear when we clearly define the skill or strategy we are teaching. If a strategy has more than a handful of steps or is too elaborate, we need to break it down. It can be difficult, but we must strive to name the strategy or skill being taught in every lesson. We want students to know what they are about to learn, but we also know that putting a strategy into words forces us to be clear and succinct about what that strategy actually is and how it can be done. For example, *being a good partner* cannot be clearly demonstrated. It is vague and means different things to different people on different days. The small steps that children need to take to become good partners, though, can be demonstrated. *Sitting hip-to-hip with the book between you* can be shown clearly and unambiguously in the space of a few minutes.

- *The demonstration is accompanied by a verbal description.* A demonstration without an accompanying description of the action is like magic. We watch the trick and are impressed and amazed but could not possibly repeat it on our own. The purpose of the accompanying description is to demystify the process of reading and writing by sharing our insider's knowledge. Imagine the magician telling his audience, "There's a hidden compartment here and that's where I get the second coin. See?" Some people call this verbal description *thinking aloud*, a phrase that aptly implies a private viewing into the mind of the expert. We are naming and describing a process that has become second nature to us but is still a challenge for our students.

- *The language is clear and consistent.* While thinking aloud, we must remember to use language that children understand. Too many metaphors or digressions will cloud the process rather than make it clear. Where possible, we must use consistent language to describe the strategies we are demonstrating. If we say sometimes, "Sound it out," and sometimes, "Get your mouth ready," and sometimes, "Think about the sound that letter makes," it can be confusing. It is easier to cue children to use a strategy when we describe that strategy with a consistent phrase.

Teaching the Units

Each unit is divided into comparable sections (with an occasional variation). We know that keeping our daily schedule consistent helps children accomplish more. The same holds true for units of study. Consistently encountering the same components, children get better at the skills of *studying* writing as well as at the skills of writing.

Understanding the Genre/Reading Like Writers

Each study begins with reading the kind of books we are going to be writing. When we know the books well as readers, we will be able to read them the way a writer might, looking at the author's craft. We look at how writers use words and punctuation and at how they put their books together. Two fantastic resources that offer information on this concept and on studying the craft of writing are *Wondrous Words*, by Katie Wood Ray (1999), and *Authors as Mentors* (from Units of Study for Primary Writing: A Yearlong Curriculum), by Lucy Calkins and Amanda Hartman (2003).

Organizing Ideas

As they get older, children start to make drafts part of their writing process. In second grade, most children are not quite ready to rewrite entire pieces into new drafts. They *are* ready, however, to plan and organize their pieces before they start writing. As a precursor to drafting, we help them make ever more substantial plans, to which they will refer as they write.

Writing

When we write, it is for a purpose and an audience. We want to communicate an idea. It is important that children discover that their voices matter and that it is for their purpose, not ours, that they learn to write well. When children consider their audience, they are motivated to convey their ideas clearly and explicitly and to pay attention to conventions. When they take this initiative, they look inside themselves for the messages they want to send, choosing topics and genres that support their needs. We teach them how to support their needs and their growth rather than how to do better on an assessment. The beauty is that most children who have a vested interest in their writing lives *do* perform better on standardized assessments.

Revision

We continue each unit by choosing the piece of writing that the children think best represents their growth as writers. They then learn a new strategy for revising this piece of writing. We often think of revision as making our writing *better*, but a more helpful and friendly definition is this: revision is the act of making the writing match more closely the ideas and feelings of the writer. In school I always thought I had to revise because my writing was not good enough the first time around. Now I tell children they revise their work because it *is* good enough. Good writing deserves to be revised. "Bad" writing is also an important part of the process, but it might not merit a lot of extra labor.

Revision is part of the process of all writers, not just adults or older children. Revision can be as simple as adding a smile to a face in a drawing to make the emotion more clear. When we teach children to revise as we teach them to write, it does not become the chore it was for many of us as we were growing up. Each unit introduces a new revision strategy, which becomes part of the children's repertoire of writing skills.

Editing

Put simply, editing is what children must learn to do to make their writing readable. Editing may mean putting spaces between words, using more letters (or the right letters) to represent the sounds in words, correcting spelling and punctuation, or making sure all of the intended words are written on the paper. As soon as children are writing (or approximating) words, they can learn to edit. Each unit contains an editing lesson, but only you will know which editing strategy is appropriate for your class at any given time. If your class is just starting to write words, it may not be appropriate to expect the children to use periods and capital letters correctly. It may be better to teach them to read their writing while pointing a finger under each word. Whatever lessons you present, it is important to get children looking at their work critically and thoughtfully.

Publishing and Celebrating

Now that their work has been revised and edited, it is ready for some final sprucing up. This could mean giving it a pretty cover, coloring the illustrations nicely, writing a dedication, telling readers about the author, or adding a blurb to the back cover. When we send our work out into the world, we make it more special than the work that stays in the folder. We are ready to celebrate! This is the reward for all our hard work.

Teachers are often overwhelmed by the thought of celebrating each published piece of writing (say, nine or ten a year). But not every celebration has to have balloons and parents and cupcakes. Most, in fact, will be simple and intimate: just the class gathering in a circle and sharing favorite pages from their writing or offering a compliment to each writer as her writing is posted on the wall or bulletin board. We may make a toast with a cup of juice, congratulating ourselves for the achievement and launching ourselves into the next challenge. Of course, sometimes (maybe twice during the year) we will want to pull out all the stops and invite the children's families and the school community to share in the joy and pride that comes from a job well done.

We shouldn't skip celebrations. Even a small celebration is important to the future of our writing communities. A celebration at the end of a unit of study is akin to graduation. We acknowledge and validate the progress we have made and name the new skills we have mastered or at least begun to master. We also prepare mentally for a new unit, unknown territory into which we can venture with the certainty that all our efforts will be rewarded with new learning. Celebrating is a way to help us be aware of our learning, and it helps children follow our lessons more fearlessly than they otherwise might.

Reflection

Sometimes as children are sharing their work and usually at the end of a unit, we need to encourage them to reflect on their learning. We might ask them questions orally or in writing. The major things we want to know are what they say they have learned, what they think they have done well, what was difficult for them, and what they wish they had done better. This tells us whether we are getting our point across and helps us understand how the children perceive our teaching. More important, it encourages the children to find words to describe what they are learning to do as writers. When they can name their intentions, it becomes possible for them to judge for themselves whether or not they are successful. Their decisions are now motivated from within, not by us.

Predictable Problems

No matter how complete our planning, how pure our intentions, how deep our knowledge, how great our experience, or how energetic our approach— no matter what—there will always be problems. Our job is not to teach without trouble, but to recognize and respond to that trouble effectively. Some problems are impossible to predict, but others are easy to imagine. The lists in the chapters are not complete. Your students may present challenges I haven't mentioned. We inevitably become frustrated from time to time, but we must remember that these obstacles are part of the work, not an impediment to it.

The way we approach difficulty will resound in the hearts and minds of our students for a long time. I try always to remind myself that my job is to help children solve their problems in a way that makes them feel loved and successful.

Assessment

Assessment of student writing is critical to effective teaching. Each unit suggests goals to keep in mind as we look at student work. Rather than thinking of our students as *high*, *middle*, and *low*, we can see them as individuals with a balance of strengths and needs. When we use this information to help us plan what we teach to the whole class, to small groups, and to individuals, we are spending our time much more effectively. Carl Anderson's book *Assessing Writers* (2005) is a great resource on the topic.

I am amazed by the things second graders are able to accomplish. The teachers and children I have worked with, in many schools, in many parts of the country, have achieved impressive results by increasing their focus on purposeful writing as part of their curriculum. The units in this book are the result of years of field testing with the help of generous teachers and children, reflecting on what worked well, and improving what could have worked better. I hope you find them helpful and that I have left room for you to find your own voice within them.

■ Professional Resources

Anderson, Carl. 2005. *Assessing Writers*. Portsmouth, NH: Heinemann.

Calkins, Lucy, and Amanda Hartman. 2003. *Authors as Mentors*. Portsmouth, NH: *firsthand*.

Cambourne, Brian. 1988. *The Whole Story: Natural Learning and the Acquisition of Literacy in the Classroom*. New York: Ashton Scholastic.

Ray, Katie Wood. 1999. *Wondrous Words: Writers and Writing in the Elementary Classroom*. Urbana, IL: NCTE.

———. 2006. *Study Driven: A Framework for Planning Units of Study in the Writing Workshop*. Portsmouth, NH: Heinemann.

www.stephanieparsons.com (author's website).

Becoming a
Community of Writers

1

Your job the first month of school—the most important thing you need to accomplish—to is turn a diverse group of individuals into a team of dedicated learners. The members of a true community care at least as much about the well-being and success of the group as they do about their own individual accomplishment. In *First Grade Writers*, I say:

In a community of writers, children

- are willing to take risks and try new things

- want to write every day

- see their daily writing as something that benefits them (rather than as something you want from them)

- cooperate in maintaining a productive environment

- may be working on different kinds of writing at different paces from one another

- know and care about what their classmates are working on

- listen to one another's writing

- comment thoughtfully on one another's work

- value one another's efforts (2005, 13–14)

I shared these thoughts about community recently to a group of teachers brand new to the writing workshop. They were excited about the mental image of a class hard at work, but they found it difficult to believe that children would work in such a focused way without constant prodding: "They won't do what I ask for long enough for me to confer with anyone!" One man, an excellent and devoted teacher, laughed outright at this (to him) pie-in-the-sky notion of the classroom as a well-oiled machine of human industry. Of course, a successful workshop *depends* on children being able to work independently for at least thirty minutes, so if you cannot envision this being true, it's hard to envision a workshop at all. The magic ingredient is community. I promise.

Children want to learn and to express themselves. What children do not want and will reject is a curriculum—any curriculum, no matter how good— that does not trust, value, or even *hear* their voices as learners. A curriculum in which you as the teacher do not feel welcome to include *your* voice is just as big a problem. You and your students *must* feel comfortable and valued in your classroom. With a true community in place, your children will live up to the high expectations you have of them.

■ Overview

Your first step in building a community of writers is to help your class identify the qualities of the community to which *they* wish to belong. When, on the first day of school, you ask children what they need in order to work and learn together this year, they will feel that their voices matter. By asking them to help you establish the norms of behavior, you are giving them an opportunity to address their fears as well as their hopes. When they say, "I don't want people to say mean things," they are letting you know that they fear an unsafe environment. When they say, "We should listen when someone is talking," they are telling you they hope to be respectful and mature. Most of the rules they want in place in the classroom are ones you would have established anyway, so why not make it a dialogue?

In this first month you will also need to establish routines and expectations for writing workshop. Children must learn appropriate ways of moving around the classroom, getting and caring for tools and supplies, coming up with ideas, putting thoughts into words, consulting with fellow writers, and staying focused. Because most, if not all, children will write stories based on their own experiences, your minilessons will be a balance between those that focus on community and those that lift the quality of personal narrative writing. At the end of the month you will have a small celebration, just for your class, acknowledging the hard work you all did to become a community. Be sure to celebrate not just the writing, or product, but also the process by which the writing was achieved. And don't be disappointed if the quality of the writing is not what you'd hoped. Now that your class is a community, it will be much easier to teach your students the many ways there are to improve the quality of their work.

■ Goals/Outcomes

As your learners become writers, there are other goals besides community that you need to address. Your shared purpose in the workshop is to learn to write better—to communicate more clearly in writing, to have a stronger sense of the conventions of written language, to begin to find your voice as a writer, and to consider the various audiences for whom you may write. Keep the following goals in mind, revising them as you get to know *these* students in *this* class.

Writing Quality

We hope children will

- choose topics that matter deeply to them
- keep their writing focused on a single idea
- choose words carefully to communicate their ideas
- write stories that make sense and engage their readers

Writing Conventions

We hope children will

- spell frequently used words correctly
- use the proper end punctuation, quotation marks, and capitalization

Writing Habits

We hope children will

- participate in class conversations about literature
- get to work quickly and remain productive for increasing amounts of time
- manage their own writing tools and supplies

- talk to one another about their reading or writing

- make and use a plan to write

- read and reread their work often

- revise their work

- edit their work

Community

We hope children will

- volunteer ideas, listen, and respond to their peers

- work with a partner to develop and improve each other's writing

- show respect for all members of the community and their work, re-gardless of ability

- express disagreement in a way that promotes conversation rather than shuts it down

- ask for help when they encounter problems and offer to help classmates with problems

■ Getting Ready to Teach

As you prepare to build a class community, you do not need to spend a lot of time and money on classroom décor. If the only thing on the walls when your students walk into the room on the first day of school is the last writing they did the year before, what better way to tell them their voices matter? You do not need prepackaged charts and displays. How do the makers of those mate-rials know what to expect of your students, anyway? You'll make what you need together.

Gathering Materials

I always get excited when I gather materials for the new school year—fresh pencils and markers, neat stacks of paper, new mentor texts I've discovered over the summer. These things will soon take on the patina of daily use, but for the moment they're pristine, waiting for a new group of kids to discover them. You don't need a lot of stuff to get started—a couple of types of paper, pencils or pens, some folders. As children become accustomed to the daily routines, you can gradually introduce new materials—tape, scissors, a stapler, a date stamp, individual word booklets, white correction tape (for covering mistakes), special ink colors for revising and editing—and teach children how to get them from a centrally located place.

Considering the Students

Before the school year even begins, you can pursue ways to help individual students become part of a learning community. Take a look at their report cards from the prior year and any anecdotal observations offered by their teacher. With this information you can introduce temporary structures, such as a seating plan and classroom jobs, with which students will be comfortable. For example, put friends at a table together. Assume they will earn the privilege of staying together and explain specifically what that means. Or put children of various academic abilities at the same table, so they will know they haven't already been categorized. Give children with low confidence a high-profile job like walking at the head of the line. As you get to know your students in the first days and weeks of school, you will discover many opportunities to help them feel successful and valuable and many ways to avoid creating situations in which they may fail or resort to destructive behavior.

This first month many children also need to build their stamina for writing. The summer has a way of inhibiting kids' productivity in the classroom. Some impediments to volume and stamina are

- being new to writing workshop
- lacking confidence
- being a perfectionist
- not knowing what is expected
- knowing what is expected and being daunted by it
- lacking hand strength or coordination
- not knowing how to get started or continue
- writing in a new language

Try to determine what is getting in your students' way so that you can address it. Often, it may look like a behavior problem, but if you address it as such—with punishments or consequences—you may unwittingly aggravate the situation. I usually behave as if my students want to do their work and do it well, working through obstacles as they arise. Make sure your expectations for individual children are realistic. Young Derek, who writes two words in thirty minutes during your first class, is not suddenly going to write a whole page. Nor is Ibrahim, who came to America the previous week and is silently observing everything that happens around him. Looking at what Derek and Ibrahim *can* do will help you decide what they can do *next*. If, on the other hand, students are writing a lot, focus your goals on meaning, structure, and voice, qualities they may be overlooking as they concentrate on volume. We, and our students, can become so proud of the quantity of work that we lose sight of the quality.

Preparing Demonstration Materials

It's important to have a few of your own texts or story ideas to use in mini-lessons. These don't need to be finished pieces, just good, solid ideas that you know you can turn into an engaging narrative. Not everyone feels comfortable writing, but we all tell stories and communicate with words. You do not need to write the great American novel! The rows upon rows of published books in your classroom library give children examples of the heights they may reach in their writing, but your demonstrations are examples of the process all writers go through. You can't get that from a book.

When you teach a new strategy, you won't have to think something up on the spot. Your bank of stories will be at your disposal. For example, say you want to teach children how to add dialogue to a story. Your lesson will be clearer if you have a story of your own that conveniently does not have dialogue but does have more than one character. The one about you and your brother sneaking into an abandoned house will do just fine! Invite children to listen in as you think aloud: "Hmm . . . I remember my brother saying, 'What if we get caught?' and I just laughed and told him not to be a baby. I'm going to add that conversation to my story!" Another day you may want to teach children how to add a character's internal thinking. You can use a version of a story in which you mention none of your thoughts and demonstrate adding them, letting your students see *how a writer decides to employ these strategies*, not just what writing that already has these qualities looks like.

■ Teaching the Unit

If you are like me, you will need to keep reminding yourself that this unit is more about teaching children how to function in a writing workshop than it is about teaching them to write better. In the third week of school, you will suddenly look at a piece of writing and wonder how it escaped your notice that *you have not taught this child a single thing*. A cold, bony hand will grip your heart. It will pass. Improving children's writing takes time and patience, faith that the fruits of your teaching will appear in their work the same way a bulb planted in the fall pops up in the spring. Be your own support group (or, better, gather an actual support group of like-minded teachers), and keep looking at the amount of growth, not the distance yet to go. Figure 1–1 shows an outline of all the teaching you might do in this unit.

We Are All Writers

We *are* all writers. We are *not* all writers of the next great novel, screenplay, or poem. But we are all people with ideas and messages worth putting onto paper so others can share them. Even after writing this book—my third—I still do not always think of myself as a writer. The feeling that I am not a real writer because I don't write novels (or memoirs or plays or essays or newspaper articles) is hard to shake. But writing is so much more than those things. If you keep an inclusive spirit in mind as you teach, you will guide children toward discovering the writers they are. You may even find the writer *you* are!

Guiding Questions

● *What do we need to have around us to be able to learn a lot and write a lot this year?* You already have ideas about the rules and routines you want in your classroom. You do not have to give these up when you ask children for input. They will want many of the same things you do. As you ask them to describe the writing environment they want, chart their responses. You may need to tweak their phrasing. Sometimes children tell us what they think we want to hear rather than what's really on their minds. If a child volunteers, "There should be no talking," you might respond, "Or if we talk in writing workshop, it should be about our writing. It would be a shame to have all these great writers in here and not be able to discuss our work." In keeping this discussion open and honest, you will help children feel comfortable about articulating their hopes for themselves as writers.

● *Who are we now and who do we want to become as writers?* From the first day of school your students need to think of themselves as writers. When you speak to them in this of-*course*-you're-a-writer way, you empower them to treat their time, environment, and classmates as a writer would. They will learn to take seriously the grand work you have planned for them this year, imagining for themselves the better, stronger writers they can become. It's even better when they think of themselves as writers with *dreams*. Their answers to this question will give you tons of information about how to reach them as you travel through a year of writing workshop. When a student says, "I want to

TIME FRAME	SECTION OF STUDY	WHAT CHILDREN DO	WHAT YOU TEACH
4–5 days	We Are All Writers	• Receive and decorate folders • Get used to writing every day • Explore writing identity, including favorite topics and genres • Learn how the classroom functions • Listen to and talk about great books together • Get to know other writers in class	Guiding questions • What do we need to have around us to be able to learn a lot and write a lot this year? • Who are we now and who do we want to become as writers? Minilessons, conferences, or midworkshop focus points • One way to start a new piece is by writing about an important thing that happened. • A good way to start a new day is by reading what we wrote before. • It's important for us to know what our favorite topics are. • Writing workshop will go the same way every day. • We must treat our work with loving care. • We need to work together to keep it quiet (not silent). • Our favorite books can inspire us. • We can make our stories more interesting by including what we were thinking, wondering, or feeling.
7–10 days	Writers Have Routines and Processes	• Learn how to move around classroom • Learn to get and care for supplies • Write for longer periods • Review oral planning • Review strategies for using time productively (chart) • Learn to manage the work in their folders • Discuss and explore the kinds of things that can be made with writing	Guiding question • What are some ways to stay productive during writing workshop (besides, of course, writing)? Minilessons, conferences, or midworkshop focus points • We can get supplies for ourselves when we need them. • We know what to do when we think we are done. • We sometimes have to push ourselves to keep writing. • Talking through a plan before writing helps keep our work clear. • As writers we should know what our trouble spots are. • Talking to writers like us can help us figure out how to work through problems. • We can work on more than one project at the same time. • The information in our pictures can also be in our words.

Figure 1–1 Becoming a Community of Writers at a Glance

TIME FRAME	SECTION OF STUDY	WHAT CHILDREN DO	WHAT YOU TEACH
4–5 days	Working with a Partner	• Learn to read a partner's writing critically and give helpful feedback • Work with different partners	Guiding question • What makes a great writing partner? Minilessons, conferences, or midworkshop focus points • Compliments are most helpful when they are specific. • People can be sensitive about their work, so it's best to ask questions or give suggestions in a gentle way. • One helpful way to listen to (or read) a partner's work is to see if everything is clear and makes sense. • If your partner has a suggestion, it may be worth trying; if you don't like it, you can always go back to the way it was. • Dialogue can bring a story to life.
2–3 days	Choosing, Revising, Editing, and Publishing	• Choose a project to publish • Revise to achieve focus • Make sure known words, onsets, and rimes are spelled correctly • Make sure end punctuation is correct • Learn to use revision and editing checklists • Participate in whole-class sharing and commenting • Celebrate	Minilessons, conferences, or midworkshop focus points • When you choose a piect to revise, you are choosing something that deserves some extra attention and work to become great. • The information in our pictures can also be in our words. • All word-wall words and spelling patterns should be spelled correctly.

Figure 1–1 *(continued)*

be a better speller," you can remind her during word study that she is learning this for herself, not for you, for the district, or for her parents.

Possible Teaching Points

● *One way to start a new piece is by writing about an important thing that happened.* In my school the second graders have heard this since kindergarten, but it needs to be repeated each year. The habit of living life as a writer, paying attention to how experiences will translate into stories, is like a muscle: it atrophies when it isn't used for, say, a whole summer. It comes back strong with encouragement, though. The examples you see in this book are those of children whose kindergarten and first grade teachers followed Units of Study in the Primary Writing Workshop, by Lucy Calkins and the Teachers College Reading and Writing Project and my book, *First Grade Writers*. If your new students have not internalized the habits of writing about important events in their lives with focus and some elaboration, consider teaching lessons on the following strategies:

- planning a story orally before writing it down

- stretching a single story across three to five pages

- keeping the story focused

● *A good way to start a new day is by reading what we wrote before.* Like the previous lesson, this should be a reminder rather than a new concept. Children should habitually reread older work as well as create new work. This is how they come to know themselves as writers. By doing this, they can learn

- which topics most interest them

- what phrases or words they use most often

- which spellings or conventions they need to work on

- how much progress they have made over time

● *It's important for us to know what our favorite topics are.* I used to get so irritated when my students would write about the same thing over and over: "If I see one more park story, I'll lose my mind." A little time and wisdom later, I see that revisiting the topic was not the problem. The problem was that they were writing the same *generalization* over and over again: "I went to the park. It was fun." What I needed to teach them was how to write specifically about experiences *at* the park. When children have a writing identity that includes certain topics (or genres or crafting techniques), they do not need to spend as much time making decisions about these things. The student who says, "I am the kind of writer who loves a good park story," can jump right into creating a narrative about a specific incident that took place there.

● *Writing workshop will go the same way every day.* It will be easier for children to internalize the workshop routines if they are in fact the same every day. Of course children will need repetition, a few days' worth, in order to make the workshop routines habitual, but an explicit outline of what these routines are will help them do it quickly. Teach and show them how to sit in the meeting area for a minilesson, get from the meeting area to their desks, get supplies, deal with dull pencils, and whatever else you want done in a specific way.

● *We must treat our work with loving care.* Children take many of their cues from adults' behavior. If you speak lovingly of your students' work, handling it with care, they will understand that you value it and that they should too. You may want to demonstrate some specific ways to treat their own work lovingly. Stacking their papers nicely and sliding them into the pocket of a folder will keep their writing safe from wrinkles and stains. Single-line cross-outs will keep their work looking nice and easy to read. Crossing out or erasing too hard can rip a paper. Not everything is a great piece of work, but it's always good enough to save for later. Teaching your children these and other good habits will help them come to value their work.

● *We need to work together to keep it quiet (not silent).* Remind children often that the classroom belongs to all of you. Your actions will speak as loud as your words here, so they must believe you. When you asked your students what they needed to succeed as writers, they probably said they needed a quiet place to work. As you remind them to keep quiet, tell them it is because *they* asked for it. As frustrated as noise or unfocused conversation may make you, respond with encouragement to keep it ever more quiet. Too much scolding (which you will also have to do from time to time; we're all human after all) will send the message that it is *your* room, not theirs.

● *Our favorite books can inspire us*. Some children in your class may have no trouble setting immediately to work on new pieces of writing. For those who have not yet discovered the great font of ideas within them, this is a strategy for starting a new piece. Show children how to use a favorite book as an inspiration for creating their own. The idea is not to copy a published piece but to try something similar—in topic, format, structure, tone, any number of ways.

● *We can make our stories more interesting by including what we were thinking, wondering, or feeling.* As you have been teaching them about the structures of writing workshop, your students have been working on stories about their lives. Remember to teach lessons that address the quality of their writing along with those that focus on routines and community. A little attention to the internal story—the thoughts, questions, or feelings a writer might associate with a memory—can make the narrative much more engaging for the reader.

Student Work

Anya, like her classmates, learned to write a personal story across three pages in first grade. Her addition of thoughts and feelings on the second page of an early second grade story make it more interesting and more specific (see Figures 1–2 through 1–4).

Lauren loved to tell her readers that something was fun or that she was happy (see Figures 1–5 and 1–6, pp. 23–24). In the second example, she shows her readers *how* she had fun.

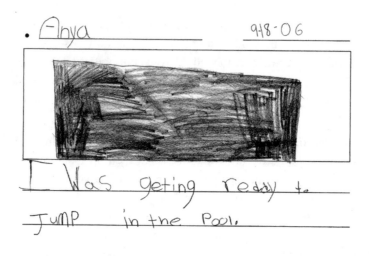

I was getting ready to jump in the pool.

Figure 1–2 Page 1 of Anya's Story

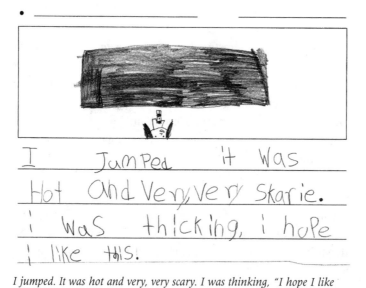

I jumped. It was hot and very, very scary. I was thinking, "I hope I like this."

Figure 1–3 Page 2 of Anya's Story

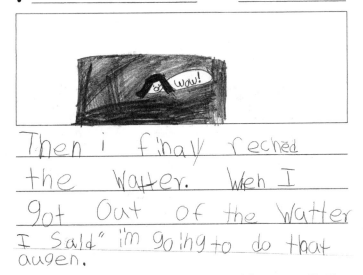

Then i finaly reched the watter. Wen I got Out of the watter I said" i'm going to do that augen.

Then I finally reached the water. When I got out of the water I said, "I'm going to do that again."

Figure 1–4 Page 3 of Anya's Story

· LAUREN   9/6/06

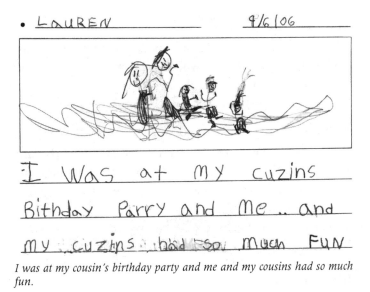

I Was at my cuzins Bithday Parry and me .. and my cuzins had so much FUN

I was at my cousin's birthday party and me and my cousins had so much fun.

Figure 1–5 Lauren's First Page

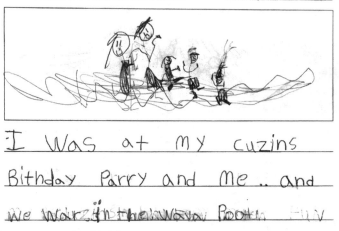

I was at my cousin's birthday party and me and we were in the wave pool.

Figure 1–6 Lauren's Second Page

David's story (Figures 1–7 through 1–8) is similar to a lot of second grade stories written during the first week of school. It tells about a really fun thing the writer did during the summer, listing several component events. His next conferences will be about focus first and then elaboration.

Writers Have Routines and Processes

Now that your students know you think of them as writers and are getting used to sitting still somewhat quietly for writing workshop, you can teach some of the routines you want them to use. Show children how you want them to move around the classroom, get and put away supplies, and work productively.

Guiding Question

• **What are some ways to stay productive during writing workshop (besides, of course, writing)?** The more options children have for using their time in a workshop, the more independent they will become, the fewer behavior problems you will need to address, and the more you can teach. If you chart your students' responses, you can refer children to the chart when they do not know what to do or they claim to be finished. Figure 1–9 (p. 26) shows some options.

Possible Teaching Points

• **We can get supplies for ourselves when we need them.** Some teachers keep a small basket of supplies on each table. Each time they add a new item—tape,

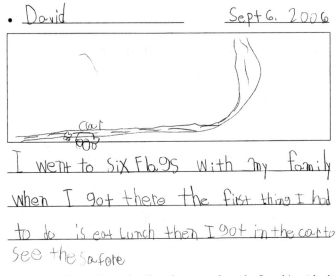

I went to Six Flags with my family. When I got there the first thing I had to do is eat lunch. Then I got in the car to see the safari.

Figure 1–7 David's "Six Flags" Story (Page 1)

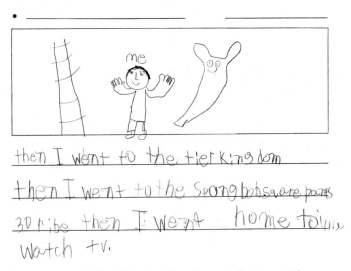

Then I went to the Tiger Kingdom. Then I went to the SpongeBob SquarePants 3D ride. Then I went home to watch TV.

Figure 1–8 David's "Six Flags" Story (Page 3)

- Read or reread your work.
    - Are word-wall words spelled correctly?
    - Are periods and capitals where they should be?
    - Is the whole story there?
    - Does it make sense?
    - Is everything in the pictures also in the words?
    - Do you like the beginning and the ending?
- Add to or rewrite an older piece of writing.
- Look at book for inspiration.
- Make a list of important memories, people, or places (these could become story topics).
- Sketch an important memory, place, or person (this could spark an idea for a story).
- Start a project in another genre (make a comic or a poem, for instance).
- Take a short walk around the classroom to clear your head (but don't bother anyone).
- Read your work to a partner.

Figure 1–9 How to Make the Most of Writing Workshop

scissors, correction tape, different-colored pens for revising—they demonstrate how to use that item properly. If you wish to keep all supplies in a central place (a writing center), show children how to use that place, as well as how to use the supplies. Students should walk there quietly without stopping to distract other children, take what they need, and walk back to their writing spot. When they have finished using the items, they should return them the same way.

- *We know what to do when we think we are done.* This concept is actually a summary of a lot of things children have already learned, rather than a new idea. Let students know that when they feel finished with a piece of writing, there are a number of things they can do other than saying, "I'm done!" Remind them to refer to the chart of ways to stay productive.

- *We sometimes have to push ourselves to keep writing.* Some young writers are very concerned with making sure that every word is spelled correctly or that their choice of words is perfect. I love the care they put into their writing. Unfortunately, this perfection sometimes hobbles them. They might stare at their paper for fifteen minutes without writing a single word! They seem to think that this is their one shot at getting it right. In a conference, try cheering them on, urging them to keep putting words onto the paper. Avoid teaching new strategies for spelling in this situation. The point is to give children the experience of getting a lot of words onto the paper so that they can internalize the feeling and begin to make it habitual.

If this needs to be a minilesson (if most of your class has the problem), demonstrate thinking aloud to yourself: "I just *have* to get this idea onto paper before I lose it. I know I can go back and fix mistakes later. It is so important to get this whole thought/story/idea down. I'm not sure how to spell this word, but I'll just put down sounds that make sense." You can also model making decisions in other lessons: "I don't love the way I said that. Let me try saying it in a different way." Over time children will come to understand that a piece of writing is a living, evolving thing.

- *Talking through a plan before writing helps keep our work clear.* Show children how to practice telling stories across three, four, or five fingers before writing them down. This helps them keep their stories focused, limited to just a few parts with a clear beginning and ending, a plan they should follow when they write.

- *As writers we should know what our trouble spots are.* My students are always surprised when I tell them, "I have such a hard time sitting still to write. I can get a lot done, but I have to keep getting up to do stuff." They think that as a teacher I must have amazing focus. I explain that I know myself and how to work within my limitations. If I get up and do a small task every so often, I can work for hours. Not everybody has a problem with focus, of course, but you can help children discover and address any of their trouble spots.

● *Talking to writers like us can help us figure out how to work through problems.* Sometimes the only person who can help a child work through trouble is another child. It helps to bring children together to be one another's cheerleaders or coaches. They can remind one another of strategies you have taught them in conferences and encourage one another to hang in there even if it feels hard. This has the added benefit of reframing a problem as a challenge, something to be overcome.

● *We can work on more than one project at the same time.* Children should be writing often and a lot. They will not finish every piece they start, at least not right away. If they lose interest in a story, or become interested in another story, they should have permission to work on the more captivating piece while it is still hot. It makes sense to teach children about this not through demonstration but by showing them a child's folder that has lots of pieces in it, some finished, some not, some that are even of a different genre or type than the one the class is studying. We want to encourage children to develop independent writing lives.

● *The information in our pictures can also be in our words.* Some children will spend lots of time on their pictures, including tons of details. Teach them how to use these amazing pictures as a source of possible revision ideas. The details some children include in the visual representation of a memory are often the ones that will make the written story more specific and complete.

Student Work

Eva was never at a loss for topics and wrote well-focused stories. Her pictures always had a lot of detail. Using the picture as a source of ideas for adding words was a perfect tool for her (see Figure 1–10). She learned this strategy in a conference and later used it in another story independently.

Sarah's writing folder says a lot about who she is as a writer. Like the rest of the class, she has written some personal stories. She also has an informational text about bats, a note to her computer at home on how to behave better (see Figure 1–11, p. 30), and some unfinished work that she seems to have lost interest in. That sounds an awful lot like my own writer's notebook.

Working with a Partner

Setting up writing partnerships requires some explicit teaching and clear management at the beginning, but it is well worth the effort. Throughout the year,

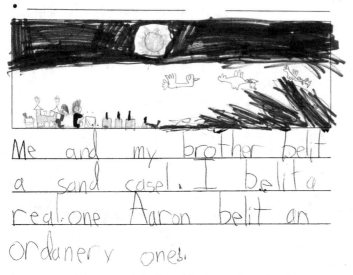

Me and my brother belit
a sand casel. I belit a
real one Aaron belit an
ordanery ones.

Figure 1–10 This page originally said, "Me and my brother built a sand castle." Eva later added, "I built a real one. Aaron built an ordinary one."

partners can help each other plan, write, revise, and edit their work. They are able to tell each other when things do not make sense and suggest appropriate ways to improve their work. Some teachers prefer to set up literacy partnerships—that is, the same partners for reading *and* writing. Start by having a discussion of what children look for in a partner. Their ideas will become the basis for your guidelines for partnership behavior.

When setting up partnerships, I try to allow children to have a choice without entirely giving up my own say in the matter. One day for homework I ask them to write down the names of three people who would be good partners for them and with whom they would be able to work well. I usually agree with at least one choice for every child. These are long-term partnerships, changing only once or twice during the year, so it's best to set them up in a way that makes both you and your class happy.

Guiding Question

- *What makes a great writing partner?* Asking this question gets children thinking about how people can work together in a mutually rewarding way. Children may use the conversation to explore their ideas about the difference between doing something for a partner and helping a partner become better at doing things for himself. Give them time to discuss and refine their answers. It is worth taking the time to map out thoughtful guidelines, as these partnerships will be in place for a long time. When partnerships experience tension,

"To computer. How not to bother a person."
Step one. You don't freeze.
Step two. You don't take a long time to load.
Step three. You don't kick someone off line.
Step four. You don't get mixed up.

Figure 1–11 One of Sarah's Many Projects

you can mediate with the chart in hand, encouraging children to reflect on their own visions of a quality partnership. Following are some examples:

- saying what is good *and* what to make better in a piece of writing

- helping you think of how to make writing better

- reminding you of favorite topics, memories, and ideas for writing

- listening to your plans and helping you make them just right

- encouraging you when you feel bad about your work or when you want to quit

Possible Teaching Points

- *Compliments are most helpful when they are specific.* We all like to be told how great our work is, but in a workshop we need to know *why* our work is so great. It helps the writer to know which parts of his writing work well and achieve what they were supposed to. Show children how "I liked your story" is not nearly as powerful a compliment as "I liked how you wrote about what the water felt like on your skin. It made me feel as if I were there in the pool too." With time, this will help children's ability to confer with each other during writing workshop.

- *People can be sensitive about their work, so it's best to ask questions or give suggestions in a gentle way.* People do not always realize what their words sound like. A child may have the best intentions when she says, "That doesn't make any sense," or "You spelled that wrong," though the writer may hear only criticism. Teach children to make their comments in a way that is less likely to hurt a writer's feelings, such as, "I didn't understand that. Can you explain it to me?" You might also mention in this lesson that those sensitive writers need not take every criticism so personally. After all, the goal is to help the writer improve the writing.

- *One helpful way to listen to (or read) a partner's work is to see if everything is clear and makes sense.* As we give children paper with more and more lines, the volume of their writing naturally increases. A side effect (or growing pain) is that children sometimes lose sight of their plans and wind up either digressing or leaving out essential parts of their story. Since children have usually lived the story they are writing about, when they reread their own work for meaning, they mentally fill in missing words or understand the context they may have left out. In other words, the story will make perfect sense to them even if it is not clear or complete. Their peers can help discover and rectify these errors.

- *If your partner has a suggestion, it may be worth trying; if you don't like it, you can always go back to the way it was.* An obstacle for primary writers is the idea that maybe they did all that hard work for nothing, which is how it sometimes feels to cross out or change words on paper. They may be more willing to revise if they know they can always return their work to its original state. They usually end up liking the revision better, but only after agreeing to risk changing it.

- *Dialogue can bring a story to life.* Some children include dialogue intuitively or remember the device from the previous year, while others habitually relate each story as a list of events. The addition of dialogue can draw readers into a story, making it feel more dynamic. While a demonstration is always helpful, showing the work of a child who has done this can be very powerful.

Student Work

Anya returned to an earlier topic, jumping into a pool. She was beginning to fill out her stories with lovely detail. Her partner helped her include dialogue and internal thinking, which make this story (see Figures 1–12 through 1–14) much richer than her first one.

With the support of a partner in the planning stage, Naglis made his story (see Figures 1–15 through 1–19, pp. 34–36) exciting. When he was finished

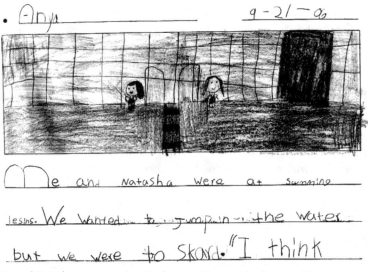

Me and Natasha were at swimming lessons. We wanted to jump in the water but we were too scared. "I think

Figures 1–12 through 1–14 Anya's Pool Story

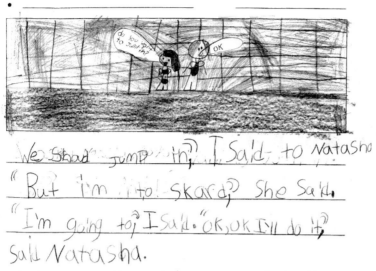

We should jump in," I said to Natasha. "But I'm too scared," she said. "I'm going to," I said. "OK, OK, I'll do it," said Natasha.

we should jump in," I said to Natasha. "But I'm too scared," she said. "I'm going to," I said. "OK, OK, I'll do it," said Natasha.

Figure 1–13

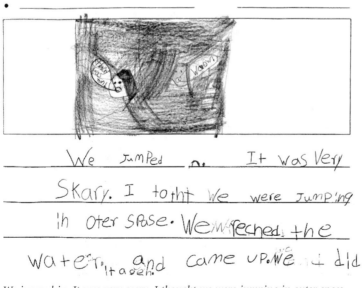

We jumped in. It was very scary. I thought we were jumping in outer space. We reached the water and came up. We did it again.

Figure 1–14

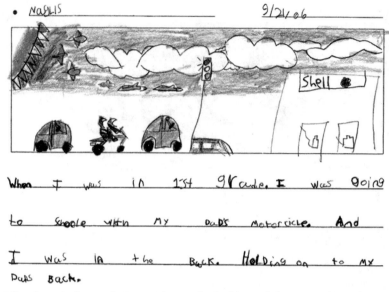

When I was in 1st grade. I was going to schoole with my Dad's Motorcicle. And I was in the Back. Holding on to my Dads Back.

When I was in first grade, I was going to school with my dad's motorcycle. And I was in the back holding onto my dad's back.

Figures 1–15 through 1–19 Naglis' Motorcycle Story

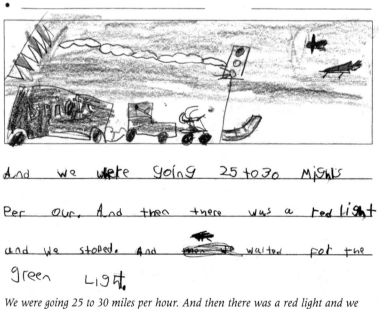

And we where going 25 to 30 Mighls Per our. And then there was a red light and we stoped. And then waited for the green Ligt.

We were going 25 to 30 miles per hour. And then there was a red light and we stopped. And we waited for the green light.

Figure 1–16

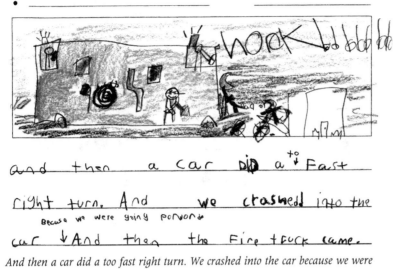

And then a car did a too fast right turn. We crashed into the car because we were going forward. And then the fire truck came.

Figure 1–17

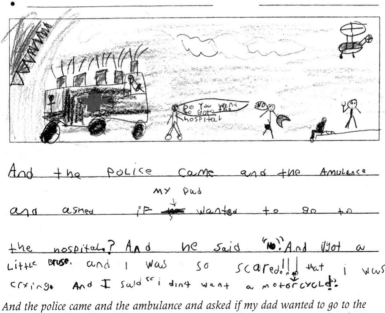

And the police came and the ambulance and asked if my dad wanted to go to the hospital. And he said, "No." And I got a little bruise and I was so scared!!! that I was crying. And I said, "I don't want a motorcycle!"

Figure 1–18

And then the police took me to school and I was crying.

Figure 1–19

writing the story, his partner gave crucial help in making his story more clear (notice his revisions on the third through fifth pages).

Choosing, Revising, Editing, and Publishing

Most children by now have written a number of stories. In this segment, they commit to a particular story and work on that piece exclusively as the one they will publish and celebrate. Though children have been revising and editing as they've been writing, you now teach specific revision and editing strategies, which are then included on revision and editing checklists. (You'll add to these checklists throughout the year.) Children can publish their work by coloring their illustrations, adding covers, or doing other final flourishes.

I have always preferred to keep the first writing celebration of the year small and intimate—just the class sitting in a circle sharing, commenting, and reflecting on their work. Other teachers make a good case for inviting friends and families and making a big party out of it. Either way, make sure to celebrate the newly forming community as much as you celebrate the writing.

Possible Teaching Points

● *When you choose a piece to revise, you are choosing something that deserves some extra attention and work to become great.* When I was in school I was taught that you revised a piece of writing because it was not yet good enough. I hated writing to begin with, and this added step was torture. I want my stu-

```
┌─────────────────────────────────────────────────────────────┐
│                                                               │
│   Revision Strategies                                         │
│                                                               │
│     ●   Information in the pictures is also in the words.    │
│                                                               │
└─────────────────────────────────────────────────────────────┘
```

Figure 1–20 The Revision Checklist

dents to see revision as the reward of creating a piece of writing that *is* good enough. Teach children how to comb through their folders in search of those magical accomplishments that represent their best thinking. These are the pieces that deserve even more care and attention.

● *The information in our pictures can also be in our words.* No, it's not déjà vu all over again. I repeat this lesson. I want children to make the connection between writing and revising, so what was originally taught as a writing lesson is now going onto the revision checklist (see Figure 1–20). Children will refer to this list for the rest of the year, and this revision strategy will help them through many units of study.

● *All word-wall words and spelling patterns should be spelled correctly.* We tend to take things for granted when they are always around, as a word wall is. Checking their spelling may not be a new habit, but your students probably need to be periodically reminded to do so. This strategy should also be charted somewhere in the classroom (see Figure 1–21). Point out that it is not just the words on the word wall that should be correct in their writing, but also any spelling patterns those words contain (such as the *ike* in *like* or the *ight* in *night*).

Student Work

Kate likes to put a lot of detail into her work (see Figures 1–22 through 1–25). She sometimes loses sight of the big picture, as on the third page, where she discusses the prices and discounts of her doll. Her teacher and I will be able

```
┌─────────────────────────────────────────────────────────────┐
│                                                               │
│   Editing Strategies                                          │
│                                                               │
│     ●   All word-wall words and spelling patterns are spelled│
│         correctly.                                            │
│                                                               │
└─────────────────────────────────────────────────────────────┘
```

Figure 1–21 The Editing Checklist

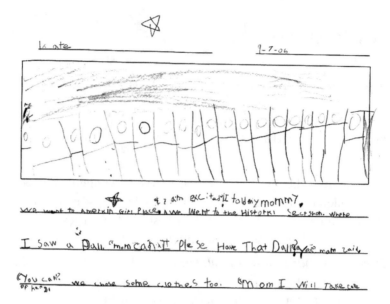

Kate   9-7-06

4 2 am ExCitasy!I told my mommy,
we went to Amerkin Girl Place & We Went to the Historki Section. where

I saw a Dull "momcan I Plese Have That Dall?"yes" mom said

"You can? of her?! we chose some clothes too. "Mom I Will Take care

We went to American Girl Place. "I am excited!" I told my mommy. We went to the historical section, where I saw a doll. "Mom, can I please have that doll?" "Yes," Mom said, "you can." We chose some clothes, too. "Mom, I will take care of her."

Figure 1–22 through 1–25 Kate's Piece About American Girl Place

2

9-8-06, 9-9-06, 9-10-06, 9-11-06   9-12-06 & 9-13-06

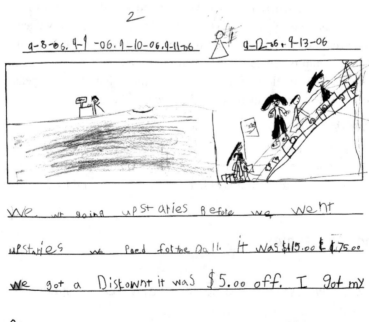

We wr going upStaties Before we Went

upStaties we Paed fot the Dall. It Was $15.00 & $.75.00

we got a Diskownt it was $5.00 off. I got my

Photoe takine.

We were going upstairs. Before we went upstairs we paid for the doll. It was $15.00 & 75¢. We got a discount. It was $5.00 off. I got my photo taken.

38   Figure 1–23

We had tea. My Doll Elizabeth and her own High chair. "Each food was made By a Doll." Elizabeth said the waitress made tea cups with vanil Puding in them. I had Chookler Puding with a candll in it. I was Happy.

We had tea. My doll Elizabeth had her own high chair. "Each food was made by a doll," said the waitress. Elizabeth made teacups with vanilla pudding in them. I had chocolate pudding with a candle in it. I was happy.

Figure 1–24

We went drawn to the 2nd flor. The amerkin girl hespiti wraped my doll in plastikn because it was raining And gave me star stikrs because it was my birthday.

We went down to the 2nd floor. The American Girl Hospital wrapped my doll in plastic because it was raining and gave me star stickers because it was my birthday.

Figure 1–25

Name_____ Date _____

We have now been in school for about a month. We have learned so much about ourselves as writers, about one another, and about writing workshop.

*How do you feel more grown-up now than you did when school started? _____

_____

_____

_____

_____

*What is your favorite thing about writing workshop?

_____

_____

_____

_____

*What is hard for you about writing? _____

_____

_____

_____

_____

Figure 1–26 Becoming a Community Reflection Questionnaire

to work with her on this in the next unit. She has a sophisticated sense of dialogue, which can be an example for other children. Notice how her additions make the story more clear for the reader.

◾ Reflection

Reflection is integral to the kind of learning that stays with us and shapes who we are. For this unit, ask children to reflect on the community you have created with them and on the writing they have done (see Figure 1–26 on previous page). The act of putting their thoughts into words will help them understand writing workshop. The information they provide will help you shape your teaching to their needs in the coming unit.

◾ Predictable Problems

At the end of this unit you may be tempted to focus on problems with spelling or the quality of children's writing. These are to be expected and you will address them over the course of the year. I encourage you to respond most urgently to troubles in the community.

PROBLEM	WHAT IT LOOKS LIKE	POSSIBLE SOLUTION/ CONFERENCE
Children lack confidence or fear taking risks.	• Children write about the same topic that the teacher used in the lesson. • Children write what seems to be the same book over and over. • Children write only the words they know how to spell. • Children stare at their paper but do not write anything.	It is especially important to compliment children who lack confidence. Be on the lookout for things they do well, because they will know if your compliment is authentic. Remind them of some of the things they know and care an awful lot about. They might not know how much they know!
	• Children discard pieces of writing with only a few words or a tiny drawing on each page.	We need to teach children to value all their attempts. We also need to teach them about process: if they make mistakes, they can continue working on the same piece of paper. If we can do this with kindness and understanding, despite being frustrated, it will help children be willing to take ever bigger risks.
	• Children distract others by talking or making noise.	When fear of taking a risk looks like a behavior problem, it is tempting to chastise the children, but we will do better to encourage them.

PROBLEM	WHAT IT LOOKS LIKE	POSSIBLE SOLUTION/ CONFERENCE
Children choose un-interesting topics.	• Children choose the same topic over and over.	Many writers return to a few topics often throughout their careers. It is not necessarily a bad thing when children do the same. They will move on when they are ready.
	• Children seem to be writing about things that have no importance to them.	We need to believe that children have many important stories to tell. Sometimes these are hidden within or disguised as mundane accounts. Instead of suggesting other topics, we can help them get at the heart of what they are trying to say. If we do not tell them we believe their stories are important, how will they know?
Children are not internalizing routines.	• Classroom remains noisy. • Children laugh, chat, play, distract others, or wander around the classroom during writing workshop.	We need to make sure that we include children in the process of setting up routines. We do not tell them to be quiet because *we* want it quiet. Rather, we ask them what *they* need in place to help them learn and grow as writers. When they tell us that they need the room to be pretty quiet, we can agree to help them achieve this. We can then tell them, "You were so clear that you wanted a quiet space to work in, so I'm happy to stop you as many times as I have to in order to help you get the room exactly how you want it to sound."
	• Children speak disparagingly about each other's work.	Model often how you want children to comment on writing. When you see a child respond to another's work in a helpful or kind way, share it with the class.
Your teaching is not reaching all learners.	• More advanced students do not appear to be working at their full potential. • Students who struggle seem un-engaged.	Keep in mind that writing quality is a separate set of skills from writing conventions. We need to address how well children are communicating their ideas as well as how well we can read what they write. You may find and acknowledge some beautiful sentiments in writing that is barely readable.

PROBLEM	WHAT IT LOOKS LIKE	POSSIBLE SOLUTION/ CONFERENCE
		Acquaint yourself with the range of students' facility with conventions early. Make sure your expectations for each child are reasonable. A child writing with mostly random letters will not benefit from being expected to use correct spelling and punctuation.
		Make sure you have mentor texts appropriate to the range of ability levels in your class. Try conferring with these children a few extra times because they may need more individualized teaching until they have a better idea of what they can expect from themselves.
A sense of community has not yet developed.	• Children make comments that make other children feel bad ("That's easy! Anyone can do that!" or "He's bad, he always does stuff like that," or "That's wrong.").	Community takes time to develop among children. Sometimes children make comments like these in an effort to be helpful to adults or to show that they are good. We can model other ways to be helpful and other kinds of comments.
	• Children do not like it when their peers have similar ideas ("You copied me!" or "She stole my idea!").	I do not know why this bothers children so much! I tell them that good ideas occur to people more often than bad ones, so it is natural we would have plenty of ideas in common.
	• Children laugh aloud or sneer at peers' work.	Unlike prior comments, these seem intentionally hurtful. We must be clear that such behavior is unacceptable and has consequences. We must also realize that wanting to hurt others usually comes from hurting or feeling inadequate. We can address these feelings with compassion at a time when the child is not being hurtful.

■ Assessment

Congratulations! You have created a perfectly structured community in which the hum of human industry rivals only the sounds of joyful collaboration! OK, I'm exaggerating. You have done a lot of work, but a community is a living, changing organism requiring periodic tune-ups. Frustrations are as much to be expected as celebrations. The chart in Figure 1–27 will help you plan your ongoing instruction. Remember to consider children's daily habits and skills as well as their published pieces. If there are things you want to address or review, incorporate them into the next unit.

STUDENT'S WORK SHOWS THAT I . . .	NEED TO TEACH OR RETEACH THIS TO THE WHOLE CLASS	NEED TO REMIND CHILD OF THIS SKILL	NEED TO TEACH THIS TO A SMALL GROUP OR IN A CONFERENCE	NEED TO CONGRATULATE CHILD FOR HOW WELL HE OR SHE DID
Child chose topics that mattered deeply to him or her.	❑	❑	❑	❑
Child kept writing focused on a single idea.	❑	❑	❑	❑
Child chose words carefully to communicate ideas.	❑	❑	❑	❑
Child began to consider his or her audience.	❑	❑	❑	❑
Child spelled frequently used words correctly.	❑	❑	❑	❑
Child used end punctuation, quotation marks, and capitalization properly.	❑	❑	❑	❑
Child participated in class conversations about literature.	❑	❑	❑	❑
Child got to work quickly.	❑	❑	❑	❑
Child remained productive for the entire workshop.	❑	❑	❑	❑
Child managed writing tools and supplies.	❑	❑	❑	❑
Child talked to classmates about reading or writing.	❑	❑	❑	❑
Child made and used a plan to write.	❑	❑	❑	❑
Child read and reread his or her work often.	❑	❑	❑	❑
Child revised his or her work.	❑	❑	❑	❑
Child edited his or her work.	❑	❑	❑	❑
Child volunteered ideas, listened, and responded to others.	❑	❑	❑	❑
Child worked with a partner to develop and improve writing.	❑	❑	❑	❑
Child showed respect for all members of the community and their work, regardless of ability.	❑	❑	❑	❑
Child expressed disagreement in a way that promoted conversation rather than shut it down.	❑	❑	❑	❑
Child asked for help with problems.	❑	❑	❑	❑

Figure 1–27 Becoming a Community of Writers Assessment Chart

■ Professional Resources

Bomer, Randy, and Katherine Bomer. 2001. *For a Better World: Reading and Writing for Social Action*. Portsmouth, NH: Heinemann.

Calkins, Lucy, and Leah Mermelstein. 2003. *Launching the Writing Workshop*. Portsmouth, NH: *First*hand.

Cambourne, Brian. 1988. *The Whole Story: Natural Learning and the Acquisition of Literacy in the Classroom*. New York: Ashton Scholastic.

Parsons, Stephanie. 2005. *First Grade Writers: Units of Study to Help Children Plan, Organize, and Structure Their Ideas*. Portsmouth, NH: Heinemann.

Peterson, Ralph. 1992. *Life in a Crowded Place: Making a Learning Community*. Portsmouth, NH: Heinemann.

Ray, Katie Wood. 2006. *Study Driven: A Framework for Planning Units of Study in the Writing Workshop*. Portsmouth, NH: Heinemann.

Ray, Katie Wood, and Lester L. Laminack. 2001. *The Writing Workshop: Working Through the Hard Parts (and They're All Hard Parts)*. Urbana, IL: NCTE.

Turbill, Jan, and Brian Cambourne. 1991. *Coping with Chaos*. Portsmouth, NH: Heinemann.

Wilson, Lorraine. 2006. *Writing to Live: How to Teach Writing for Today's World*. Portsmouth, NH: Heinemann.

2 | Writing for Change

ortfolio assessments in second grade often include a piece of persuasive writing. My first few attempts to teach second graders to write persuasively resulted in watered-down "essays," since an essay seemed the most logical forum for arguing a point, but the form wasn't appropriate for such young writers. The students and I were alternately frustrated and bored to tears. There were no clear criteria specifying what these pieces should contain and how to make them meaningful. I was stumped.

When I approached second grade teacher, Jeremy Manger, about developing a unit on persuasive writing that did not merely simplify an upper-grade unit, he was enthusiastic. He knew that the pieces had to be authentic and heartfelt and that we needed to include forms of writing other than traditional essay pieces. He also knew that his class was blossoming into an amazing community of learners with a strong sense of social responsibility. He suggested we angle the unit toward writing to effect social change or at least social awareness.

I knew immediately that this was the tone that had been missing from my prior attempts to teach persuasive writing. I had been teaching a kind of writing without creating the burning need to use that kind of writing. One of the things I have come to love about this unit is that it centers on the *reasons* children are writing rather than on the form they are using. This sense of purpose needs to be at the heart of persuasive writing.

■ Overview

This unit can last three or four weeks. Spend the first few days becoming familiar with some examples of good-quality persuasive writing. Choose books that share a sense of social responsibility but that are written in different genres and styles, and then, along with your students, discover how the authors use words to effect change and how their choices differ depending on the intended audience. Students can then plan, organize, write, and edit their own pieces. At the end of the study, celebrate the good work and send it out into the world: if at all possible, get the pieces into the hands of their intended audiences.

■ Goals/Outcomes

This unit introduces children to the concept of writing for a definite purpose. Most of the new goals are about making writing decisions geared to influencing readers. These goals should build on, not replace, the goals of the prior unit.

Writing Quality

We hope children will

- keep their writing focused on its purpose
- clearly state an opinion or desire
- choose a genre or form for exploring this opinion or desire
- consider the audience for their work
- organize their thoughts to support their ideas
- choose words carefully to communicate their ideas
- continue to develop their voices as writers

Writing Conventions

We hope children will

- spell frequently used words correctly
- spell words particular to their topics correctly
- use end punctuation, quotation marks, and capitalization correctly
- use commas, even if not always correctly

Writing Habits

We hope children will

- participate in class conversations
- get to work quickly
- manage their own writing tools and supplies
- talk to one another about their writing
- articulate the job they want their writing to do
- read and reread their work often
- revise their work
- edit their work

Community

We hope children will

- volunteer ideas, listen, and respond to others
- work with a partner to develop and improve writing
- show respect for all members of the community and their work, regardless of ability
- ask for help when they encounter problems and offer to help classmates with problems

■ Getting Ready to Teach

As you prepare to teach, look over your rubrics from the last unit and decide whether there are any whole-class or small-group lessons you will need to incorporate into this one. Gather a set of books with which to begin the unit (you can add more as you discover them), making sure to represent the full range of your students' reading abilities.

Gathering Materials

Collect as many books as you can that have a social message or that emerge from a desire to make the world a better place. The most important qualities these mentor books must have are being accessible to second grade minds and enjoyable for everyone to read. If texts meet these conditions, they will be good teaching aids. This unit is about writing for a specific reason but is not limited to a single genre. Mentor texts that encompass a variety of levels, genres, and formats will open your children's eyes and minds to the vast possibilities of what they can create.

As always, the paper you provide will play a role in children's writing. The size of the picture box and the number of lines above or below it give children cues about how much writing you expect from them and how important a picture is in representing their ideas. You will have to make this decision based on your assessment. (Sample templates are included in the Appendix.) Later in the unit, children will attempt different kinds of writing. If you can, allow them to design paper that meets their needs, and copy it for them.

Considering the Students

As you go over your assessment notes from the last unit, decide which concepts you will need to reinforce and whether this should be done with the whole class or just a few individuals.

Preparing Demonstration Materials

Next prepare the demonstration pieces you are going to write for your class in the first few lessons. You'll begin with sticky notes and short jottings and then, as the unit goes on, create new, longer demonstration texts or amplify your earlier ideas, depending on the lesson. If your lesson is about trying a new way to write about a topic, demonstrate writing a new piece. When you teach children to add examples to their work, use a piece you wrote earlier. Although you will write these in front of your class, as if you are just coming up with the ideas, plan what you will write so that it clearly matches what you are trying to teach.

Demonstration is vital to learning. A clear explanation is good, but nothing compares with a strong physical demonstration with accompanying commentary. You need to write pieces of the quality you expect from your class. As a new teacher I almost never wrote the kind of writing I was teaching my students about. Although I felt I was explaining things clearly, I had much difficulty lifting the quality of their work. As soon as I started to write in front of them, I got better results. My demonstrations accomplished several things. First, only when writing my own piece did I discover the specific strategies and skills I wanted to see in *their* writing. Second, I was able to plan a few ways to challenge children in the class who needed it. Finally, only I could create an example accessible to my class, one within their zone of proximal development (Vygotsky's term). Your demonstrations will be a key factor in the success of this unit.

■ Teaching the Unit

The unit is broken up into four sections: reading like writers, exploring ideas that matter, writing and revising, and getting ready to publish. I have provided general time guidelines, but they are flexible (see Figure 2–1).

TIME FRAME	SECTION OF STUDY	WHAT CHILDREN DO	WHAT YOU TEACH
2–3 days	Reading Like Writers	• Read good books with a social message for meaning, craft, and voice and discuss their thoughts • Help record observations on a chart	Guiding questions • How is this writer using words to make the world a better place? • What tools is the writer using to do this job? Minilessons, conferences, or midworkshop focus points • When we read a model piece of writing, we must make sure we understand it. • It will help our writing to look at choices authors make in their work.
2–3 days (ongoing)	Exploring Ideas That Matter	• List some issues that matter deeply to them • Talk about how these issues affect them and ways to improve the situation • Orally rehearse supporting a cause • Jot supports that seem to work persuasively	Guiding question • What matters to us enough to argue for it? Minilessons, conferences, or midworkshop focus points • We can try to change things that drive us nuts. • It helps to make a list of possible causes and audiences. • We can talk out an idea as if we were talking to our readers. • Writers jot down good ideas right when they come to mind so they won't forget them. • Our writing will go more smoothly if we organize our supporting ideas. • A good partner can help by refuting our arguments.

Figure 2–1 Writing for Change at a Glance

TIME FRAME	SECTION OF STUDY	WHAT CHILDREN DO	WHAT YOU TEACH
5–7 days	Writing and Revising	• State cause clearly • Support cause (reasons, anecdote, bargaining) • Consider the audience • Adopt a clear voice • Read aloud to peers and help one another fine-tune their work • Keep writing focused • Refer to revision checklist	Minilessons, conferences, or midworkshop focus points • Writers try different genres, forms, or tools to help them support their cause. • Our beliefs should be clear in our writing. • Our writing will do its job if we include clear support. • Doing research can help us find the words to make our case. • We can elaborate on our supporting ideas by describing them in more detail. • As we start to write, we must think about our audience and what is most likely to get them on our side. • We can make our supporting ideas more personal by including a little story, or *anecdote.* • It sometimes helps our cause to describe a reward, or to *bargain.* • Our writing voice can help (or hurt) our cause. • When we listen to others' work, we can tell them if they are persuading us (and if not, why not). • One thing we can do when we get stuck is look at our revision checklist.
2–3 days	Getting Ready to Publish	• Learn a new revision strategy • Learn a new editing strategy and add it to checklist • Reflect on work in class • Mail or display work • Celebrate	Minilessons, conferences, or midworkshop focus points • When it is time to publish, writers choose their most promising work to revise and edit. • One way to revise is to make sure our piece really says what we want it to. • Sometimes revising means taking away parts that don't help our piece say what we want it to. • We should correctly spell words that are important to our topic or come up often in our work.

Figure 2–1 *(continued)*

Reading Like Writers

I begin most units of study by offering some clear guidance on how to read like writers. Sometimes my students and I look generally at the work of a number of authors and name some of their writing moves. Other times, as in this unit, I focus our inquiry around a few specific qualities that I want to highlight in the form or genre we will be writing (see Figure 2–2).

Guiding Questions

- *How is this writer using words to make the world a better place?* Ask your students to consider what a piece of writing is doing. You might say, "Sometimes you can really tell that a piece of writing is trying to do a job. For instance, when I read *Common Ground*, by Molly Bang, I can see that the writing has a purpose—to get everyone to take better care of the earth." Give students a chance to explore the purpose of some other texts. The way they articulate the intent, the job, of the pieces they read will help you form a good working definition of *writing for change*. Understanding the concept that a piece of writing can set out to accomplish something will focus how you guide your students to look at the author's craft.

WAYS TO USE WRITING TO MAKE THE WORLD A BETTER PLACE	TITLES	HOW IS THE WRITING DOING ITS JOB? (TOOLS OR MODES)	HAVE ANY OF US TRIED THIS?
Convince people to change the way they do something	*Common Ground*, by Molly Bang *Dear Children of the Earth*, by Shim Shimmel	Warning Telling a story Giving examples Describing details Describing a problem Begging Writing a letter	
Describe the beauty of something worth protecting	From *Sky to Sea*, by Joy Cowley *Dear World*, by Takayo Noda (poems)	Describing details Using poetry	
Describe the benefits of doing something more often	*The Smile*, by Joy Cowley *Why Should I Recycle?*, by Jen Green and Mike Gordon	Using a repeated pattern Describing benefits or rewards	
Send a message about how to treat people	*The Peace Book*, by Todd Parr *The Meanest Thing to Say*, by Bill Cosby	Using a repeated pattern Telling a story with a message	
Inspire people to be brave	*The Librarian of Basra*, by Jeanette Winter	Telling a story with a message	

Figure 2–2 Qualities of Persuasive Writing

- *What tools is the writer using to do this job?* If writing can have a purpose, an angle, it follows that an author will use tools to accomplish that purpose. For instance, in *Dear World*, Takayo Noda attempts to get readers to protect the earth by celebrating its beauty in poems. In *Common Ground*, Molly Bang tells a story, warns, explains, teaches, questions, and challenges her readers as she makes her case. Demonstrate for children how you can reread a book to look specifically at how the author makes the writing do its job, jotting your observations on a sticky note. Send children off in pairs to do the same with books they can read comfortably.

Possible Teaching Points

- *When we read a model piece of writing, we must make sure we understand it.* In the past you may not have had to state this explicitly. By this point in a unit of study, you have already read the mentor texts aloud several times. If any of them are particularly difficult or challenging, this is a good opportunity to teach children that when they want to learn from a writer, they must first concentrate on what the writer means before examining the techniques he uses to convey that meaning.

- *It will help our writing to look at choices authors make in their work.* This is, of course, what you are working on in this whole section. Encourage students to notice lots of choices an author can make: topic, structure, words, tone, repetition, to name just a few. It's helpful to think of these choices as tools that authors use to help their writing do its job.

Student Work

The randomly selected sticky notes in Figure 2–3 show the different ways children approach reading like writers. Some primarily pay attention to the content, or what the writing is about. Others are better able to focus on craft decisions writers make. Over the course of the school year, with your guidance, children will get better at looking at a writer's craft.

Exploring Ideas That Matter

This is the time for children to try on different ideas, topics, and styles of communication. Lots of things make them tick, and they will benefit from having time to explore issues freely. Some children are drawn to global issues, while others have more personal concerns. Allow room for everyone's ideas in your conversations. Students need to feel safe digging into the issues that preoccupy them if they are to write about them honestly.

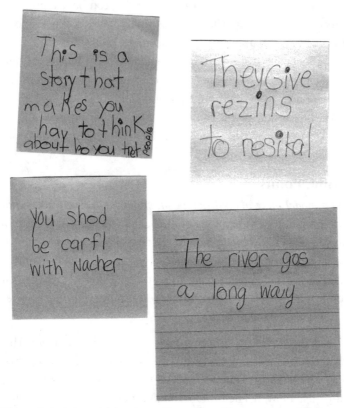

Figure 2–3 A Few Sticky Notes Show the Different Ways Children Read Texts Like Writers

Guiding Question

● *What matters to us enough to argue for it?* Sometimes children begin identifying their burning issues before you get to this section of the study, inspired by the great reading they've been doing. Other times, you need to empower children to discover what matters most to them. They may think, "Of course a published author has important things to say, but not me." When you ask, "What matters to you enough to argue for it?" you are telling children they have a right to care deeply about something in the world that needs to be changed, addressed, or at least recognized. A chart of their responses becomes a resource for the rest of the unit.

Possible Teaching Points

● *We can try to change things that drive us nuts.* It's natural for children to want to embrace the issues of the times, or the ones they hear their parents talking about. And it's important for them to discuss war, famine, global warming—the issues that shape our world. It helps them learn to consider multiple perspectives and develop opinions based on their observations. However, some students may feel somewhat disconnected from topics and ideas like these that are still abstract, often happening in what might as well be another world. If you find children writing unconvincingly about worthy and important topics, you may need to help them zero in on things nearer at hand. Give children permission to care about noisy neighbors, local litterbugs, or inconsiderate schoolmates. They need to have a strong emotional attachment to what they write.

- *It helps to make a list of possible causes and audiences.* Although it is certainly not necessary, many teachers have their students make a list of all the topics they can imagine writing about in a given unit. This way when children finish a piece of writing or no longer want to work on it, they can immediately choose another topic from their list. If you do this, having children determine the audience as well will help them rehearse arguing their point before they start writing.

- *We can talk out an idea as if we were talking to our readers.* You will discover a lot about children's writing voices when you give them a chance to talk about their topics with their literal voices. Uninhibited by conventions, spelling, penmanship (the handwork of writing), they can try different ways of making their arguments (the mind work of writing). During these oral rehearsals, children can revise instantly, changing their tone or their content without having to write and rewrite. Let them work with a partner so that they can give and receive feedback.

- *Writers jot down good ideas right when they come to mind so they won't forget them.* If you have taught children the concept of *jotting*, show them how to record their more compelling arguments on sticky notes. Otherwise, you may need to teach them the difference between writing down a whole idea and jotting just the main words.

- *Our writing will go more smoothly if we organize our supporting ideas.* Show children how they can put their jotted notes in the order they think best before starting to write. When they write about each jotted idea, they can say as much as they want to say about it before moving on to the next jotted idea. This will keep them from getting too scattered and will help them remember all of the great ideas they have.

- *A good partner can help by refuting our arguments.* You have talked to children about being gentle and considerate partners. You have also talked to them about being helpful partners, even if it means giving criticism. Here you can teach children to listen to one another's ideas as if they were the intended audience. In other words, Anya could pretend that she is a smoker as she listens to Naglis' work. If she forces him to think about her point of view, his writing will be more targeted to the very people whose behavior he wishes to change.

Student Work

Kate had a lot of interests. When she spoke to the class about the noise her neighbors made when they threw their trash down the chute (located adjacent to Kate's bedroom wall), she was so animated and outraged that we recommended she pursue the topic. "It's so rude! Why do they have to take their trash out at ten o'clock at night? Don't they know kids are *sleeping*?" She explored the argument, rehearsing it orally and jotting down notes (see Figure 2–4), before choosing another topic.

Anya jotted her notes about water conservation on a sheet of loose-leaf paper (see Figure 2–5). She later decided to do some research to see if there were more reasons to protect our water.

Do not waste water because human beings need water to stay alive.
- *Because other countries have no water at all.*
- *Because almost all of our food has water in it.*
- *We should keep our water clean so animals that live in the water that we eat can live.*

Andaiye explored the idea of breaking dolls. She did not know how far she could go with it, but she wanted to try. In the end, she decided to follow another line of thought, but she needed the freedom to write this without having an adult try to dissuade her.

Saschael's piece (Figure 2–6, p. 59) came straight from her heart. The country had been at war for almost half her life. She needed to write down her feelings before moving into note taking and organizing. Her approach reminded me that we do not all follow the same process and that this kind of expressive writing is essential to the creative process.

Writing and Revising

In this section, children commit to making something of their writing. They need to finalize their topic and decide the genre or form their writing will take. Your lessons will guide them through a lot of writing and should be determined by what you see your students need.

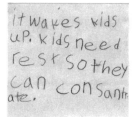

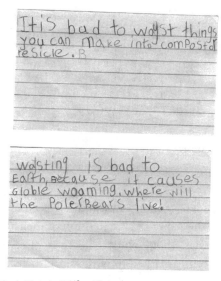

Figure 2–4 Kate's Sticky Notes

Possible Teaching Points

● *Writers try different genres, forms, or tools to help them support their cause.*
Now that children have had a chance to talk through their ideas, they are ready
to start writing. If most children are going to write pieces that ask readers directly to change a particular behavior, remind them of other ways they can make
their point: a story with a moral, a poem, an exposition, and so on. Charting
how model texts did their jobs should have helped children see the ways they
could make *their* writing do a job. Remind them to open their minds to the many
ways they can get their readers to come around to their way of thinking.

● *Our beliefs should be clear in our writing.* Readers should know what the
writing is asking them to do or believe. Some of the mentor books students have
read state a point of view explicitly, while others imply a message. Sometimes

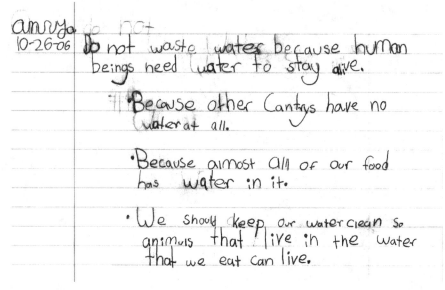

anrya to not
10-26-06 Do not waste water because human
beings need water to stay alive.

• Because other Cantrys have no
water at all.

• Because almost all of our food
has water in it.

• We should keep our water clean so
animals that live in the water
that we eat can live.

Figure 2–5 Anya's Notes on Water Conservation

young writers forget that their readers cannot peer into their head and know what they are thinking. They see the paper as an extension of their thinking, sometimes leaving out words or even whole sentences. This is, of course, entirely natural for children who recently learned to write, since their thoughts and speech move so much faster than their pencils. Teach them to read their work, looking specifically for evidence they have used to support their point. This is also a good job for partners.

● ***Our writing will do its job if we include clear support.*** If during their oral rehearsal children have grasped the concept of supporting ideas and have several thoughts on sticky notes, you may be able to skip this lesson now. Otherwise, remind them that their argument is not going to carry much weight without some support. It will help to give an example from your own writing: "I could just say to my neighbors, 'Pick up your trash,' but I don't think they'd really be convinced. I'd have to give them reasons, or some support, for my idea. What if I told them that their trash makes rats want to come to our street? Or that they could get a fine from the city for having too much trash outside their building? They'll need reasons if I am going to convince them."

● ***Doing research can help us find the words to make our case.*** Children's arguments will be more convincing if they know a lot about their topic. Teach them how to look in books for answers to their potential readers' question *Why*

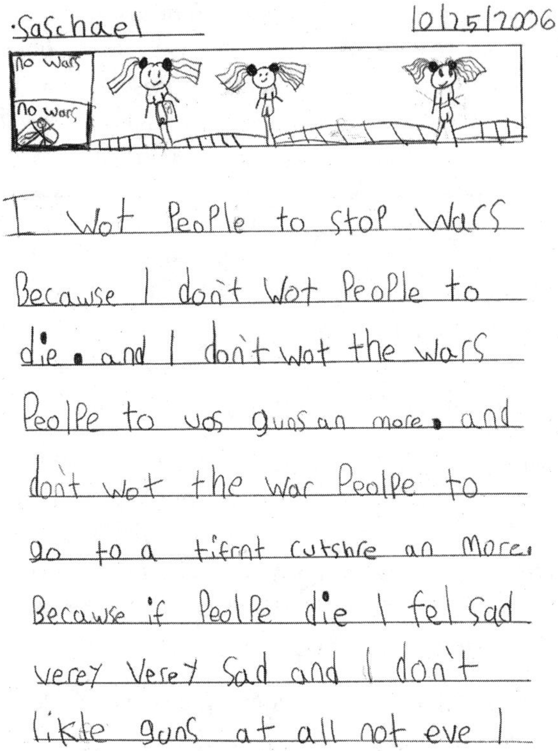

·Saschael   10/25/2006

I wot People to stop wars
Because I don't wot People to
die. and I don't wot the wars
PeolPe to uos guns an more. and
don't wot the war PeolPe to
go to a tifrnt cutshre an more.
Because if PeolPe die I fel sad
verey verey sad and I don't
likle guns at all not eve l

I want people to stop wars because I don't want people to die. And I don't want the war people to use guns anymore. And I don't want the war people to go to a different country any more. Because if people die I feel sad, very, very sad, and I don't like guns at all . . .

Figure 2–6 Saschael's Jottings About War

should I believe you? This lesson can help writing that feels like a repetitive rant become a solid persuasive piece.

● *We can elaborate on our supporting ideas by describing them in more detail.* For some children it will be a big enough challenge to keep their piece focused on one topic and to include supports for their arguments. Other children will be ready to challenge themselves to expand on or elaborate their supporting ideas. Refer to some of your mentor texts as examples of how this might sound. (Molly Bang says a lot about how the world will be if we continue to exhaust out natural resources. And look at what happened to Shel Silverstein's Sarah Cynthia Sylvia Stout, who would not take the garbage out, or Maurice Sendak's Pierre, who didn't care.)

- *As we start to write, we must think about our audience and what is most likely to get them on our side.* You have guided your students to think about the jobs of your mentor texts. Now you can show them that their own writing can do a job. Writers will use different tools to get that job done, depending on the audience. Show children how you choose your tools based on who your audience is and what you know about them.

- *We can make our supporting ideas more personal by including a little story, or anecdote.* While reading like writers, you and your students may have noticed that some mentor books used narratives to illustrate their points. Molly Bang uses narrative to great effect in persuading her audience to take an interest in protecting the planet's natural resources.

- *It sometimes helps our cause to describe a reward, or to bargain.* In this part of the study you may notice, as I did, that many of the pieces rely heavily on the words *don't* and *stop.* As a way to avoid sounding so negative, children can write about the benefits of following their advice. It is important to outline the dangers of wasting water or throwing trash all over the place, but readers may want to see how changing their actions can have positive results.

- *Our writing voice can help (or hurt) our cause.* Students are familiar (at least we hope they are) with the concept that whining or demanding does not get good results. In writing, being bossy or insulting to the reader does not go over well, either. On the other hand, being clear and authoritative or treating the reader as a possible partner in making a change is an effective way of getting a message across.

- *When we listen to others' work, we can tell them if they are persuading us (and if not, why not).* When children listen to others' work, they should know what they are being asked to do or believe. They can let the writer know whether or not they are feeling sympathetic to the cause. Most of the time they will agree with the message but may feel the writer is not making a strong enough argument. Partners can help each other include more evidence, support, or research to make their arguments as strong as they can be.

- *One thing we can do when we get stuck is look at our revision checklist.* I usually teach a revision lesson near the end of every unit, adding the new strategies to an ever growing list. However, I don't want children to get the idea that revision comes only after working on a piece for a while or only when they are ready to publish. For writers, revision is almost indistinguishable from writing. The two processes happen together as a piece of writing develops, whether or not it eventually gets published. If you remind children often to consult the chart of revision strategies, they will come to see it equally as a resource for writing new pieces and for revisiting pieces that are already written. This will help them internalize the habit of writing and revising as a joined activity as they develop their own processes for writing.

Student Work

Coley and Natasha had both worked on projects independently but decided to make an alphabet book together about protecting the environment. Because twenty-six pages is a tall order, they decided some pages would be longer than others and only some would be based on research. Despite differences in work styles, they created an interesting project (see Figures 2–7 and 2–8).

I is insecticide. When people send planes over banana farms they spray insecticide on the insects. But they do not care if the people get hurt.

Figure 2–7 Coley's *I* Page

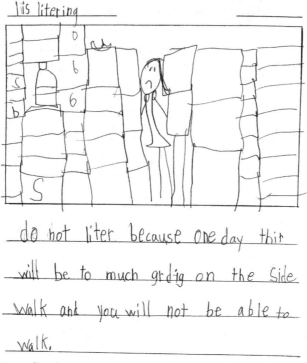

Do not litter because one day there will be too much garbage on the sidewalk and you will not be able to walk.

Figure 2–8 Natasha's *L* Page

A few children chose to write a story with a moral. In one, also by Coley, a man likes to shoot animals for no reason. After a hard lesson from Mark, the hero, the man's feelings for animals change (see Figures 2–9 and 2–10).

For some children this writing will be cathartic. Robert played around with several ideas at the beginning of the study but soon found a topic, noise pollution, to which he could commit. He said the point of his piece was to help people realize there was a problem rather than to suggest solutions. This shows an impressive awareness of the job he wanted his writing to do. Ordinarily calm and even tempered, he tells his readers how he is driven mad by noise problems: cars (*beep too much*), dogs (*as loud as cars when they beep*), workers (*the loudest people I have ever heard*), and sanitation crews (*as loud as workers*). His final chapter brings it all home.

> Chapter 5. The city bothers me too because of all that noise. The city bothers me because of ladies screaming and cars beeping and fire trucks. The city is two times louder than workers.

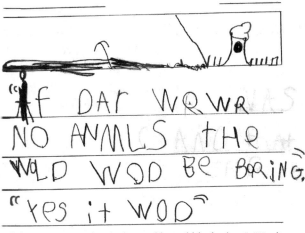

"If there were no animals the world would be boring." "Yes it would."

Figure 2–9 Excerpt from Coley's Story

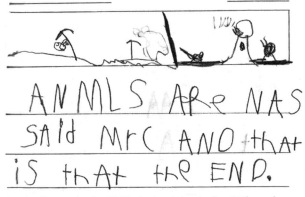

"Animals are nice," said Mark, "and that is that." The end

Figure 2–10 Excerpt *(continued)*

Getting Ready to Publish

Children have been writing and revising for a while and now choose a piece to publish. Remind them about the revision and editing checklists, and teach them new strategies for each. You might want to ask them how they wish to publish their work. After an in-class celebration, some children will need help giving or sending their pieces to the appropriate audience.

Possible Teaching Points

● *When it is time to publish, writers choose their most promising work to revise and edit.* This is probably a point best made in a conference or a small-group lesson. Help those children who have not been able to settle on a topic choose a piece from their folder to bring to completion. They should feel that the piece represents some of their better thinking and that it is worthy of putting in a bit more effort. Some children may be utterly unenthusiastic about all of their work. This can be exasperating in the third week of a unit. Try to channel your frustration into generating excitement about how great these pieces can become with a little effort. (A revision checklist is shown in Figure 2–11; an editing checklist is shown in Figure 2–12.)

● *One way to revise is to make sure our piece really says what we want it to.* Revision is so much more than just changing some words here and there. It is looking at our work with fresh eyes and making sure it really says what we

---

Revision Strategies

● Information in the pictures is also in the words.
● My piece really says what I want it to.
● I took away parts that did not belong.

Figure 2–11 The Revision Checklist

Editing Strategies

● All word-wall words and spelling patterns are spelled correctly.
● Important words related to my topic are spelled correctly.

Figure 2–12 The Editing Checklist

had hoped to say. This unit of study, because it is about sending a clear message, is a great one for teaching children to read their writing with this specific question in mind: *Does this piece really say what I want it to?* If they need to reword a part or add some information to make the message clearer, they should do so.

● **Sometimes revising means taking away parts that don't help our piece say what we want it to.** This is the complementary lesson to the previous one. Now that children are reading their work critically, they can ask themselves whether there are parts that do not belong with the rest. They can cross out (with a neat single line) or cover with white correction tape anything they no longer want in the piece. If you are teaching this unit before March, don't ask students to rewrite a clean final draft: it takes too long.

● **We should correctly spell words that are important to our topic or come up often in our work.** Long before children are ready to use a dictionary for spelling, they are able to find the correct spelling of words particular to their topics. Teach children how to decide which words are the most important or occur most frequently in their work. Then show them how they can find books or resources in the classroom library that are likely to contain those words. This is much easier than using a dictionary when children have not yet mastered the concept of alphabetizing beyond the first letter of a word.

Student Work

Brianna (who one day early in the unit had blurted out in frustration, "I have a lot of issues!") wrote a book on cleaning up after pet dogs. As an extra feature, she included a how-to page (see Figure 2–13).

Naglis did not know a name for the kind of writing he was doing, so he invented a new term: a reason book. His book (see Figure 2–14) had three full pages of reasons to quit smoking, some based on research and some based on his personal experience of watching a family member struggle with a smoking-related illness.

Gia also wrote about smoking. She initially gave three reasons to quit, but she wrote about them in a disorganized way, going back and forth from one to another. With the help of a partner, scissors, and tape, she reworked her writing into a clear argument (see Figures 2–15 and 2–16, p. 68).

Reflection

For this unit, it will be helpful to know how children think and feel about writing with a strong sense of purpose. You can use the questionnaire in Figure 2–17, p. 69, to find out.

1. Bend over and pick the poop up.
2. Take the bag off your hand.
3. Tie it up.
4. Then put it in the garbage.

Figure 2–13 Brianna's Dog Piece

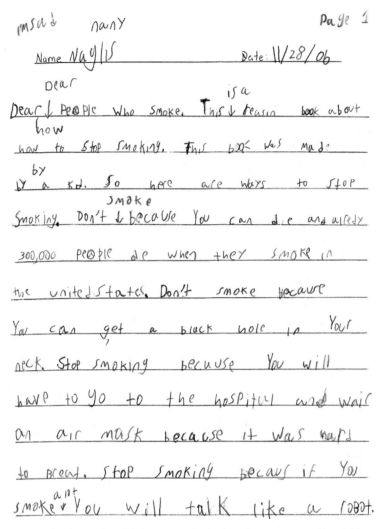

Dear people who smoke, This is a reason book about how to stop smoking. This book was made by a kid. So here are ways to stop smoking. Don't smoke because you can die and already 300,000 people die when they smoke in the United States. Don't smoke because you can get a black hole in your neck. Stop smoking because you will have to go to the hospital and wear an air mask because it was hard to breathe. Stop smoking because if you smoke a lot you will talk like a robot.

Figure 2–14 First Page of Naglis' Book About Quitting Smoking

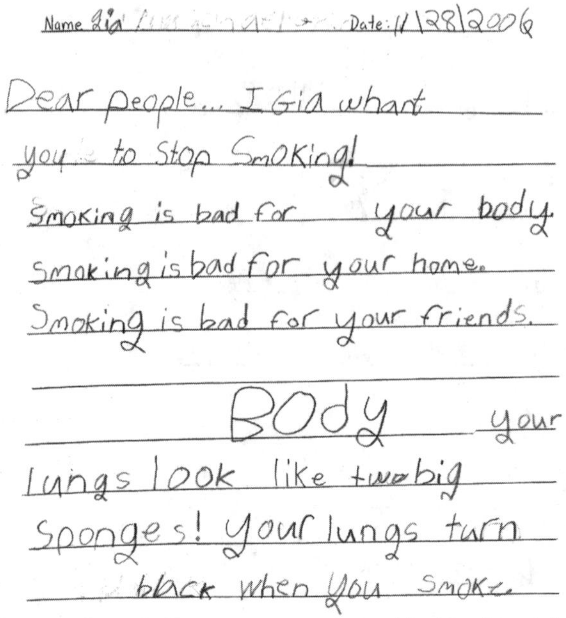

[Handwritten:]

Dear people... I Gia what
you to stop Smoking!
Smoking is bad for your body.
Smoking is bad for your home.
Smoking is bad for your friends.

BODY your
lungs look like two big
sponges! your lungs turn
black when you smoke.

Dear people . . . I, Gia, want you to stop smoking! Smoking is bad for your body. Smoking is bad for your home. Smoking is bad for your friends.

 Body: Your lungs look like two big sponges! Your lungs turn black when you smoke.

Figure 2–15 Gia's Piece About Quitting Smoking

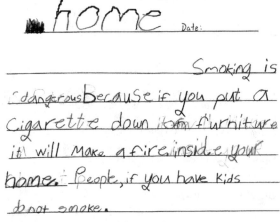

[Handwritten:]

home Date:

Smoking is
dangerous Because if you put a
cigarette down on furniture
it will make a fire inside your
home. People, if you have kids
do not smoke.

Home: Smoking is dangerous because if you put a cigarette down on furniture it will make a fire inside your home. People, if you have kids, do not smoke.

Figure 2–16 Gia's Piece *(continued)*

Name_____ Date _____

What job do you think your writing will do?	What tools did you use to make your writing do its job better?
What did you learn about thinking of the people who might read your writing?	Did you like this unit of study? Why or why not?

Figure 2–17 Writing for Change Reflection Questionnaire

■ Predictable Problems

In this unit you will probably still need to address children's difficulty with internalizing routines. It may take a while for children to get used to your expectations, especially with newly forming partnerships. Take time to reinforce your routines, making sure they are consistent. You may also notice children having trouble connecting to a strong purpose for their writing. Guide them to topics that matter deeply to them and demonstrate how *you* find purpose within the topics that most engage you.

PROBLEM	WHAT IT LOOKS LIKE	POSSIBLE SOLUTION/ CONFERENCE
Children are not choosing topics that matter to them.	• Children keep choosing new issues to write about, never settling on one.	The first thing to figure out is the reason children are having trouble settling on a topic. If they do not think that what matters to them could possibly be worth writing about, let them know that it is. Even what seems to be the most trivial thought can lead to bigger ideas. Sometimes this lack of commitment stems from a fear of not being able to write well. It is frustrating, but we need to treat it with gentle encouragement and realistic expectations.
	• Children seem to have chosen issues that have no importance to them	If the problem is that they do not seem to care about anything, remind them to explore the things that drive them nuts. You may have to do some detective work, talking to parents or whoever watches them at recess. It may be as simple as giving them permission to care a lot about something.
Children do not yet have a lot of stamina for writing.	• Children work quietly for a while but not as long as you would like.	You must stop the class every time it gets too loud, reminding the children to stay productive. You will feel like a nag, but it works. They will get so tired of being stopped that they will respond. Tell them, "You were so clear that you wanted a quiet space to work in, so I'm happy to stop you as many times as I have to in order to help you get the room exactly how you want it to sound."

PROBLEM	WHAT IT LOOKS LIKE	POSSIBLE SOLUTION/ CONFERENCE
Partners are not working well together.	• Children criticize each other's work.	Partnerships will become stronger with time and patience. Remind children of helpful ways to give feedback. Teach them how to give a compliment before a criticism.
	• Children do not follow partners' suggestions.	If children are uncomfortable changing their work, urge them to try the change orally or on a sticky note. They should change the original only if they like how the piece sounds with the revision.
	• Partners talk about everything except their writing.	It is a privilege to work with a partner. Let children know what kind of talk is productive during the workshop and what kind of talk inhibits productivity. Have the chatting partners spend fifteen minutes observing a productive partnership, writing down how they behave and what they discuss.
		A partnership that chats too much can be temporarily assigned seats far from each other for most of the workshop and allowed to meet briefly at the very end to discuss their work. If all else fails, switch the partners. This is a last resort because it means splitting up at least one other partnership, which may be working well.

■ Assessment

Before you look over the assessment chart (Figure 2–18), go back over the one in the previous unit and check the items you were not satisfied with at the time. Building a strong reading and writing community can take a few months and span a few units of study. Take note of any concepts you want to continue to address in the next unit. Then look at this unit's chart, adding and removing items based on what your class needs and is ready for.

STUDENT'S WORK SHOWS THAT I . . .	NEED TO TEACH OR RETEACH THIS TO THE WHOLE CLASS	NEED TO REMIND CHILD OF THIS SKILL	NEED TO TEACH THIS TO A SMALL GROUP OR IN A CONFERENCE	NEED TO CONGRATULATE CHILD FOR HOW WELL HE OR SHE DID
Child kept his or her writing focused on its purpose.	❑	❑	❑	❑
Child clearly stated an opinion or desire.	❑	❑	❑	❑
Child chose a genre or form for exploring this opinion or desire.	❑	❑	❑	❑
Child considered the audience for his or her work.	❑	❑	❑	❑
Child organized his or her thoughts to support the ideas.	❑	❑	❑	❑
Child chose words carefully to communicate his or her ideas.	❑	❑	❑	❑
Child continued to develop his or her voice as a writer.	❑	❑	❑	❑
Child spelled frequently used words correctly.	❑	❑	❑	❑
Child spelled words particular to the chosen topic correctly.	❑	❑	❑	❑
Child used end punctuation, quotation marks, and capitalization properly.	❑	❑	❑	❑
Child used commas, though perhaps not always correctly.	❑	❑	❑	❑
Child participated in class conversations about literature.	❑	❑	❑	❑
Child got to work quickly.	❑	❑	❑	❑
Child managed writing tools and supplies.	❑	❑	❑	❑
Child talked with peers about his or her writing.	❑	❑	❑	❑
Child articulated the job he or she wanted the writing to do.	❑	❑	❑	❑
Child read and reread his or her work often.	❑	❑	❑	❑
Child revised his or her work.	❑	❑	❑	❑
Child edited his or her work.	❑	❑	❑	❑
Child volunteered ideas, listened, and responded to others.	❑	❑	❑	❑
Child worked with a partner to develop and improve writing.	❑	❑	❑	❑
Child showed respect for all members of the community and their work, regardless of ability.	❑	❑	❑	❑
Child asked for and gave help with problems.	❑	❑	❑	❑

Figure 2–18 Writing for Change Assessment Chart

■ Professional Resources

Bomer, Randy, and Katherine Bomer. 2001. *For a Better World: Reading and Writing for Social Action*. Portsmouth, NH: Heinemann.

Wilson, Lorraine. 2006. *Writing to Live: How to Teach Writing for Today's World*. Portsmouth, NH: Heinemann.

Writing a Book Review | 3

A confession: I used to avoid asking second graders to respond to literature in writing. "They'll do it next year," I thought, much to the chagrin of my upper-grade colleagues. I have awful memories of having to write summaries and book reports in second grade, which seemed to have no other purpose than to allow Mrs. W. to use her red pen, slashing my breathless run-ons to bloody ribbons. Of course, her real reason for these assignments was to make sure I had read the book. She didn't know about my talent for writing a great book report without jumping that particular hurdle. I never wanted to subject my own students to this waste of time. Luckily, there are richer, better ways to respond to literature in writing.

The good news is that second grade writers *can* respond to what they read in thoughtful and meaningful ways. A key factor is an effective reading workshop with an emphasis on comprehension and discussion as well as on decoding and fluency. (For information and inspiration on setting up a great reading workshop, refer to the resources at the end of this chapter.) Read aloud a variety of books, taking time to talk about them. Make sure that your book talks do not turn into question-and-answer sessions, but leave room for children to develop their ideas about literature. Give reading partners time to talk about their books together, teaching them strategies to develop ideas together.

A book review is just one way to respond to reading. We can have children write and produce plays based on favorite stories, write jacket copy (blurbs) for books, create graphs or time lines that correspond to a character's emotional journey, or all of the above. Whatever we choose to do, our introduction to reading response must be gentle, with lots of support and encouragement. We must explain what we expect children to do clearly and with simple demonstrations.

■ Overview

This unit is approximately four weeks long. At the beginning of the study have children participate in whole-class conversations about familiar texts (a common activity during a read-aloud). During these conversations, help children develop ideas about literature by looking at a few common story elements, such as character development, conflict, or plot. You will also read some book reviews with your students, discussing their qualities and how they are written. Children then choose a book or two to review. Give them time to write expressively about their impressions of the book, encouraging them to discover new thoughts and feelings. They can then plan their review orally with a partner. As children start to write their own reviews, they should refer to the mentor texts for inspiration. Each student should also decide the purpose of her review and how best to publish it. You might create a book review newsletter to distribute to other students, teachers, parents, pediatricians' offices, after-school programs, or anywhere else young readers might be found.

■ Goals/Outcomes

It is important to have a clear idea of what you want the children's work to look like before starting the unit. If your students met (or were close to meeting) the goals of the last unit, you will want to stretch them a little further in this one. The new challenge here is writing expressively or using writing to discover what they are thinking. While in prior units you expected your students to hash out their ideas orally, you are now prompting them to do some of this discovery work in writing. You want children to understand that sometimes their best ideas come *after* writing about them for a while.

Remember to consider not just the writing but also the students' work habits and their sense of community. Continue to raise your expectations of the way children approach their writing and one another.

Writing Quality

We hope children will

- clearly state an opinion or idea about a text

- organize their thoughts to support this statement

- keep their writing focused

- support their ideas with evidence from the text, using quotes appropriately

- use some elements of a book review

- choose words carefully to communicate their ideas

- continue to develop their voice as a writer by trying to make the work engaging

Writing Conventions

We hope children will

- spell frequently used words correctly

- spell words particular to their topic correctly

- use end punctuation, quotation marks, and capitalization properly

- use commas, perhaps not always correctly

- try to attend to grammar conventions, such as subject-verb agreement

Writing Habits

We hope children will

- participate in class conversations about literature

- get to work quickly

- manage their own writing tools and supplies

- talk to one another about their reading or writing

- make and use a plan to write

- read and reread their work often

- refer to their reading as they write

- revise their work independently as they write

- edit their work

Community

We hope children will

- volunteer ideas, listen, and respond to others

- work with a partner to develop and improve writing

- show respect for all members of the community and their work, regardless of ability

- express disagreement in a way that promotes conversation rather than shuts it down

- ask for help when they encounter problems and offer to help class-mates with problems

▪ Getting Ready to Teach

Start assembling a collection of good book reviews well before the study. Include some written by and for adults about books with which your students are familiar, planning how to simplify or paraphrase them (perhaps leaving out portions) so that your class will understand them. Search the Internet for reviews written by children. Ideally you should find enough reviews at appropriate reading levels so that each partnership in your class can have one.

Gathering Materials

Set up an easel and chart paper on which to itemize the conventions of a book review. Make sure you have plenty of sticky notes and paper. Children will do some of their early work on plain paper, sticky notes, and sentence strips. Later in the unit, they will need lined paper, some sheets of which include room for a picture.

Considering the Students

Your observations and rubrics from the last unit will help you determine how to teach this one. If a majority of your class had trouble with particular concepts, review them in this unit instead of moving on to something new. As you glance over the possible teaching points for this unit, decide which are appropriate for minilessons, which to spread over a few days, which to use in conferences with individuals, and which to ignore.

Preparing Demonstration Materials

Choose one or two favorite books that you've read aloud to your class several times and, on sticky notes, make notes about how you will use them in your demonstrations and as you write a shared review with the class. Practice retelling the book in different ways: concise, detailed, interpretive, personal response. Doing this ahead of time ensures a smooth demonstration.

Expressive writing is probably new to your students, and it may be new to you, too! If you try some of this kind of writing yourself ahead of time, it will be easier for you to understand what your students will experience. Settle down in a comfortable place and write whatever comes to mind about your book. Keep pushing thoughts onto the paper. If you do not know what to write, write *that*. Give yourself permission to write stuff that does not make sense or sound elegant and to repeat yourself. It's for your eyes only. As your mind loosens up, ideas will bubble to the surface, ideas you may not have known you had! Writing like this also helps when you have an idea but do not quite know how to put it into words. Your children will not be able to do this as quickly or voluminously as you, but now that you have done it, you will be able to teach expressive writing clearly. (Figure 3–1 is a bit of my expressive writing about *Pretzel*, by H. A. Rey.)

■ Teaching the Unit

This unit begins with some work on reading comprehension and discussion and moves into understanding and identifying key features of book reviews. You are asking children to do two kinds of reading: reading for enjoyment and reading like writers. It may be tricky balancing these, so your students will need clear demonstrations and support. They will then plan, organize, write, revise, edit, and publish a review of one of their favorite books. Figure 3–2 shows one way to organize this unit.

Reading for and with Ideas

A dynamic, efficient reading workshop is vital to the quality of children's written responses to literature. This section of the study depends on how comfortable

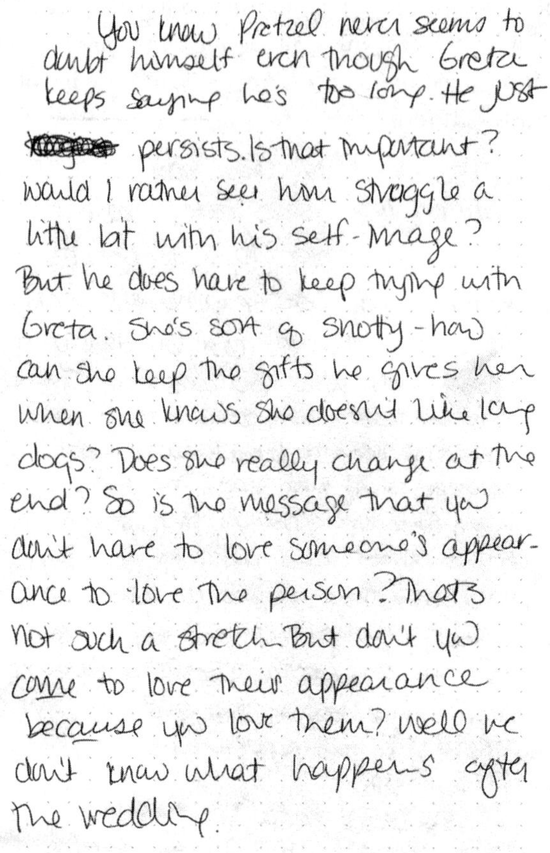

You know Pretzel never seems to doubt himself even though Greta keeps saying he's too long. He just ~~the~~ persists. Is that important? Would I rather see him struggle a little bit with his self-image? But he does have to keep trying with Greta. She's sort of snotty - how can she keep the gifts he gives her when she knows she doesn't like long dogs? Does she really change at the end? So is the message that you don't have to love someone's appearance to love the person? That's not such a stretch. But don't you come to love their appearance because you love them? Well we don't know what happens after the wedding.

Figure 3–1 Expressive Writing Sample

students are with talking thoughtfully about literature and the experience they have had doing so. You will teach them to talk about books as an oral rehearsal for their written work. They will then need to flesh out their ideas, explain them clearly, find supporting details in the text, retell parts of the text as needed, compare or contrast the text with another one, or draw connections between the text and their own lives. While they might have done all of these things in past conversations, they now need to learn to do them in writing.

Start by reading aloud a richly evocative story, such as *Jamaica's Find*, by Juanita Havill, and have the children discuss their ideas about it as a class. Ideally, the book will already be familiar so you can move beyond content and talk about its qualities. You might show the class some of your expressive

TIME FRAME	SECTION OF STUDY	WHAT CHILDREN DO	WHAT YOU TEACH
3–5 days	Reading for and with Ideas	• Deepen conversational skills to include adding to classmates' thoughts and combining several comments into an umbrella idea • Learn more sophisticated ways of discussing a story, such as how a character responds to issues, conflict, or change • Listen to and enjoy a few great stories • Understand, think about, discuss, and re-tell these stories • Notice themes, issues, styles, or authors' messages • Choose a book or two to review • Write to explore and discover ideas about books • Jot thoughts on sticky notes	Guiding question • What makes our favorite books so good? Minilessons, conferences, or midworkshop focus points • In a conversation about literature, we may learn more by adding to one another's ideas than by bringing up lots of new ideas. • Writing down (and talking through) all the things we think about a book can help us discover more ideas. • People who write about books know how to retell in a way that is both con-cise and complete. • Writing down (and talking through) the big things we remember happen-ing in a book can help us discover our own thoughts and feelings about the book. • Keeping track of themes, issues, styles, or authors' messages helps us develop ideas. • Telling about changes in the story can help us explain our idea.
2–3 days (ongoing)	Organizing Ideas	• Read and discuss book reviews • Plan how their review will go • Sort and group thoughts that support elements in their review • Find examples in text that support their comments	Guiding question • What do good book reviewers do (and not do) in their writing? Minilessons, conferences, or midworkshop focus points • When we write about a big idea, it helps to describe the steps that got us to that big idea. • It helps to decide, before we start writ-ing, which elements of a review we want to use and how they might sound. • Right before starting to write the re-view is a good time to sort through our sticky notes.

Figure 3–2 Writing a Book Review at a Glance

TIME FRAME	SECTION OF STUDY	WHAT CHILDREN DO	WHAT YOU TEACH
4–5 days	Writing and Revising	• Craft a review from their plan • Write a lead that hooks readers • Write a closing that captures the essence of the review in an engaging way • Refer to the text to confirm, support, or add details • Use some juicy extras (quotes from the book, a direct address to the reader, connections between text and self, world, or another text, and so on) • Keep writing focused on purpose • Refer to the revision checklist (one new item)	Minilessons, conferences, or midworkshop focus points • A good review says what the book is about without giving too much away. • A good review gives readers a feeling for the book. • Retelling part of the story or giving specific examples can help us explain our idea. • We can let the reader hear a bit of the author's voice by quoting from the book. • Readers of book reviews want to know for whom the book is written. • We can open our review with a hook that makes our readers want to keep reading. • Some reviewers end their reviews by summing up their opinion of the book. • If we look at the book review chart, we might see elements we did not use but would like to.
2–3 days	Editing and Publishing	• Consult editing checklist (one new item) • Reflect on learning • Celebrate	Minilessons, conferences, or midworkshop focus points • Book reviewers give strong evidence for their opinions. • Writers of book reviews try to use the most correct grammar they can.

Figure 3–2 *(continued)*

writing about this text and ask them to try some. It will be interesting to see how differently everyone thinks about the same book.

Guiding Question

● ***What makes our favorite books so good?*** It may seem limiting to focus only on good reviews. After all, some books do get bad reviews out in the world and we *are* teaching children about writing for a real purpose. Nevertheless, it is easier to start with books children like. They can identify what makes a book enjoyable, valuable, and worth the time it takes to read it. Knowing this will eventually enable them to write negative reviews, too, but not just yet. Invite, challenge, and guide them to try to name the qualities of the books they love. This discussion will help them develop a language for talking about books beyond "I liked it." If you make a chart like the one in Figure 3–3, add to it

Things We Love About Books

- Characters who surprise us

- Characters who are active, who think and change

- Characters who do things their own way

- Details that help us see the story inside our mind

- Something crazy or unexpected that happens

- Characters who talk back and forth

- Vividly imagined things that couldn't really happen

- Not knowing what's going to happen

We love different kinds of books

Funny books

Books that express strong feelings

Factual books

Mysteries

Adventure stories

Figure 3–3 Chart of Book Qualities

throughout the study as children read more and develop a more specific or sophisticated vocabulary for talking about books.

Possible Teaching Points

● *In a conversation about literature, we may learn more by adding to one another's ideas than by bringing up lots of new ideas.* The art of conversation sometimes eludes enthusiastic young readers. Make sure your students know how proud you are that they have so much to say about what they read (or what you read and they listen to). Gently suggest plumbing one topic in depth rather than floating on the surface of many topics. They can write down ideas they'd like to discuss in future conversations about the same text.

● *Writing down (and talking through) all the things we think about a book can help us discover more ideas.* It can be so hard to write without having an image of what it is we are supposed to be writing. Usually most of us sit down to write something specific, such as a note, list, or plan. Those of us who keep journals have an easier time making sense of this. The idea is that children sit down and just write what they are thinking about a book and see where it takes them. The quality of this writing may not be great. It may meander from one idea to the next without a clear order or structure. However, the point is not to make sense to a reader but to help the writer shape ideas. Many children will find that after a bit of writing, they'll get to a sort of *aha* moment. These discoveries become the basis for writing that *is* meant for readers. (Children who have a hard time getting a lot of words onto paper quickly can do this same work orally.)

● *People who write about books know how to retell in a way that is both concise and complete.* When asked what a story is about, children sometimes say things like "a boy" or "being good." When pressed, they can often say much more. If they are going to learn how to respond to literature in writing, you need to help them say much more *without* being pressed. In this lesson and the next, you will show them a couple of good ways to say what a story is about. Giving the plot of a story means telling, in sequence, the main events. You could demonstrate how you might do this with *Jamaica's Find*: "One day in the park, Jamaica finds a toy dog. She wants to keep it, but her mother tells her she should turn it in to lost and found. She is sad to give up the dog, but she does it anyway. Jamaica sees the dog's owner, Kristen, get her toy back. The girls become friends and are both happy in the end." Point out that this kind of retelling is short and leaves out most of the details.

- *Writing down (and talking through) the big things we remember happening in a book can help us discover our own thoughts and feelings about the book.* While some children retell a story in a word or two, others retell every single detail and the plot gets lost. It will take more than one lesson for your students to reach a happy medium: Have children practice a few retellings, with feedback and support. Once they can do a basic, no-frills version, children can learn to include certain important parts of the book in greater detail. A character's struggle or change, the introduction of a new character or setting, and the evocation of strong feelings are story elements that require a more detailed retelling.

- *Keeping track of themes, issues, styles, or authors' messages helps us develop ideas.* Instead of sticking to the plot, children can talk about what ideas or themes they think the story addresses. This skill will be especially important for texts without a real plot, like nonfiction articles and poems. In relation to *Jamaica's Find*, you might say, "This story is about how important it is to do what's right," or "Sometimes it's hard to do the right thing, but you should anyway," or "You feel better about yourself when you are honest than you do when you are selfish." In order to identify themes or ideas, children must get beneath the surface of a book, go beyond literal comprehension into more interpretive and responsive thinking.

- *Telling about changes in the story can help us explain our idea.* Many of the ideas that strike readers most strongly in stories have to do with the changes that take place. In *Jamaica's Find*, the change that Jamaica has in her attitude toward returning the toy dog is closely connected with the big ideas children tend to have about the story. You could say, "After I say what my idea is, I can talk about the change. Here's my idea: *Jamaica's Find* is about how doing what's right even when you don't want to makes you feel better than being selfish does. Now I'll talk about the change: In the beginning, Jamaica doesn't want to do what's right. She knows she should return the dog, but she wants to keep it. Soon, looking at the dog makes her kind of sad. I think that's where she starts to change. In the end, Jamaica is happy when Kristen gets her dog back. She learns that doing what's right can make you feel happier than having something you want. That's what this story is really about. See how talking about the change helps me make my idea more specific?"

Student Work

Athena wrote her thoughts on sticky notes as she read her book. After reading each chapter, she pulled them out to write more about her ideas (see

Figure 3–4). She used these to build a strong theory about the character of Ramona.

Athena built a web based on the plot of her book (see Figure 3–5). She focused on one of Ramona's problems: having no friends.

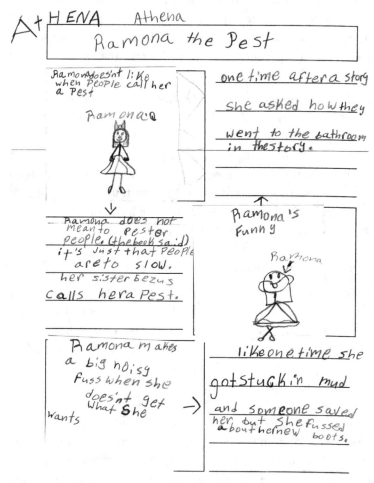

Ramona the Pest

  Ramona doesn't like when people call her a pest. Ramona does not mean to pester people. (The book said.) It's just that people are too slow. Her sister, Beezus, calls her a pest.

  Ramona's funny. One time after a story she asked how they went to the bathroom in the story.

  Ramona makes a big, noisy fuss when she doesn't get what she wants. Like one time she got stuck in mud and someone saved her but she fussed about her new boots.

Figure 3–4 Athena's Thoughts on *Ramona the Pest*.

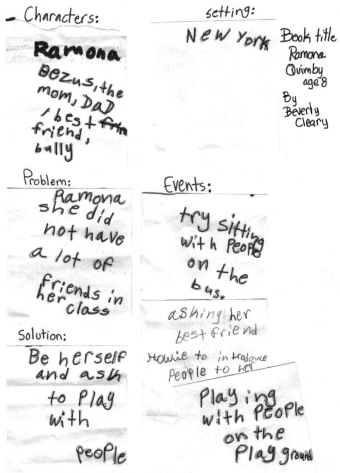

Characters: Ramona
Beezus, the mom, Dad / best friend, bully

Setting: New York

Book title Ramona Quimby age 8

By Beverly Cleary

Problem: Ramona she did not have a lot of friends in her class

Events: try sitting with people on the bus. asking her best friend Howie to introduce people to her. Playing with people on the play ground

Solution: Be herself and ask to play with people

Ramona Quimby Age 8, *by Beverly Cleary.*
 Characters: Ramona, Beezus, the mom, Dad, best friend, bully.
 Setting: New York.
 Problem: Ramona, she did not have a lot of friends in her class.
 Events: Try sitting with people on the bus. Asking her best friend, Howie, to introduce people to her. Playing with people on the playground.
 Solution: Be herself and ask to play with people.

Figure 3–5 Athena's Web for *Ramona Quimby, Age 8*

Organizing Ideas

In this section of the unit you guide children through the essential step between conceiving an idea and putting the idea into writing for others to read and understand. Only part of a writer's work is writing. So much of it is preparing to write. Give children a chance to read some book reviews, naming their qualities and pointing out some optional elements. Then have them gather and sift through all their notes to decide what potential readers must know about the book they are reviewing. Your job is to help them articulate their ideas, gather text support, and plan a way to help their readers follow their line of thinking.

Guiding Question

● *What do good book reviewers do (and not do) in their writing?* Gather some good book reviews at a level that your students can read (or understand if you are reading them aloud) and help them identify qualities of the writing. I choose some short and long reviews of children's books from the *New York Times* and various websites, parts of which I paraphrase as I read them aloud. (I use published reviews of children's books by and for adults because these reviews are more likely to have the qualities I want children to notice.) I also find reviews by children, so students can see examples that are closer to the kind of writing they will be able to produce on their own. Demonstrate how you read a review as a writer, underlining parts of the review you think are important. Have partner teams do the same. Their charted responses (see Figure 3–6) will be a resource as they write their own reviews.

Possible Teaching Points

● *When we write about a big idea, it helps to describe the steps that got us to that big idea.* The conversations children have had so far are good preparation for this section of the unit. Steps that may lead to an idea include the things that happen in a book, inferences children make about events or characters, comparisons of characters in the book, comparisons with other books, or connections to real life, to name a few. Separating these elements allows readers to look at each one in isolation. If the big idea in *Jamaica's Find* is that doing what's right even when you don't want to makes you feel better than being selfish does, the parts leading up to it could include what happens at the beginning, middle, and end of the story and how Jamaica changes because of the things that happen.

● *It helps to decide, before we start writing, which elements of a review we want to use and how they might sound.* Encourage children to plan ahead how they want to incorporate certain elements of a book review into their work. If they know, for example, that they want to use a quote to retell part of the book or to illustrate the book's voice, they can take some time now to find just the right one. Making these decisions in advance will make their writing go more

Book Reviews . . .

- Give the title and author of the book

- Give a sense of the book's style

- Let readers know if they should read the book
  (or avoid it)

- May let readers know if it is like another book

- Have some actual words from the book (quotes)

- Tell what a book is about but do not give away the
  ending or the best part

- Tell how the book feels

- Have beginnings that make you want to keep reading

Figure 3–6 Qualities of a Book Review

smoothly—they won't have to consult their notes or the book as often while they are writing. (However, remind them that the decisions they make now are a guide and may need to change.)

● *Right before starting to write the review is a good time to sort through our sticky notes.* Now that children have a rough idea of how their review will go, what they want to communicate to readers, and what elements of a book review they want to use, they can sort their notes. Show them how to determine which notes support what they want to say and which ones aren't helpful. They can then sort the helpful notes into categories: *what happened, feelings, quotes, character, change, best part,* and whatever others they can think of. Sorting the notes makes them easier to refer to and therefore more likely to inform the final product.

Student Work

Figure 3–7 shows a cluster of notes having to do primarily with retelling.

Kalen has sorted his sticky notes into categories (see Figure 3–8). Some retell events, some address feelings and help him think about how the character changes in the story, and one is an interpretation of the author's message.

Writing and Revising

Though a few children may already have started to write their reviews, it's now time for the whole class to put all their reading and planning to work. As children work, you may need to remind them to keep their notes, plans, and books nearby for reference.

Possible Teaching Points

● *A good review says what the book is about without giving too much away.* Chances are that children noticed this in the reviews you read together, but you might need to remind them as they work on their own reviews. Their enthusiasm for sharing their thoughts about a favorite book can overshadow the rational planning and organizing they did. An excellent way for children to help each other in this unit is to have them say whether their partner hasn't told enough of the plot to make sense, has given away too much, or has struck a good balance.

● *A good review gives readers a feeling for the book.* Readers want to know how a writer approaches what he or she is writing about. A funny book about the importance of self-confidence is different from a poignant one. A good way

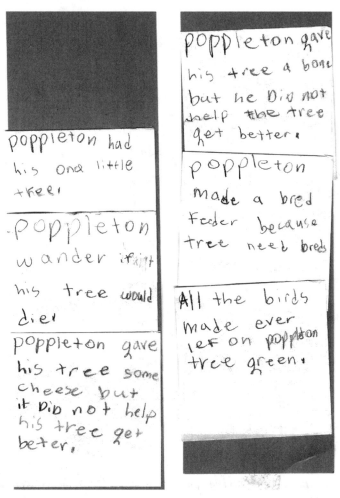

Poppleton had his own little tree. Poppleton wondered if his tree would die. Poppleton gave his tree some cheese but it did not help his tree get better. Poppleton gave his tree a bone but he did not help the tree get better. Poppleton made a bird feeder because the tree needed birds. All the birds made every leaf on Poppleton's tree green

Figure 3–7 A Student's Notes About *Poppleton Forever*, by Cynthia Rylant

to help children learn to do this independently is to practice with books you have read aloud to them. Pull out a few familiar books with a range of different feelings—funny, sad, hopeful, serious. Show children how, even though these books evoke different feelings at different points, you can still name the overall sense of each book.

Figure 3–8 Kalen's Notes

● *Retelling part of the story or giving specific examples can help us explain our idea.* Many children do this automatically, but it is still worth demonstrating. You might tell children how you can go back and forth between your own idea and what actually happens in the book: "In the beginning, Jamaica doesn't want to do what's right. She wants to keep the dog even though it's not hers. She knows she should turn it in to the lost and found, because that's what she does with the hat. And she seems to feel guilty at home when she hears her mom say that the dog probably belongs to a child just like Jamaica. My idea carries a lot more weight when I back it up with stuff that happened in the story."

● *We can let the reader hear a bit of the author's voice by quoting from the book.* Although one reason book reviews contain quotes is to retell part of the plot, the skillful reviewer chooses a quote that lets reader hear the author's voice as well. Consider these two quotes from *Jamaica's Find:*

> Jamaica ran to the park house and plopped the stuffed dog on the counter.

and

> Her mother came in quietly, sat down by Jamaica, and looked at the stuffed dog, which lay alone on the chair. She didn't say anything. After a while she put her arms around Jamaica and squeezed for a long time.
>
> "Mother, I want to take the dog back to the park," Jamaica said.
>
> "We'll go first thing in the morning." Her mother smiled.

Both passages convey the information that Jamaica returns the dog. The second one does this while also giving a feeling for Juanita Havill's voice. Children will understand this better if you demonstrate choosing between two quotes like these, thinking aloud that one quote just gives the facts while the other shows more of the author's voice.

- *Readers of book reviews want to know for whom the book is written.* The purpose of a book review is to let readers know if they should invest in the book being reviewed. Some of the books your students review may be aimed at a particular audience, such as girls, sports fans, or mystery lovers. If this is the case, they should certainly say so in their reviews. When reviewing books that do not target a specific kind of reader, children can indicate circumstances under which a reader might choose the book. For example, "If you have a new baby brother or sister, you should definitely read *Julius, Baby of the World*, by Kevin Henkes."

- *We can open our review with a hook that makes our readers want to keep reading.* Beginning a piece of writing is always hard for me. I find it much easier to write the beginning after most of the piece has been written. (As I wrote these words, I had not yet written the beginning of this book.) So it makes sense to me to have a lesson about beginnings this late in the unit. Now that children know what their review is going to say, they can create a beginning that will draw their readers in. Take another look at your review examples, focusing on the leads. Here are some interesting ones my students and I discovered:

  - questioning the reader ("Have you ever wondered what would happen if you could go back to ancient Greece?")

- giving a quote ("'Bah, go away!' wouldn't make you think Frog and Toad are such good friends, but they are.")

- playing with the title ("What makes *A Good Day* so good?")

You can repeat this lesson with endings.

- ***If we look at the book review chart, we might see elements we did not use but would like to.*** Earlier in the study, children identified elements of a book review they might use in their work. Now that they are pretty much finished writing their reviews, encourage them to take another look at the chart. They may see something they had not noticed or cared for before but now want to try. Sometimes our vision for our writing changes as we write it. Giving children room to make changes to their plans reinforces the idea that writing and revising are part of the same process.

Student Work

Before Natasha began revising and editing, she was aware that her piece (see Figures 3–9 and 3–10) was a little hard to understand. Her next step was to work with a partner to clear up some of the confusion. She took more time to explain how the original story has Chicken Licken claiming that the sky is falling, but in this story the narrator warns everyone that the table of contents is falling.

In her review (see Figure 3–11, p. 95), Kate does a nice job of explaining what the book is like. Her voice is beginning to develop as she tries to make the piece engaging and informative. As a final revision, she decided to add a quote (where the star is) and to make her ending a little more satisfying. The rating system is a nice touch.

Editing and Publishing

Revision and editing checklists are provided in Figures 3–12 and 3–13, p. 96. This unit lends itself to publishing a newsletter of reviews. If you have a parent volunteer or some other kind of help, ask him or her to type the reviews. (A computer-savvy helper might even be able to use a fancy newsletter template.) Then arrange for the newsletters to be photocopied and distributed to children in kindergarten through third grade, posted in the school library, or brought to other places where consumers of children's books are likely to be found.

Name __Natasha__   Date _____

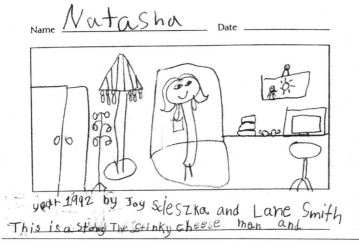

~~ year 1992 by Joy Scieszka and Lane Smith
This is a story The Stinky cheese man and

rather Fairly Stupid Tales makes me fill

crasy, Dissy, and it macks my tong twist

up. It macks me Dissy becouse i'm Saying

the same thing agin and agin, Chicken

Licen gos with her friends and

Jack Narrator said waita

a minute! wait a minute!

"I forgot The Table of content

This is a story The Stinky Cheese Man and Other Fairly Stupid Tales *makes me feel crazy, dizzy, and it makes my tongue twist up. It makes me dizzy because I am saying the same thing again and again. Chicken Licken goes with her friends and Jack Narrator said, "Wait a minute! Wait a minute! I forgot the table of contents!"*

Figure 3–9 and 3–10 Natasha's Review Before She Revised It

Possible Teaching Points

● *Book reviewers give strong evidence for their opinions.* You will probably notice that most children have included support for their ideas from the text they reviewed. The purpose of this lesson at the end of the study is to teach children how to reread their work with a specific critical lens: "Have I made a

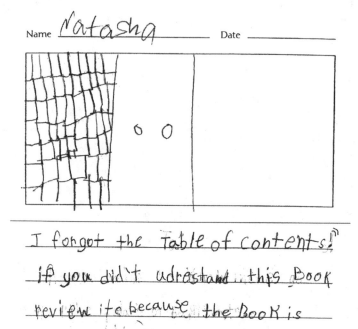

I forgot the Table of contents!
if you did't udrostand this Book
review ite because the Book is
Konfewsing if you want to
Know more go to the lidray or
Book Stori

"I forgot the table of contents!" If you didn't understand this book review, it's because the book is confusing. If you want to know more, go to the library or bookstore.

Figure 3–10

strong case for my opinion? Will a reader trust me?" If their evidence does not entirely match their opinion or seems not to belong in the review, they can change it to be more fitting.

● ***Writers of book reviews try to use the most correct grammar they can.*** Like spelling and word study, grammar needs to be taught as a special part of the curriculum. In writing workshop, children apply what they've been taught in these isolated lessons, and it takes them a while to make the transfer. (To use a sports analogy, it's easier to get a basketball into the net when given a free throw than it is in the confusion of actual play.) For example, children who

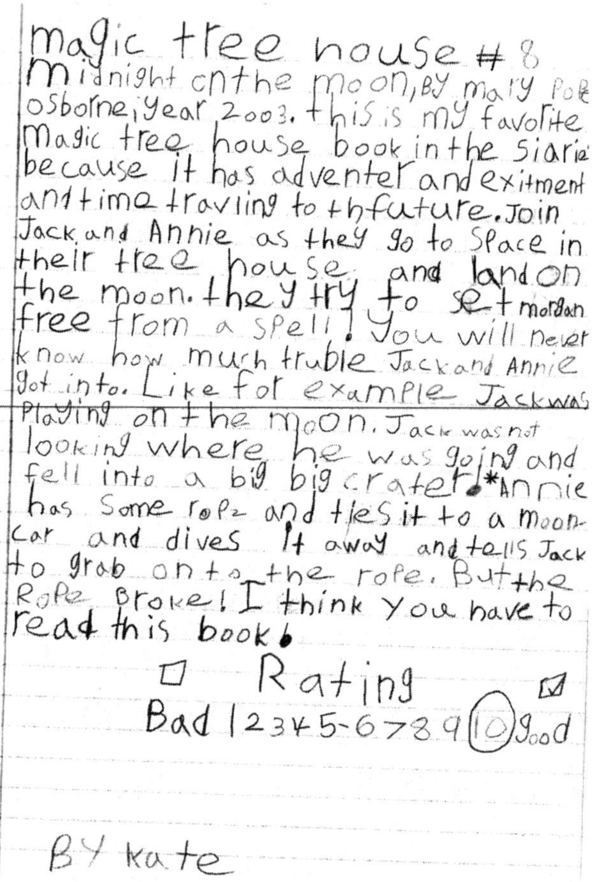

magic tree house #8
Midnight on the moon, by mary Pop
Osborne, year 2003. this is my favorite
Magic tree house book in the siarie
because it has adventer and exitment
and time traviing to thfuture. Join
Jack and Annie as they go to Space in
their tree house, and land on
the moon. they try to set morgan
free from a spell! You will never
know how much truble Jack and Annie
got into. Like for example Jackwas
Playing on the moon. Jack was not
looking where he was going and
*fell into a big big crater!*Annie*
has Some rope and ties it to a moon-
car and dives It away and tells Jack
to grab on to the rope. But the
Rope Broke! I think you have to
read this book.

☐ **Rating** ☑
Bad 1 2 3 4 5 6 7 8 9 ⑩ good

BY Kate

Magic Tree House #8, Midnight on the Moon, *by Mary Pope Osborne, year 2003. This is my favorite Magic Tree House book in the series because it has adventure and excitement and time traveling to the future. Join Jack and Annie as they go to space in their tree house and land on the moon. They try to set Morgan free from a spell! You will never know how much trouble Jack and Annie got into. Like, for example, Jack was playing on the moon. Jack was not looking where he was going and fell into a big, big crater!* Annie has some rope and ties it to a moon car and drives it away and tells Jack to grab on to the rope. But the rope broke! I think you have to read this book.*
  Rating. Bad 1 2 3 4 5 6 7 8 9 ⑩ Good.

Figure 3–11 Kate's Review

Revision Strategies

- Information in the pictures is also in the words.
- My piece really says what I want it to.
- I took away parts that did not belong.
- I gave support or evidence for my ideas.

Figure 3–12 The Revision Checklist

Editing Strategies

- All word-wall words and spelling patterns are spelled correctly.
- Important words related to my topic are spelled correctly
- I tried to use my best grammar.

Figure 3–13 The Editing Checklist

spell every word correctly on a test will misspell the same words in their writing. An added difficulty is that many children's instinctual grammar is not textbook grammar. I sometimes explain the difference between home language and school language. Your students' work will tell you what you need to teach. Choose one small grammar convention you have taught in isolation, such as subject-verb agreement or the difference between *a* and *an*. Ask children to comb through their writing, looking for places where they need to make the necessary correction.

Student Work

Figure 3–14 shows three reviews on the front page of a newsletter. The typist did correct some spelling (after children had corrected what they could inde-

The 2-309 Review of Books

Ramona Quimby, Age 8

By Beverly Cleary, reviewed by Athena

Julius Baby of the World

by Kevin Henkes

This book will teach you that just because there is a baby in the house does not mean that your parents don't like you. When you read this book you might change your mind about your baby sister or brother. The you might like your baby sister or brother a lot. Then you might have an opinion on your sibling like Lily did, "His eyes are sparkly and his fur smells like perfume." You might like her or his eyes. I recommend this book because it has an important lesson.

-Saschael

In the book Ramona Quimby, Age, 8, Ramona does not think her life is an easy life. Her father smokes, her sister's a grouch, her mother works a lot, and she has a hard time at school, and a lot of other things are wrong. Like one time her mother said she was going to pack Ramona a hard boiled egg, but...something else happened! "At last it was time for the egg. There were many different ways of cracking the eggs. The most popular, and the real reason for bringing an egg to school, was knocking the egg against one's head." And guess what happened. It EXPLODED right on Ramona's head! This book makes me feel excited because you don't know what's going to happen next. I recommend this book because it's funny and about a girl who is just trying to be herself. Please read this book!

BABYMOUSE, QUEEN OF THE WORLD, BY JENNIFER L. HOLM AND MATTHEW HOLM

Babymouse, Queen of the World is a very good comic book about a young mouse who dreams about being queen of the world. "But everyone knew who the REAL queen was...Felicia Furrypaws."

Is Babymouse going to get an invitation to Felicia's slumber party?

I liked this book so I bet you would, too. Babymouse would love to be Queen of the World. Or is she already? Find out in this book.

-Anya

PAGE 1

Figure 3–14 Book Review Newsletter

pendently) and neatened up the punctuation and grammar, but the words are essentially as the children wrote them.

■ Reflection

The questionnaire in Figure 3–15 will tell you how children think and feel about reading as well as what they learned about writing book reviews.

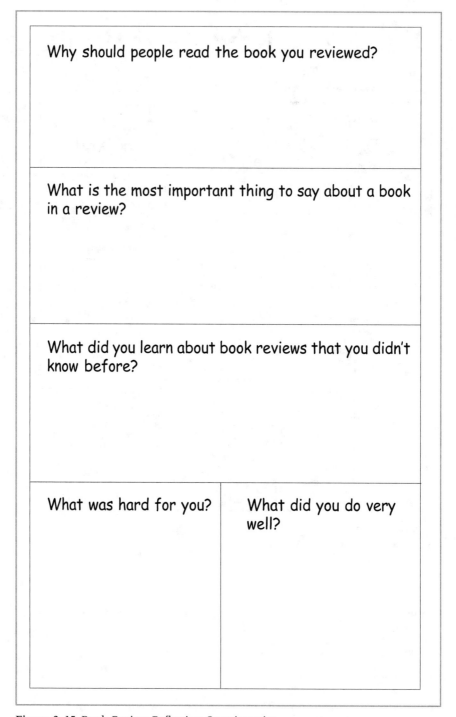

Why should people read the book you reviewed?

What is the most important thing to say about a book in a review?

What did you learn about book reviews that you didn't know before?

What was hard for you?

What did you do very well?

Figure 3–15 Book Review Reflection Questionnaire

Predictable Problems

You may still be running into problems with topic choice and stamina if you are teaching this unit in the fall. Be on the lookout for children having a hard time organizing their ideas in this unit, also. Take note of which students have difficulty with this so you can give them extra attention in the planning stages of the following units.

PROBLEM	WHAT IT LOOKS LIKE	POSSIBLE SOLUTION/ CONFERENCE
Children have not chosen books well.	• Children are able to discuss only the plot of a book, nothing deeper. • Children misunderstand or misinterpret parts of the book.	If children have trouble going beyond literal comprehension, have them choose books they are more familiar with. They could write reviews of past read-alouds or books they have read several times. Another possible solution is to have them review books that are a level or two below their regular independent reading level.
	• Children choose books they do not care for or have read only part of.	Children may do this because they believe they have to write reviews of the books they have read most recently. Remind them of books you know they have loved in the past. These can also be unconventional books, like graphic novels or joke books.
		Sometimes this lack of commitment stems from a fear of not being able to write well. It is frustrating, but we need to treat it with gentle encouragement and realistic expectations.
Children have not planned enough.	• Pieces are scattered. • Children include random quotes. • Examples from text do not support opinion.	Before they get far along in writing their reviews, make sure you have seen children's plans. If you cannot get to everyone before the students begin to write, prioritize. First see the children who have had difficulty planning in other units.

PROBLEM	WHAT IT LOOKS LIKE	POSSIBLE SOLUTION/ CONFERENCE
		Remember that, like many of the skills children acquire in second grade, planning can come slowly. Accept that some pieces will not flow as well as others in this unit. Schedule a time to meet with children in a small group to go over the key planning and organizing strategies.
Children have poor stamina.	• Children work quietly for a while, but not as long as you would like.	You must stop the class every time it gets too loud, reminding the children to stay productive. You will feel like a nag, but it works. They will get so tired of being stopped that they will respond. Tell them, "You were so clear that you wanted a quiet space to work in, so I'm happy to stop you as many times as I have to in order to help you get the room exactly how you want it to sound."

■ Assessment

Remember to consider children's daily work habits—that will tell you how much control they have over the necessary skills. (Published work logically shows a mastery of more skills and strategies than daily writing does, because the published work has gone through more revision and editing.) If children had any trouble with reading comprehension and discussing ideas at the beginning of the unit, keep in mind that they will need support with the reading they are asked to do at the beginning of the unit on writing about research. Figure 3–16 has an assessment guide for this unit.

■ Professional Resources

Angelillo, Janet. 2003. *Writing About Reading*. Portsmouth, NH: Heinemann.

Calkins, Lucy McCormick. 2001. *The Art of Teaching Reading*. New York: Addison-Wesley Educational.

STUDENT'S WORK SHOWS THAT I . . .	NEED TO TEACH OR RETEACH THIS TO THE WHOLE CLASS	NEED TO REMIND CHILD OF THIS SKILL	NEED TO TEACH THIS TO A SMALL GROUP OR IN A CONFERENCE	NEED TO CONGRATULATE CHILD FOR HOW WELL HE OR SHE DID
Child clearly stated an opinion or idea about a text.	❑	❑	❑	❑
Child organized thoughts to support this statement.	❑	❑	❑	❑
Child kept the writing focused.	❑	❑	❑	❑
Child supported ideas with evidence from the text, using quotes appropriately.	❑	❑	❑	❑
Child used some elements of a book review.	❑	❑	❑	❑
Child chose words carefully to communicate ideas.	❑	❑	❑	❑
Child continued to develop voice as a writer by trying to make the work engaging.	❑	❑	❑	❑
Child spelled frequently used words correctly.	❑	❑	❑	❑
Child spelled words particular to the chosen topic correctly.	❑	❑	❑	❑
Child used end punctuation, quotation marks, and capitalization properly.	❑	❑	❑	❑
Child used commas, though perhaps not always correctly.	❑	❑	❑	❑
Child tried to attend to grammar conventions, such as subject-verb agreement.	❑	❑	❑	❑
Child participated in class conversations about literature.	❑	❑	❑	❑
Child got to work quickly.	❑	❑	❑	❑
Child managed writing tools and supplies.	❑	❑	❑	❑
Child talked to classmates about reading or writing.	❑	❑	❑	❑
Child made and used a plan to write.	❑	❑	❑	❑
Child read and reread his or her work often.	❑	❑	❑	❑
Child referred to his or her reading as he or she wrote.	❑	❑	❑	❑
Child revised his or her work.	❑	❑	❑	❑
Child edited his or her work.	❑	❑	❑	❑
Child volunteered ideas, listened, and responded to others.	❑	❑	❑	❑
Child worked with a partner to develop and improve writing.	❑	❑	❑	❑
Child showed respect for all members of the community and their work, regardless of ability level.	❑	❑	❑	❑
Child expressed disagreement in a way that promoted conversation rather than shut it down.	❑	❑	❑	❑
Child asked for help when he or she encountered problems.	❑	❑	❑	❑

Figure 3–16 Writing a Book Review Assessment Chart

Collins, Kathy. 2004. *Growing Readers*. Portland, ME: Stenhouse.

Harvey, Stephanie, and Anne Goudvis. 2000. *Strategies That Work*. Portland, ME: Stenhouse.

Miller, Debbie. 2002. *Reading with Meaning: Teaching Comprehension in the Primary Grades*. Portland, ME: Stenhouse.

Zimmermann, Susan, and Ellin Oliver Keene. 1997. *Mosaic of Thought*. Portsmouth, NH: Heinemann.

4 | Exploring Humor

When I was much younger (back in the seventies) there was a television game show called *Make Me Laugh*. The contestant (an ordinary person, not at celebrity) would sit in a chair as, one after another, stand-up comedians performed their routines in front of him or her. All the contestant had to do was not laugh. It was hard not to, though, because the comedians were funny and any contestant able to keep from laughing at the humor usually gave in to the infectious laughter of the live audience. It was a brilliant game because very few people won but it was fun to watch nevertheless. My family tuned in regularly.

One night at our dinner table someone suggested we play *Make Me Laugh* during dessert. Thus was born a joyful dinnertime tradition. We each had a turn to make up some jokes and try to get the rest of the family to laugh. We tried it all—bathroom humor, physical humor, one-liners, story jokes. Soon we were planning our routines during the day, workshopping jokes on our friends. We learned that the comedienne depends on her audience. Our purpose was not to please ourselves, but to get a laugh. If the audience doesn't laugh, the work is not successful. It's that simple.

I originally wanted to teach this unit of study because I thought it would be fun. I knew there would also be some instructional value but was unable to say what kind. It was the children who showed me the way. First, I came to know (or remember) that having fun *is* an instructional value. This unit gave them something to invest in joyfully. They learned the power of asking the mind to think differently, of having a deliberate purpose to their work, and of being able to see for themselves whether they had been successful at achieving that purpose. They learned the importance of working to come up with specific language rather than settling for general language. The pride they felt after completing the unit motivated them to work hard in other units. Our writing workshop took on a joyful tone; we were reminded to keep finding things to laugh about in the midst of hard work.

■ Overview

This unit takes approximately three weeks. In the beginning, children explore what they think is funny. You read and discuss funny books together, and children open their eyes to funny things happening in the world around them. You then help them develop some of the humorist's skills by giving them writing exercises that challenge them to think in new ways. They eventually choose one of these exercises to expand into a bigger piece, learning some strategies to make it more fun for the reader. Finally, they edit and publish their piece. Some may want to read their piece aloud; others may want to create a humor magazine to distribute around the school.

I should warn you that you'll be dealing with bodily function humor. If you try to forbid it, it will be that much more desirable for children to explore. Nevertheless, as you teach the specific strategies and skills of humor, most children will move beyond the toilet. Those who do not will at least use this kind of humor in a more creative way.

■ Goals/Outcomes

In teaching this unit several times, I learned not to put too much emphasis on *comedy*, *jokes*, or *funniness*. The more pressure one feels to be funny, the less funny one becomes. Instead, I came to value writing that was clever, unconventional, or inventive. Keep in mind that the goal is not so much that children produce funny work, but that they think creatively. In other words, emphasize the process, not the product.

Writing Quality

We hope children will

- understand some basic principles of humor
- consider the audience for their writing

- choose a vehicle that works for them (narrative, parody, comic strip, and so on.)
- try a variety of humor exercises
- choose words carefully to communicate their ideas
- choose and commit to a writing voice
- understand that humor is best when it's not hurtful

Writing Conventions

We hope children will

- spell frequently used words correctly
- spell words particular to the chosen topic correctly
- use end punctuation, quotation marks, and capitalization properly
- use commas, though perhaps not always correctly
- attend to grammar conventions, such as subject-verb agreement
- write appropriate-length sentences (rather than one long one with a lot of *and*s)
- correct more of their own errors independently

Writing Habits

We hope children will

- participate in class conversations about humor
- get to work quickly
- stay at work or know what to do when they encounter problems
- manage their own writing tools and supplies
- workshop jokes together, trying multiple deliveries
- make and use a plan to write
- read and reread their work often
- revise their work
- edit their work

Community

We hope children will

- volunteer ideas, listen, and respond to others

- work with a partner to develop and improve writing

- show respect for all members of the community and their work, regardless of ability

- express disagreement in a way that promotes conversation rather than shuts it down

- ask for help when they encounter problems and offer to help classmates with problems

- be aware of what their classmates are working on

■ Getting Ready to Teach

Prepare to teach this unit by collecting or making all the materials you will need, going over your assessment notes from the last unit, and planning your demonstrations for the first few exercises.

Gathering Materials

Ask your students to help you pull together a collection of books they think are funny. Consider designating a special basket of funny books that children can read during the unit. Children's reading diets influence what they write, so you want a lot of humor in their system. Buy or make little memo books, one for each member of your class. (You can make a book by cutting two pieces of blank paper into quarters, folding the quarter sheets, and stapling them; see Figure 4–1.)

Make a few kinds of writing paper with different combinations of picture boxes and lines for writing. (Samples of paper templates are in the Appendix.)

Considering the Students

This unit is fun for everyone and is an opportunity to invite reluctant or struggling writers to feel more successful. Look over the exercises in the second section of the unit with these children in mind. Think of ways to give them

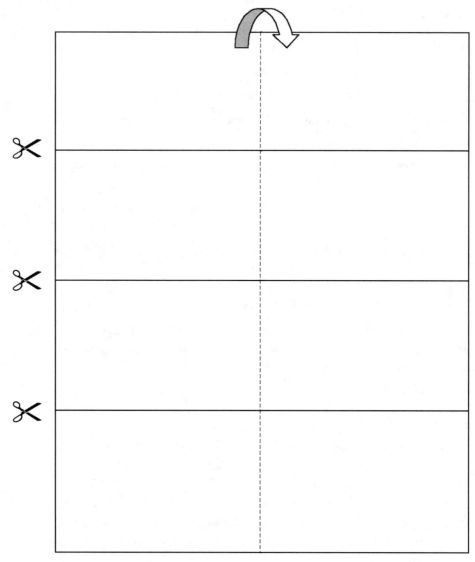

Figure 4–1 To make a memo book out of plain paper, cut along the solid lines and fold at the dotted line.

extra support so that some of their work can become examples in your lessons and share sessions. These exercises tend to be short and less daunting than, say, a book review. As always, use your assessment notes from the last unit to inform your teaching of this one.

Preparing Demonstration Materials

Buy or make yourself a memo book in which to record things that make you laugh. If you start making entries before the unit, you will have an example to show the children when you give them their memo books. Look over the exercises in the second section of the unit and create examples for each one, using whichever type of paper you will provide for your students. You may still want to write them in front of your class, as if you are just thinking of them, so that the children can hear how you think aloud about your decisions.

■ Teaching the Unit

Remember to emphasize thinking creatively rather than producing funny work. The most successful pieces are written in a low-pressure environment in which the focus is on the process rather than the product. See Figure 4–2 for one way to structure this unit.

Exploring What Is and Isn't Funny

Either before or at the beginning of the study, hand out the small memo books that you have either bought or made. Ask children to carry these with them for a few days, recording everything that makes them laugh. They can also record things that make other people laugh, even if they themselves do not find them funny. You may want to exclude things they see on television, as these can be difficult for them to retell and tend to be unsavory or obvious. Making entries in your own funny memo book will help you make decisions as you teach this unit.

Figure 4–3 is a page from my funny book (which I started keeping about fifteen years ago). As you see, not all of this is suitable for children. They would not appreciate some of the things I find funny. Nevertheless, it's valuable for me to record the things that make me laugh, because it helps me begin to understand my own sense of humor, which helps me guide children to discover *their* sense of humor.

Figure 4–4, p. 110, is a chart one of my classes created recently. The gray items were added later in the study, as we got better at naming what was funny to us.

Guiding Questions

● *What makes something funny?* This is a time both to read like writers and analyze what children have recorded in their memo pads. Even adults find it difficult to articulate what makes something funny. You will have to help

TIME FRAME	SECTION OF STUDY	WHAT CHILDREN DO	WHAT YOU TEACH
2–3 days	Exploring What Is and Isn't Funny	• Read and talk about humorous literature • Name some principles of humor • Collect (in a small notebook or memo pad) things that make people laugh • Begin to develop a personal taste in humor • Discuss what is funny and what is not at all funny	Guiding questions • What makes something funny? • What are some different kinds of funniness? • Are there some things that just are not funny?
3–4 days	The Humorist's Tools	• Try several exercises that ask the mind to think in new ways • Workshop jokes and funny lines	Writing exercises • What Would It Say? • It's Hard Being . . . • Odes to Objects • Write the Caption • Role Reversal • Not What I Expected • Just Deserts
4–5 days	Writing and Revising	• Try different voices and kinds of humorous writing • Try multiple ways of making a joke, story, poem, or line funny • Read writing aloud, practicing delivery • Work with timing • Give and accept feedback from partners	Minilessons, conferences, or midworkshop focus points • One way to make something funnier is to exaggerate, go over the top. • If a piece has a lot of dialogue, it might work better as a comic strip. • Specific words are funnier than general ones. • Some words sound funnier than others. • Reading our work aloud with a partner will tell us how well it works. • We can make our work more or less funny in the delivery.
2 days	Editing and Publishing	• Refer to the editing checklist • Distribute funny stories and poems around the school • Celebrate with a comedy show or reading	Minilessons, conferences, or midworkshop focus points • Our work will be more successful if it does not try to do too much. • Instead of having one long sentence with a lot of *ands*, use several sentences.

Figure 4–2 Exploring Humor at a Glance

children put their thoughts into words. Record the responses to this question on a chart, leaving room to add more ideas as the unit progresses.

● **What are some different kinds of funniness?** This question is of particular interest to me, so I always have children think about it first. I usually give an example to help them understand what I'm after. I might say, "One kind of humor

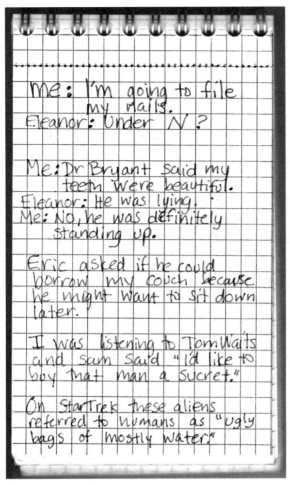

Figure 4–3 Page from My Funny Memory Book

is physical humor, when it is funny to watch someone do funny things with his body. Another kind of humor is jokes that make your brain twist up a little bit. This guy Steven Wright has a joke that goes "I bought some powdered water. What do I add?" That doesn't make me crack up like crazy, but it gives my brain a satisfying little stretch. What are some other ways to be funny? Some responses I have gotten include "jokes," "funny stories," "mean funny versus nice funny," "funny that you see versus funny that you read," and "gross funny."

● **Are there some things that just are not funny?** If your students have an intuitive sense of this, you may want to skip the question, addressing the issue only if it arises. If, on the other hand, you want to address inappropriate jokes

What's So Funny?

- Talking objects can be funny

- Some things are funny because you expect something else

- Some words just sound funny

- When bad things happen to people who deserve it

- Farts and burps, and things like that

- When people use words in a different way than usual (puns)

- When characters act crazy or weird

- Specific words

- Going over the top (exaggerating)

What's NOT So Funny?

- Making fun of people

- Making people feel bad or sad

- Hurting people

Figure 4–4 Chart of What We Think Is Funny

preemptively, a class discussion is a good forum. Help children talk about keeping the classroom safe for everyone during this unit. Jokes that make people feel bad, are about things people cannot help, embarrass people, or are in any way at someone's expense are not funny.

Student Work

In her memo book, Anya focused on funny things she heard people say (see Figure 4–5). The one about the crocodile is a helpful example of why context is important to humor.

Figure 4–6 shows two entries from Naglis' memo book. It is amazing to me that thirty years after it first cracked me up, children still say, "Guess what? Chicken butt!" More interesting, Naglis wrote the word *ukulele*. This led to a discussion about how some words are funnier than others and prompted other children to record funny words or phrases as well as funny incidents. *Ukulele* is just funnier than *guitar*, right?

The Humorist's Tools

This section of the study is a departure from how workshop teachers usually do things. I found as I was teaching the unit that children benefited from a more structured curriculum, which included exercises designed to develop

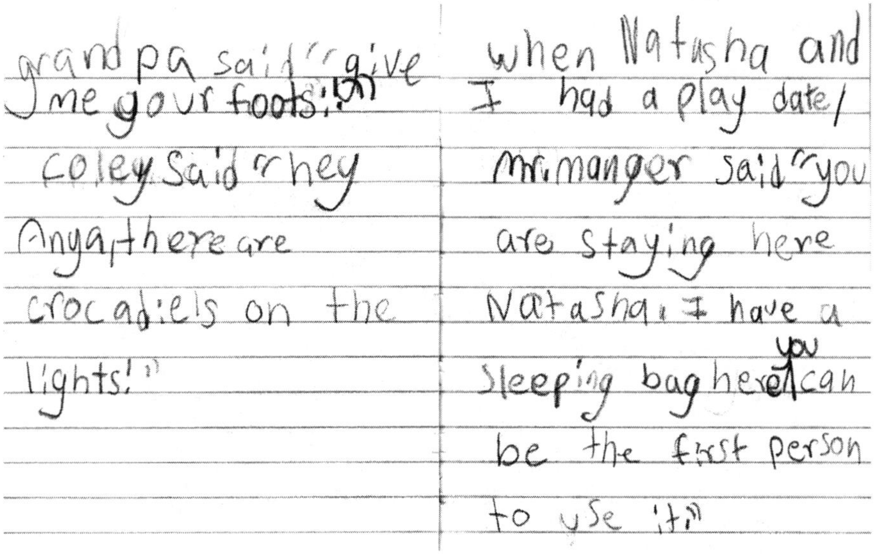

grandpa said "give me your foots!"
coley said "hey Anya, there are crocadiels on the lights!"

when Natasha and I had a play date, mr. manger said "you are staying here Natasha, I have a sleeping bag here you can be the frist person to use it"

Figure 4–5 Pages from Anya's Memo Book

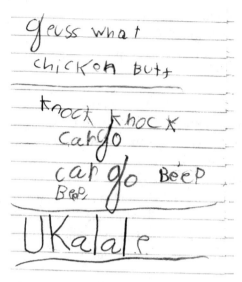

Figure 4–6 Page from Naglis' Memo Book

©2007 Christina Kelly

A) *I can't believe I fell for Grandma's socks in the giant box trick. Again.*
B) *I told Billy not to mess around with that genie! Now he'll never go to college.*
C) *I'll paw wrestle you for it.*
D) *You can't wear pants, can you?*

Figure 4–7 Drawings I Gave Children and Some of Their Captions

certain ways of thinking. Without these, children were having a lot of trouble creating a context for their humorous events, which made them more painful than funny. Far from limiting students, as a traditional prompt might, these exercises allowed their minds to explore new territory.

Introduce the idea of *workshopping* humor. First of all, for every successful joke there are at least ten that fail. Second, most successful jokes have been shaped and tweaked before they became funny. Children need to know this if they are to continue without getting discouraged.

Writing Exercises

● *What Would It Say?* In this exercise, children endow objects with the power of speech. Encourage them to imagine what a wide variety of things would say if they could. Some will be funny and some will not. Remind the children that the point is not always to be funny, but to think creatively.

● *It's Hard Being . . .* A logical continuation of the prior exercise, this one has children giving objects the power to complain. The challenge of these two exercises is in bending the mind to think of objects as beings with their own perspective, rather than as things that serve us. Children have probably never thought about how hard that piece of gum really has it.

● *Odes to Objects.* When children get used to imagining their stuff talking, they sometimes start to talk back. Explain to children that an ode is a lyrical poem that praises a beloved person or object. Since they now know how hard it is to be a chair or a pencil, they can write odes to these poor downtrodden things. The humor here comes from elevating something ordinary to an exalted status.

● *Write the Caption.* This exercise is borrowed from the *New Yorker* magazine's caption contest. Give children a few drawings and ask them to think of captions. The drawings can be simple but should set up an expectation of a certain family of responses. The more successful captions play on that expectation, turning it on its head. The samples in Figure 4–7 show how, within the limitations of the exercise, children take diverse approaches.

● *Role Reversal.* This is a different way to get children to look at familiar objects in a new way. Ask children to think of their relationships to certain objects and then turn them around: the TV watches me, my dog takes me for a walk. The best responses to this exercise are usually not as much funny as captivating, as when Finn said, "The water drinks me," or when Eva said, "The ocean swims in me." (This is a great exercise to repeat in a poetry study.)

- *Not What I Expected.* If you start paying attention to comedy, you'll see that so much of what makes us laugh does so by defying an expectation. But before you can defy it, you have to set it up. Even this is too broad of an exercise, so you will need to provide children with a few specific scenarios from which to choose. Talking to a parent or teacher, opening a gift with great excitement, stirring an aromatic pot, and going on a trip are all good fodder. Here's an example of how this might play out:

> A: Can I stay up late to watch a program? It's educational.
> B: Sure, Dad, but not too late. Tomorrow's the big meeting.

- *Just Deserts.* When my students and I first started thinking about some of the funny books in our classroom, children noticed that it can be funny when something bad happens to a character. It's important to guide children to think more specifically about this. Is it always funny when a bad thing happens to someone? Obviously not, so what makes it funny? Most students tend to agree that the recipient of bad luck has to deserve it in some way. It is funny for a character to eat so much candy that she throws up only if she has refused to share the candy with a single soul.

Student Work

Zaire's What Would It Say? piece (see Figure 4–8) has some promising beginnings and some attempts that she did not end up pursuing. She was successful in brainstorming enough possibilities to give her mind some exercise.

David wrote from the perspective of an apple (see Figure 4–9). He thought about all the hardships an apple might have to endure. At the end he started to explore giving the apple more of a voice.

Writing and Revising

In this section of the study, which is a bit shorter than in other units, children choose something they wrote in an exercise that could become something bigger and fuller. Here you'll need to teach them some strategies for turning up the volume on the humor, so to speak. They will also need to reread their work more than usual and work closely with a partner to stay on track. You will also want to go over the idea of *delivery*. They probably already practice reading their work fluently before every writing celebration. In this unit, fluency, expression, and timing work together to make the piece sound its best.

The pants say, "Your butt is too fat!"
The paper says, "Hey, hey, that tickles!"
The tree says, "Stop staring at me!"
The candy says, "You suck me too much and I like it!"

Figure 4–8 Zaire's What Would It Say? Exercise

Possible Teaching Points

● *One way to make something funnier is to exaggerate, go over the top.* A well-placed bit of exaggeration can make a big difference. Many of the exercises from the prior section will be much funnier with some exaggeration. Explain to children that there is an expected amount of description or emotion

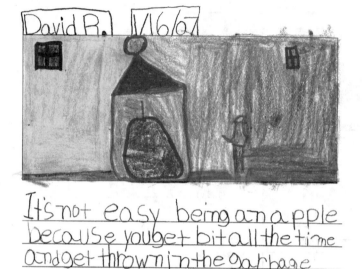

It's not easy being an apple because you get bit all the time and get thrown in the garbage when you're rotten. And you get cut up with a knife and get peanut butter on you. And if you're making apple pie, don't even ask. You get baked.

Figure 4–9 David's Apple Piece

relative to most situations and that going far beyond this expectation can be quite funny.

● *If a piece has a lot of dialogue, it might work better as a comic strip.* Lots of children write pieces that depend heavily on dialogue, so much so that there is often nothing else on the page. These pieces are difficult to follow without any information about the context or even who is talking. If you encounter this situation, give children paper divided into boxes and show them how to convert their dialogue into the balloons of a comic strip.

● *Specific words are funnier than general ones.* In the first *George and Martha* book, by James Marshall, George does not know how to tell Martha that he does not like pea soup. He pours the soup not into his *shoe*, but into his *loafer*. Show children how to reread their work, looking for places where they have used nonspecific language. Words like *thing* and *stuff* are good candidates for replacement. The habit of using specific language is vital to good writing and will benefit children in everything they write.

- **Some words sound funnier than others.** It is a widely documented phenomenon that /k/ is a funny sound, which explains why Naglis wrote *ukulele* in his memo book. Beyond this, some words just sound funny or feel funny in the mouth. *Octopus* is funnier than *squid* and *bouillabaisse* is funnier than *chicken noodle soup*. A good activity for partners is to read each other's work, suggesting words to replace with funnier ones.

- **Rereading our work aloud with a partner will tell us how well it works.** Partners are indispensable in this unit. Like tickling oneself, being able to tell if your own writing is funny can be hard. Partners can, gently, give one another feedback about how their writing is working. Show them how to use each other as a sort of test audience for their work, trying out different ways to make it funny. Remind them to give and accept suggestions and to try ideas orally before committing to them.

- **We can make our work more or less funny in the delivery.** Children need to practice reading their work aloud in every unit so they can do so with fluency. In this unit, children need to work particularly on phrasing and timing. Demonstrate the difference by reading aloud something you know the class thinks is funny. Read it once word by word, without any fluency. Read it again too quickly, and a third time with no expression. Then read it as you think it should be read to maximize the humor. Point out to children how fluency, timing, and expression worked together to make the piece sound better. Send them off with a partner to practice reading their work aloud. Teach them how a good partner will listen carefully to the piece, telling the writer where it sounds right and where it needs to be read differently.

Student Work

What I love about Sarah's comic strips (see Figures 4–10a through 4–11, pp. 118–120) is that she truly visualized each scene before putting it down on paper. These would not be nearly so funny as a narrative, but they work perfectly as a storyboard. In Figure 4–11 especially, the reader needs to see the character trying so hard to get his head through the neck of his shirt.

Eva dove into her piece very thoroughly, creating a five-page biography of a soccer shoe. She clearly allowed herself to explore the plight of her subject. Her second page is shown in Figure 4–12, p. 121.

Harry and Tod and the Bathtub

Tod wanted to tell Harry a secret. I have to tell you a secret. Come here. All right. *Tod told Harry to come closer.* Closer. *Then he told him again.* Closer. *Harry fell into the bathtub.* Aaaaaaaaah! My trick worked! Haha! *Harry jumped out of the tub, dragging Tod.* Errrr! Hey! *Harry took Tod outside.* What are you doing, taking me outside? Yes. *Everyone was staring at Tod.* Step up and see the naked boy! Hahahaha. *Tod was mad. Harry was happy.*

Figure 4–10a A Comic Strip by Sarah

Figure 4–10b

Editing and Publishing

In this section, teach children about focus and about avoiding run-on sentences. Then have them edit their work (see the checklists in Figures 4–13 and 4–14, p. 122) and ask them how they wish to publish their pieces. I recommend a performance or reading of their work: they'll be excited about performing for their families or for other classes. You can collect pieces that work

Mini Comic with Tod
In this comic, Tod finds a shirt and struggles to get it on. His head pops through and he says, "Phew." He then looks at a pair of pants and says, "Uh-oh."

Figure 4–11 Another Comic Strip by Sarah

well without being read aloud in a humor magazine and distribute copies to other classes.

Possible Teaching Points

● ***Our work will be more successful if it does not try to do too much***. Focus is important in all writing. In this unit, children focus by committing to their humor without trying to overdo it. Show them how to fine-tune the jokes they have written by reviewing some of the principles of humor. These revisions will vary. Some children will need to shorten their work; others will need to add a little to some of their jokes or change general words to specific ones, for example.

● ***Instead of having one long sentence with a lot of*** **and**s, ***use several sentences***. We have all encountered the page-long sentence containing ten *and*s. It is part of children's natural writing development. They get to the point of being able to write a lot in one sitting but do not yet know how to handle the volume they are able to produce. The magic of being able to write so quickly has taken over, and the sentences just pour out of them like speech. Remember to love their enthusiasm as you address this habit. Show them how to read their work,

Then the feet run away. I was
glad the stinkiey feet were
out of me. Then I see another me,
He dose not look happy. "What is
wrong" I asck. When we are worn out
we well get thrown away the other
me says. I wish I was back at the
shoe store. The other me tells me
"when we are worn out two things
will crush us." I am scard. I cannot
sleep that night. In the moning
I am tierd. Then those
Sinkey feet get Put into me agin

*Then the feet run away. I was glad the stinky feet were out of me. Then
I see another me. He does not look happy. "What is wrong?" I ask.
"When we are worn out we will get thrown away," the other me
says. I wish I was back at the shoe store. The other me tells me,
"When we are worn out two things will crush us." I am scared. I
cannot sleep that night. In the morning I am tired. Then those stinky
feet get put into me again.*

Figure 4–12 Excerpt from Eva's Soccer Shoe Biography

looking specifically at the word *and*. It will be easier if you use one of their
pieces as an example or create one of your own. Each time you see the word
and, stop and think aloud, "Should I start a new sentence here by replacing
this *and* with a period? Or does it make sense how it is?" Not every *and* will
be a problem, so they need to know how to judge which ones to change and
which ones to keep.

Revision Strategies

- Information in the pictures is also in the words.
- My piece really says what I want it to.
- I took away parts that did not belong.
- I gave support or evidence for my ideas.
- My piece is focused.

Figure 4–13 The Revision Checklist

Editing Strategies

- All word-wall words and spelling patterns are spelled correctly.
- Important words related to my topic are spelled correctly
- I tried to use my best grammar.
- Instead of having one long sentence with a lot of *ands*, I have several sentences.

Figure 4–14 The Editing Checklist

■ Reflection

Children's responses to questions about the unit (see Figure 4–15) will give you important insights. The things children find important or are proud of will tell you how your teaching affected them. It will also tell you what they think of themselves as writers. You will know what you need to be clearer about in the next unit and whose confidence needs a boost.

Name_____ Date _____

What are you most proud of in this unit?	Which humor exercises did you like best?
What did you learn about humor?	Did you like this unit of study? Why or why not?

Figure 4–15 Humor Reflection Questionnaire

■ Predictable Problems

One of the biggest problems you will contend with in this unit is in trying to maintain some seriousness about writing in the midst of all this merrymaking. Don't hold the reins too tightly, but do talk to children seriously about the purpose of humor—to get a laugh. A writer may find his own work hilarious, but if his audience doesn't, he needs to keep working on it.

■ Assessment

As you prepare for the next unit, complete the form in Figure 4–16 and decide which concepts you will need to address and how you will do so. Remember

PROBLEM	WHAT IT LOOKS LIKE	POSSIBLE SOLUTION/ CONFERENCE
Children get their ideas of humor from television.	• Their writing is all dialogue with no setting or character development.	You gave children little notebooks in which to record things that struck them as funny specifically to avoid this problem, but the television is a powerful influence. One way to deal with humor that is all dialogue is to create a comic. Show children how to provide the setting and other details in the pictures.
	• Their humor seems visual, but there is not enough description to understand it.	Children cannot just keep making comic after comic. Some of the exercises require descriptive writing in order to be successful. Have some good examples at hand, especially ones written by students. Show children how the descriptive parts actually can make physical comedy come to life on the page.
	• Many jokes are violent.	I can see why some children enjoy this. I guess it is funny when a steamroller flattens the roadrunner or Yosemite Sam shoots a hole through himself because we always know they'll be back, miraculously unharmed. Help children use blood and guts not just for the sake of being gross, but to make their work funny.

to evaluate any information that tells you how well children responded to the models you provided. Giving children time to explore examples fully before starting to write is very important.

STUDENT'S WORK SHOWS THAT I ...	NEED TO TEACH OR RETEACH THIS TO THE WHOLE CLASS	NEED TO REMIND CHILD OF THIS SKILL	NEED TO TEACH THIS TO A SMALL GROUP OR IN A CONFERENCE	NEED TO CONGRATULATE CHILD FOR HOW WELL HE OR SHE DID
Child understood some basic principles of humor.	❏	❏	❏	❏
Child considered the audience for his or her writing.	❏	❏	❏	❏
Child chose a vehicle that worked for him or her (narrative, parody, comic strip, and so on).	❏	❏	❏	❏
Child tried a variety of humor exercises.	❏	❏	❏	❏
Child chose words carefully to communicate ideas.	❏	❏	❏	❏
Child chose and committed to a writing voice.	❏	❏	❏	❏
Child understood that humor is best when not hurtful.	❏	❏	❏	❏
Child spelled frequently used words correctly.	❏	❏	❏	❏
Child spelled words particular to the chosen topic correctly.	❏	❏	❏	❏
Child used end punctuation, quotation marks, and capitalization properly.	❏	❏	❏	❏
Child used commas, though perhaps not always correctly.	❏	❏	❏	❏
Child tried to attend to grammar conventions, such as subject-verb agreement.	❏	❏	❏	❏
Child wrote appropriate-length sentences (rather than one long one with lots of *and*s).	❏	❏	❏	❏
Child corrected more of his or her own errors independently.	❏	❏	❏	❏
Child participated in class conversations about humor.	❏	❏	❏	❏
Child got to work quickly.	❏	❏	❏	❏
Child stayed at work or knew what to do when he or she had trouble.	❏	❏	❏	❏
Child managed writing tools and supplies.	❏	❏	❏	❏
Child workshopped jokes with classmates, trying multiple deliveries.	❏	❏	❏	❏
Child made and used a plan to write.	❏	❏	❏	❏
Child read and reread his or her work often.	❏	❏	❏	❏
Child revised his or her work.	❏	❏	❏	❏
Child edited his or her work.	❏	❏	❏	❏
Child volunteered ideas, listened, and responded to others.	❏	❏	❏	❏
Child worked with a partner to develop and improve his or her writing.	❏	❏	❏	❏
Child showed respect for all members of the community and their work, regardless of ability.	❏	❏	❏	❏
Child expressed disagreement in a way that promoted conversation rather than shut it down.	❏	❏	❏	❏
Child asked for help with problems and offered help to peers.	❏	❏	❏	❏
Child was aware of what classmates were working on.	❏	❏	❏	❏

Figure 4–16 Exploring Humor Assessment Chart

■ Professional Resources

Lane, Barry. 2003. *Wacky We-Search Reports*. Shoreham, VT: Discover Writing.

The following books for adults about writing comedy may also be helpful, but the exercises need to be modified heavily for young writers.

Kachuba, John B. 2001. *How to Write Funny: Add Humor to Every Kind of Writing*. Cincinnati: Writer's Digest.

Macks, Jon. 2003. *How to Be Funny*. New York: Simon and Schuster.

Writing About Research | 5

As an elementary school student, I never had the pleasure of being part of a writing workshop. I did, however, get to write many research reports. I do not remember all of them, but at least one was copied directly from the encyclopedia, with a few words changed so it would sound more like a child wrote it. I know this not because I remember doing it, but because I still cringe at the tongue-lashing I got when my father got wind of it. Most of my early writing instruction was based on prompts and formulas: topic sentence + (3 × supporting sentence) = paragraph and so forth. So it was that by the world-weary age of nine I was a sworn hater of writing. Just in time, along came Mrs. Talbert, who allowed us to choose our own topics and then allowed herself to get caught up in our excitement to learn about them.

Intoxicated by the power of choosing my own topic, I settled on *the impact of the navel orange on the development of Riverside*, my hometown. I later had to broaden it to include other varieties of citrus. Bless my mother for taking me to the library whenever I needed to look at books that could not be checked out and for driving me to see the first two navel orange trees in California, conveniently growing next to my orthodontist's office. Bless the woman in the little room full of rare historical books for helping me learn about my topic, setting aside books and photographs for me in between my visits. Bless me for choosing such an annoying topic and then falling in love with it. Most important, bless Mrs. Talbert for rescuing me from an otherwise certain fate as a sullen, bored teenager. She gave me the room to explore what interested me and trusted me to learn what I was supposed to learn from the process. She opened doors and pushed me through.

The study was magical for me for three important reasons. First, I saw the work as my own. Choosing the topic and gathering research materials was a lot of responsibility and left a lot of room for error, but it also raised the stakes and motivated me to do well. Second, I approached the material as a writer, not as a kid with an assignment. The difference is that I wanted the material to be clear and instructive and interesting to the reader rather than good enough for a decent grade. Finally, I believed my work might have an audience other than the teacher. The woman at the library asked for a copy, as did my next-door neighbor, a citrus grower. I hope I've infused this unit with these qualities.

■ Overview

You will want your students to spend a good five weeks writing about research, which will give them time to sink their teeth into some juicy material. In the beginning, children will consult a wide variety of nonfiction, learning to take notes on what they notice. As they develop interests in specific aspects of their topic, they will begin to sort and organize their notes in preparation for drafting. They will need time to read like writers so that they can decide what kind of project they will create from their research and how they want to present their information.

Next they will turn their notes into a draft. During this time they will learn to focus their topic, getting rid of notes that do not fit and doing more research to fill in gaps in the material. Most children will then be ready to make a clean draft from their revised and edited (messy) one. Illustrations will be important to this piece, and they should be both found and created, photographed and drawn.

■ Goals/Outcomes

You may have taught a nonfiction unit of study earlier in the year that was not based on research. If so, many of the lessons you taught about organization and structure will resurface in this unit. Children's work in the earlier unit will alert you to how they will respond to this one. If your students do not have much prior experience writing nonfiction, you will want to spend more time looking at published literature. Children will need time to explore and discuss the qualities of the kinds of books they will soon be creating. If you know that you need to incorporate goals of organization, planning, or structure into this unit, do so.

Writing Quality

We hope children will

- choose topics that excite them
- teach the audience with their writing
- keep their writing focused
- organize their work
- use features of nonfiction (diagrams, charts, indexes, and so on) effectively
- choose words carefully to communicate their ideas
- write in an authoritative voice

Writing Conventions

We hope children will

- spell frequently used words, onsets, and rimes correctly
- spell words particular to their topic correctly
- use end punctuation, quotation marks, and capitalization properly
- attend to grammar conventions, such as subject-verb agreement
- write appropriate-length sentences (rather than one long one with a lot of *and*s)
- use commas correctly in lists

Writing Habits

We hope children will

- participate in class conversations about literature
- get to work quickly
- keep working or know what to do when they have trouble
- manage their own writing tools and supplies
- work with partners to express themselves clearly
- make and use a plan for what to write
- read and reread their work often

- refer to their research as they write
- revise their work
- edit their work

Community

We hope children will

- volunteer ideas, listen, and respond to others
- work with a partner to develop and improve each other's writing
- show respect for all members of the community and their work, regardless of ability
- express disagreement in a way that promotes conversation rather than shuts it down
- ask for help when they encounter problems and offer to help their classmates with problems
- be aware of what classmates are working on and share research materials
- help one another find ways to put ideas from a text into their own words

■ Getting Ready to Teach

Before beginning, it helps to have a vision for what kids can create. The class may be dealing with a single big topic (like *animals* or *Antarctica*), but children should choose smaller topics or interests within it (like *gorillas* or *animals that use camouflage for survival*). The freedom to choose topics that matter to them offers children many more ways to approach the writing. Before launching the unit, be sure you gather (from the library or the Internet) the materials you will need to help children find a focus within your umbrella topic. All of these resources will fuel your and your students' imagination for what they can create.

Gathering Materials

Make sure you have a good supply of nonfiction books on a variety of topics. Prepare yourself for the inevitable fact that if you have only one book on platypuses, at least two children will have a burning desire to research that and only that. Encourage children to bring books from home or the library, to use magazines such as *Ranger Rick*, and to explore the Internet.

If your children keep reading logs, they can use them to organize and explore their notes, thoughts, observations, questions, and ideas. If you do not use reading logs or notebooks, make sure you have plenty of plain paper on hand that can be used for the same purpose. (Samples of writing paper, text layouts, and illustration options are included in the Appendix.) Students will also need a lot of sticky notes.

Considering the Students

Now is a good time to go over your assessment notes from the last unit to see who will need extra support in meeting the unit's challenges: finding and using resources, jotting down notes, putting information into one's own words, or presenting information using graphic organizers. Also identify children who may need more of a challenge. This will help you group students for focused lessons or conferences along the way.

It is always important to have mentor texts on hand that represent the range of reading levels in your class. In this research unit, you don't need to limit yourself to this range if you teach children how to get good information out of a nonfiction book that is otherwise too difficult for them. By applying prior knowledge to pictures, diagrams, or captions, for example, children learn useable information even though most of the book is far too hard for them to read independently. Nonetheless, children must also be able to consult books they can read fluently and understand easily.

Preparing Demonstration Materials

You will need to demonstrate most of the strategies you'll teach during this unit. Before you start, choose a topic for yourself and plan some of the ways you will write about it. While you should not complete a final version ahead of time, you do want a vision of how your piece can turn out. Then, when the time comes to demonstrate certain strategies, you will be prepared to do so clearly and specifically. Make sure you have enough resources and materials nearby.

■ Teaching the Unit

This unit assumes that students have written nonfiction in the past. They are probably familiar with books that are *all about* a particular topic and with the ways such books are organized. If your students have not written much non-fiction, spend some additional time looking at published books and talking about how these books tell about their topics so effectively.

If any of the lessons or concepts seem too difficult for children to grasp, modify how you teach them or leave them out. While preparing to write this book, I cotaught this unit in several classes. One teacher decided not to have an umbrella topic, allowing children to write about anything that interested them. Another teacher decided she would teach children to use only one type of graphic organizer. One class made dummy books, while another went straight into drafting. The children in these classes all benefited because their teachers tailored the plan to meet their needs. Figure 5–1 shows one way to organize the unit.

TIME FRAME	SECTION OF STUDY	WHAT CHILDREN DO	WHAT YOU TEACH
3–5 days	Reading to Learn, Reading to Teach	• Review nonfiction reading strategies • Choose a topic to teach their audience about • Find what, for them, is the heart of their subject • Gather materials (not just books, but also websites, physical objects, pamphlets, and so on.) • Jot down ideas	Guiding questions • We are studying [a large, umbrella topic]. What passions of ours are we beginning to identify within this topic? • What about our favorite nonfiction books makes them so helpful in teaching us? Minilessons, conferences, or midworkshop focus points • Nonfiction writers focus on a topic they know and care a lot about. • Writers prepare to write nonfiction by gathering all the important materials they can find. • Researchers jot down notes about something in the text that captivates them rather than about every single fact. • Sorting notes can help us understand our topic. • Sometimes a fact in a book makes us ask a question, which guides further research. • Sometimes a fact in a book gives us an idea. • Writing what we know, think, feel, or wonder about a topic can help us discover the heart of our subject.

Figure 5–1 Writing About Research at a Glance

TIME FRAME	SECTION OF STUDY	WHAT CHILDREN DO	WHAT YOU TEACH
2–3 days	Planning and Organizing Projects	• Divide subject into manageable parts • Create headings for their project • Share materials	Minilessons, conferences, or midworkshop focus points • Nonfiction writers help their readers learn by dividing their subjects into smaller parts. • Headings help our readers learn, just as they help us learn when we read. • It is OK to get rid of notes that are not helpful.

4–5 days	Writing and Revising	• Envision their audience and what they need to learn
		• Write in a knowledgeable or teaching voice
		• Write material in their own words
		• Choose specific words to teach about their topic
		• Refer to research materials when necessary
		• Read work to partners often
		• Use features such as diagrams, labels, or cross sections to make their topic clear
		• Learn to use one or two kinds of graphic organizers
		• Keep their writing focused on the topic
		• Refer to revision checklist (new items added)
			Guiding question
			• What tools do good nonfiction writers use to teach about their topic?
			Minilessons, conferences, or midworkshop focus points
			• We can design paper to help our readers learn about our topics.
			• Writers have many ways of presenting information:
			  • web, or semantic map
			  • diagram
			  • T-chart
			  • Venn diagram
			  • list
			  • flowchart
			  • cross section
			  • close-up
			  • graph
			• Research writers think about what their readers really need to know.
			• Research writers make sure all the information in a section belongs there.
			• Research writers put sentences in an order that flows well.
			• If a fact sounds fishy, we should double-check it.
			• We should make sure the heading matches what we write under it.
			• Some nonfiction writers include fun extra bits.
			• Our partner can help us determine whether our work makes sense.

2–3 days	Editing and Publishing	• Refer to editing checklist, with new items added • Create cover and table of contents (if not already done) • Reflect on learning • Celebrate	Minilessons, conferences, or midworkshop focus points • Nonfiction writers give information in the clearest possible way, using words, pictures, and diagrams. • Commas are used to separate items in lists.

Figure 5–1 *(continued)*

Reading to Learn, Reading to Teach

In order to do good factual research, children need to be good readers of nonfiction. Take time either before launching this unit or at the beginning of it to teach or review nonfiction reading strategies. It helps to list them on a chart (see Figure 5–2) so children can remind themselves of effective nonfiction reading habits. *Growing Readers*, by Kathy Collins (2004), *Reality Checks: Teaching Reading Comprehension with Nonfiction*, by Tony Stead (2006), and *Nonfiction Matters*, by Stephanie Harvey (2006), are great resources for more information on these types of reading skills.

Encourage children to read without a filter first, taking in and jotting down notes about anything that grabs their attention. They can then go back to these notes, look for particularly captivating information, and thus arrive at the specific focus of their research organically. That is, as they are reading about a big topic, they will find themselves drawn to specific aspects of that topic. Some children will need help narrowing down their choices. You or a proficient peer can help them sort through their notes in search of a focus. Once they have a focused topic, their reading will be targeted to learning more about it and deciding what they want to teach their own readers about the topic.

Guiding Questions

● *We are studying [a large, umbrella topic]. What passions of ours are we beginning to identify within this topic?* From the beginning of the study you want children to understand that they will be writing about one interesting aspect of your larger topic. As they narrow down their interests, eventually choosing a suitable subject for their own writing, record their choices on a classroom chart. This will help them stay on topic, help you keep track of their topics, and help children decide whom to ask for help or with whom to share resources. As they choose topics, allow children with the same interests to sit and work together, sharing resources.

● *What about our favorite nonfiction books makes them so helpful in teaching us?* As the class reads a lot of published nonfiction, discuss and chart the qualities that make these books good learning resources (see Figure 5–3). Guide them toward noticing how writers present information to make it clear to the reader. In past units, your charted observations about books probably focused more on how authors used words. In this unit, look closely not just at the words but also the illustrations. You might even photocopy interesting things you notice in books so that children can refer to these photocopies as they look for the best ways to present their information. Remember to keep adding to the chart as the unit goes on.

NONFICTION READING STRATEGIES

Getting Ready to Read
- Preview text (cover, title, a few pages).
- See how book works (sections, continuous, features, easy, hard).
- Name topic (what book seems to be mostly about).
- Activate prior knowledge.
- Any questions about topic?

Reading
- Visualize information (even if there are pictures).
- Chunk text into sections (for longer texts).
- Summarize in own words.
- Sketch or physically act out parts that seem confusing.
- Determine importance (for longer texts).
- Use context to better understand new vocabulary.
- Stop often and ask, *What am I learning?* or *What did I just learn?*
- Ask, *What new information am I learning?*

Thinking While Reading
- Connect new learning to prior knowledge.
- Think about how pictures and words go together.
- Allow new information to change or expand your prior knowledge.
- Connect each page, section, or chunk to prior one.
- Connect each page, section, or chunk to overall topic of whole book.
- Compare or contrast information, format, style, and so on to another book.
- Make connections from page to page (Does information build on itself? Does information seem to contradict itself?).
- Put chunks or sections together to form new ideas about topic.
- Question text or pictures.
- Study pictures closely.
- Connect graphic information with body of text and overall topic.

Using Text Features
- Table of contents
  - Read as a way of learning about topic.
  - Read to see how book works.
  - Decide what to read about next.
  - Look up information.
- Headings
  - Determine which text falls under a heading.
  - Circle back to heading at end of section.
  - Reread heading and ask, *What did I just learn about this?*
- Drawings, photos, diagrams
  - Ask how these fit with body of text.
  - Study carefully.
  - Know what you are looking at.
  - Do new questions arise?
- Captions and labels
  - Read them.
  - Use them to understand picture or graphic.
- Print styles (bold, italic, highlighted, large, and so on)
  - Stop and think about why this part needs to stand out.
  - Use styles to help determine importance.
- Index
  - Know how to use it.
  - Imagine where in alphabet your word is before using the index.
- Pronunciation guides

Figure 5–2 Nonfiction Reading Strategies You May Need to Teach

Nonfiction Observations

Even the hard books have lots of pictures.

We can learn a lot from the pictures, even when the words are hard.

Some pictures are photographs and some are drawings.

The words are easy to understand, not complicated.

Things in the pictures are labeled.

Some pages have a lot of pictures, so you can look at them for a long time.

Some books have clear plastic pages so you can see through them.

Some books show you the insides of things or animals.

Figure 5–3 Nonfiction Observations

Possible Teaching Points

● *Nonfiction writers focus on a topic they know and care a lot about.* As children read widely about the larger topic, help them gravitate toward smaller topics within it. In a minilesson, demonstrate how you weigh the attractions of certain topics over others. The topic you choose for yourself can become the subject of your writing demonstrations for the rest of the unit. Point out that you are choosing a topic with which you are already familiar but that is interesting enough that you want to learn still more about it.

● *Writers prepare to write nonfiction by gathering all the important materials they can find.* You have made lots of books and other materials available, but your students need to build their own text sets from which to do their research. This includes gathering books and combing through magazines for relevant material. If your classroom has computers, they can find websites that have pictures, video clips, or written information. Your school or community librarian may also help them find documentary films or episodes of educational television programs. Your enthusiasm for finding cool resources will be infectious and will be reflected in the quality of the work your students do.

● *Researchers jot down notes about something in the text that captivates them rather than about every single fact.* The nonfiction materials you and your students have assembled will be packed with exciting information and interesting facts. You don't want to rain on anyone's parade, but you also don't want children losing sight of the big picture because they are stopping to note every detail. Taking notes on the facts that interest them most will help children find a specific focus within your umbrella topic and will hone the important skill of determining the relative importance of information.

If you have already demonstrated jotting down notes, commenting on how you write just active words or fragments rather than complete sentences, your students may not need an isolated minilesson on this skill. Sometimes, though, we do such a good job of teaching children to write in complete sentences that they need to be taught explicitly when and how it is useful *not* to do so. Use their work as a guide.

● *Sorting notes can help us understand our topic.* What did we do before sticky notes? Children are now able to take notes without having to look away from the book, thus keeping their focus on reading rather than shifting back and forth between reading and writing. Sorting notes into groups can become an end-of-workshop routine for a few days, or you can teach individual students to do it when they finish with a particular resource. Either way, this is an important step. First, it forces them to reread notes they may have forgotten since writing them, which solidifies comprehension. Second, it helps them begin to envision how they will teach others about their topic.

- *Sometimes a fact in a book makes us ask a question, which guides further research.* This teaching point and the next one encourage children to think while they read, or read with a wide-awake mind. Reading is a dialogue between writer and reader, with the reader's thoughts and questions being his side of the conversation. When children pay attention to their mental activity as they read, they participate in their learning. When we encourage children to ask questions about what they read, we give them a reason to return to a book (or find a new resource) with the new focus of finding answers to those questions.

- *Sometimes a fact in a book gives us an idea.* I have avoided overusing the word *report* with regard to research writing because I want children to go beyond reporting facts. As children sort their notes, show them how to reread each note and respond to it in some way. Instead of simply absorbing and cataloguing facts, they can stop and say, "Gee, that reminds me of this," or "Hey, that must mean thus-and-so." This kind of thinking will prompt them to approach their writing with a fresh voice, making what they write much more engaging for their audience.

- *Writing what we know, think, feel, or wonder about a topic can help us discover the heart of our subject.* By the end of this segment many children will have found a specific topic for their research and writing. Others may still feel overwhelmed or otherwise unable to choose a focus. Having some time in which to write or sketch expressively can help them find the heart of what really interests them about the topic, especially when they don't want to focus on a subject in a predictable way. For example, if the class is studying animals, most children will choose a specific animal to study. Other children might have two or three animals that interest them. Instead of choosing between their interests, they can explore a common characteristic that draws them to these animals (being endangered, using camouflage, and so on) and *that* can become the focus.

Student Work

Amen had taken a note about hibernation, which did not seem to belong with any of his other notes. He decided to keep the note on a page by itself temporarily. This prompted his teacher and me to teach a small-group lesson on devoting a page of the notebook to those notes that seem interesting but do not belong with any others.

In Sabine's earliest notes on prairie dogs, she often mixed opinions (*Prairie dogs have big, cute eyes* and *Prairie dog babies are cute*) in with her facts. While we didn't dissuade her from doing this (we loved her fondness for the topic), we did try to steer her toward digging into the meatier questions she might want to answer about such cute animals.

How long do prairie dogs live?

What do prairie dogs think of people?

What do prairie dogs do to keep warm?

Do prairie dogs have thick hair?

How do prairie dogs live in the wild?

Figure 5–4 shows the many kinds of thinking Devin was doing. He empathized with frogs, visualized the topic, inferred and predicted information. He also suggested something that was not true, that some dinosaurs evolved into frogs. While we always watched out for misinformation, we also wanted to teach Devin to do his own fact checking.

Planning and Organizing Projects

Some children will be ready to start writing within a day, while others may need more time to plan and organize their projects. Different working styles demand different degrees of preplanning. It is impossible to be aware of every child's work at all times. That said, as you see children getting ready to move from planning to writing lots of text, try to ensure that they are using a clear, solid plan. A disorganized or unclear plan will lead to disorganized and unclear writing.

Possible Teaching Points

● *Nonfiction writers help their readers learn by dividing their subjects into smaller parts.* If children start writing everything they know about their topic, it will quickly become overwhelming and hard to read. They must first plan how to deliver their content in bite-sized pieces. This is an extension of the work they did when they sorted their notes. If they fully grasped that concept, you may need to teach this idea only in small groups or conferences.

● *Headings help our readers learn, just as they help us learn when we read.* When children were beginning to read nonfiction books, you probably taught them that a heading is like a title for a small section of a book. Good readers

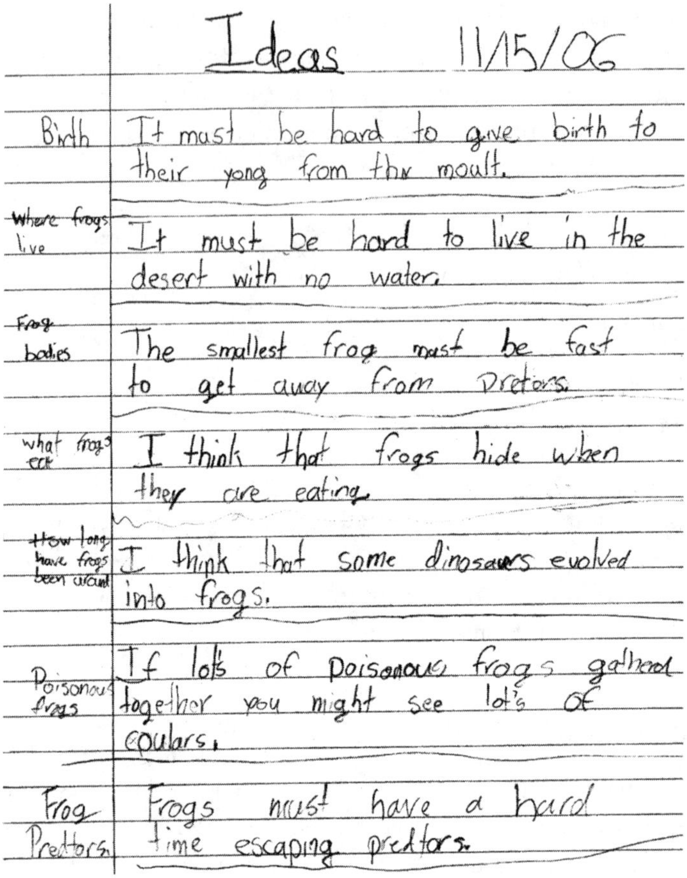
Ideas 11/15/06

Birth — It must be hard to give birth to their yong from thr moult.

~~Where frogs~~ live — It must be hard to live in the desert with no water.

~~Frog~~ bodies — The smallest frog must be fast to get away from pretors.

what frogs eat — I think that frogs hide when they are eating.

~~How long~~ have frogs been around — I think that some dinosaurs evolved into frogs.

Poisonous frogs — If lot's of poisonous frogs gatherd together you might see lot's of coulars.

Frog Pretors — Frogs must have a hard time escaping predtors.

Figure 5–4 Devin's Ideas About Frogs

know they can use a heading as a sort of mental file in which to place the information that comes after the heading. Now, as writers, students can use headings the same way. Children should be able to name the notes they have grouped together, and these names will become the basis for their headings. Some children will want to create more amusing or imaginative headings. Teach them how to make sure that a section heading applies to everything underneath it.

- ***It is OK to get rid of notes that are not helpful.*** We do children a service by letting them know that all the writing they do is valuable, even if it doesn't make it into the final published piece. Many children will have notes that don't fit into their topic as they have chosen to focus on it. For example, Amen decided he did not want to include information on hibernation in his frog book.

It was hard to do, but he put that note in the discard pile. (Some of these oddball notes pertain to facts that are weird or surprising, and children may put these into a *cool facts* page or inset.)

Student Work

Henry's plan (Figure 5–5) is a list of headings he wanted to have in his book. He would check off each one as he wrote the corresponding section. Henry was articulate and knew his topic well, but writing was physically difficult for him. Because it took him a long time to write, we did not want him to have to rewrite anything. This is an option for those children who are still mastering the manual dexterity required for writing.

Nidhi folded a piece of plain paper into eighths, planning how each page of her book would look (see Figure 5–6). She returned to this plan often throughout the rest of the unit.

Taylor organized her notes in a dummy book (a page of which is shown in Figure 5–7). She was able to move her notes from one page to another as she finalized the order in which she would present her information.

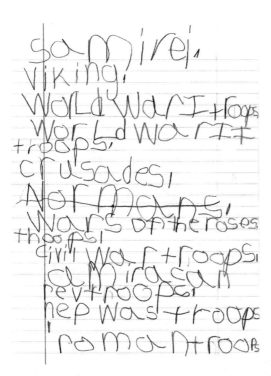

Figure 5–5 Henry's Plan

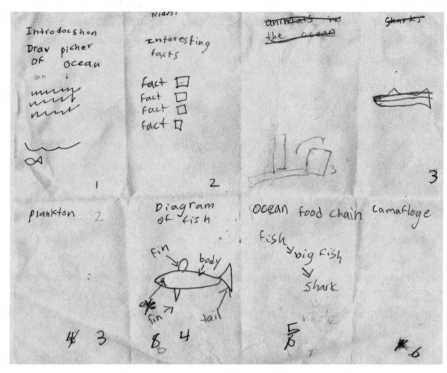

Figure 5–6 Nidhi's Layout

Writing and Revising

Having conducted focused research and prepared a solid plan, children are now ready to write the text, working mainly from the plan but perhaps returning occasionally to their research material for additional information or help with spelling. Encourage them to read their own and their partner's writing often, making sure it makes sense and says what they want it to.

Guiding Question

● *What tools do good nonfiction writers use to teach about their topic?*
Children's responses to this question can be added to the chart of nonfiction writing observations (see Figure 5–8). At some point during this segment of the unit, I call the children together and ask them to look again at the stack of nonfiction books we have been using to do our research. I demonstrate putting a sticky note on an interesting way that a nonfiction writer has presented information and send children off to do the same. I try not to give them

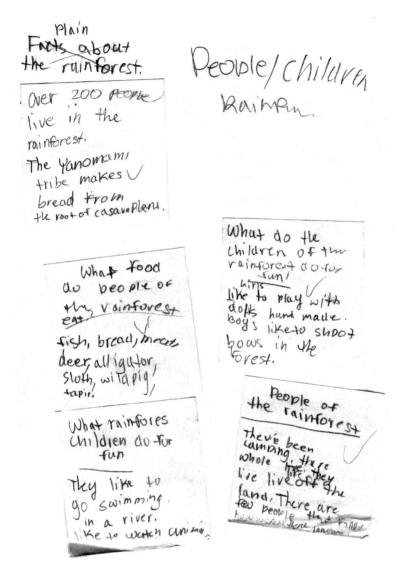

Figure 5–7 A Page from Taylor's Plan Booklet

books on the topics they are writing about, because I want them looking at books with fresh eyes. After about fifteen minutes, I call them back together to share their findings. After they have gone home for the day, I go through the books and photocopy the things they noticed. I attach these photocopies to the chart, along with their observations. As they continue writing their own books, they refer to this chart for ideas on how to present their information effectively.

Figure 5–8 Nonfiction Tools

Possible Teaching Points

● *We can design paper to help our readers learn about our topic.* This and the next teaching point relate directly to the tools nonfiction writers use. Children notice a lot of text features and graphics and want to try these in their own writing. It's not necessary to have children design paper, but it's lots of fun and helps them make the connection between using a cool feature or layout and conveying information.

Inviting children to create some layouts that will work well with their ideas can build enthusiasm and yield some exciting results. This also encourages critical thinking about how best to teach their readers about their topics. After they have designed the layout, you can copy it for the whole class to use. I usually neaten it up by creating a version of it on the computer. Figures 5–9 through 5–11, pp. 146–148, are just a few examples of student-designed paper. All of them have a box at the top for a heading. Each of these is also included in the Appendix.

● *Writers have many ways of presenting information.* One of the fun things about reading and writing nonfiction is that information is communicated visually as well as verbally. Of course, this is not done just for fun. Nonfiction writers use a variety of graphics to illustrate most clearly the concepts they want to teach their readers about. As children look through nonfiction books or refer to the chart of nonfiction writing tools, they will see possibilities for their own writing. They will have to think critically about the type of graphic that will best illustrate the information they are presenting. Some choices are

- web, or semantic map
- diagram
- T-chart
- Venn diagram
- list
- flowchart
- cross section
- close-up
- graph

● *Research writers think about what their readers really need to know.* Before they get too deep into their writing, ask children to start thinking about what it is that makes them care about their topic. Each person who writes about frogs does it differently. Otherwise books about frogs wouldn't keep getting published. Children should feel empowered to write about their topic in a way that is individual to them.

● *Research writers make sure all the information in a section belongs there.* Although children have sorted and organized their notes, when they begin writing they may fill out their notes with other information or ideas they have picked up along the way or think they know. Things can sneak in where they

Figure 5–9 This paper is meant for a large illustration or diagram. The inset is for a magnified section of the larger picture or an internal view.

Figure 5-10 This is a versatile paper design. It can be for two aspects, kinds, or stages of a thing.

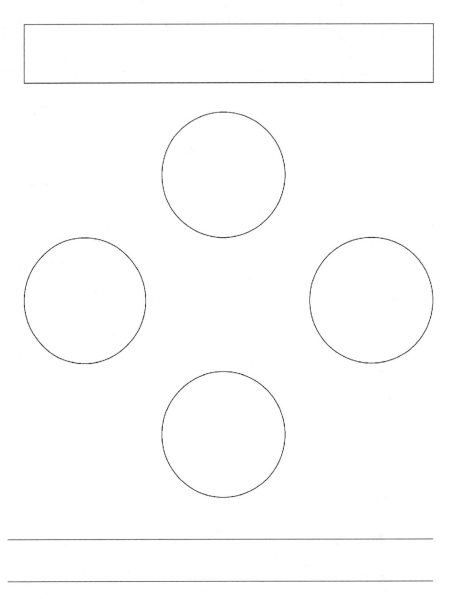

Figure 5–11 This paper was adapted from a page in a book describing a life cycle. Children who wanted to use it to illustrate a cycle connected the circles with arrows. Some other ingenious children drew arrows to the circles from the center and used this paper to make a web.

don't belong. Teach children to read and reread their own writing with a critical eye, asking, "Does all of this go together?"

- **Research writers put sentences in an order that flows well.** This is a difficult idea to teach and to learn. I am not suggesting teaching children about topic sentences and supporting sentences just yet. Rather, I think second graders can benefit from reading their own words with their inner ears attuned. Teach them to ask themselves, "Does it sound right? Do I like how it goes?" and even, "Did I make my writing sound like that book I love so much?"

- **If a fact sounds fishy, we should double-check it.** There are a several reasons misinformation can find its way into children's nonfiction writing. It could be the result of faulty reading or a long-held belief that has become fact in the child's mind. Regardless of how misinformation gets there, it can be hard to teach children how to get rid of it. Telling them to check their work for information that is not true doesn't work, because they think the information *is* true. Another way to approach this task is to make it a partner activity. Partners can flag facts that sound suspect, sending the writers back to their research for evidence. If they can't find any evidence, they should ask an adult for help, rephrase the fact, or just remove the information entirely.

- **We should make sure the heading matches what we write under it.** If you taught earlier lessons on headings, you may not need to make this point again. However, children may forget to move to a new heading when they are ready to write about a new idea. It is easy to get carried away writing interesting information and forget to attend to the organizational plan. Sometimes children *have* put all of their information where they meant to, but the heading still doesn't quite work. They may need to change the wording to make it match the information underneath. Remind children that part of writing is reading what they have written and making sure that it really says what they want it to say.

- **Some nonfiction writers include fun extra bits.** You can make this option available to everyone or use it as a way for children who finish their work ahead of schedule to make their projects even more special. When you were studying published nonfiction books, your students might have noticed things like a puzzle page, insets with bizarre facts, an accompanying poem or song on the topic, jokes related to the topic, or other interesting tidbits. It is essential that their books be informative, and even better if they are fun and engaging for the reader.

● *Our partner can help us determine whether our work makes sense.* If children have not worked much in pairs during this project, now is a good time to have them read each other's work. As in prior units, remind them to make their comments specific and considerate.

Student Work

Zachary's plan for a page about meat-eating and plant-eating dinosaurs (see Figure 5–12) was a good idea. He wrote quickly, so a couple of spots do not make sense. In the final version (see Figure 5–13), he has corrected this with the help of his partner and chosen a type of paper that complements the content.

Henry's book was about different kinds of soldiers in history. As a bonus feature, he decided to include instructions for how to fire a caplock (see Figure 5–14), which he explained was a gun used during the Civil War. Henry's partner was an invaluable part of Henry's process of making his work clear, particularly when it came to defining unfamiliar vocabulary.

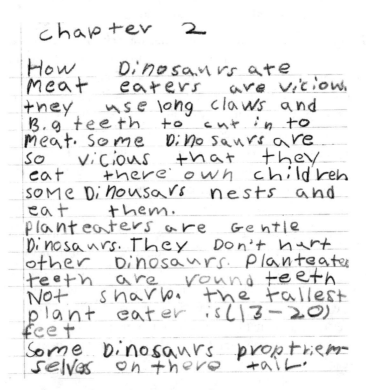

Figure 5–12 Zachary's Plan for a Page About How Dinosaurs Ate

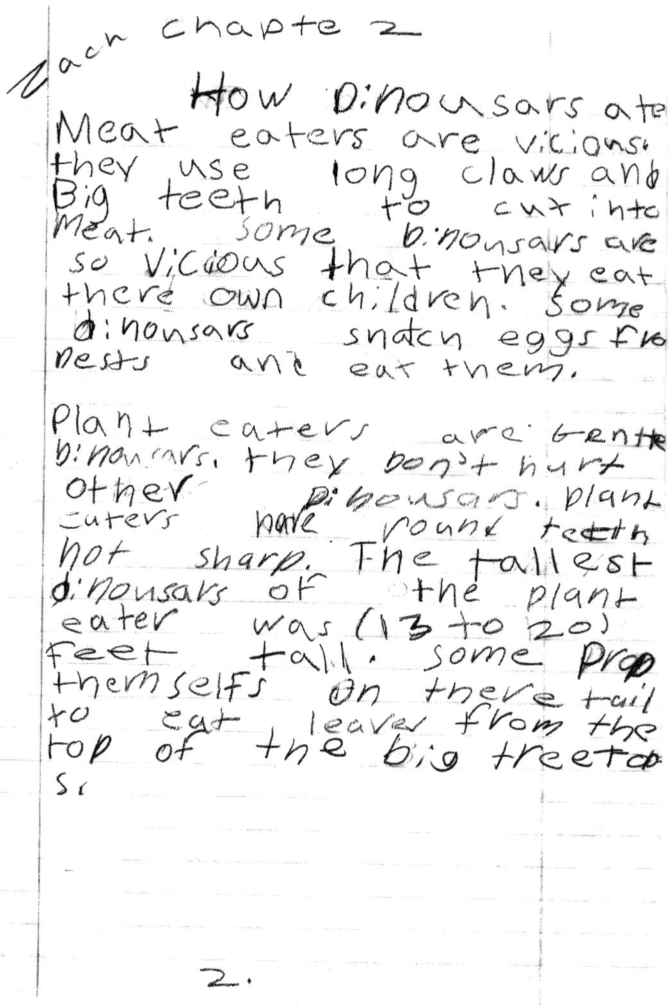

Zach chapter 2

How Dinousars ate

Meat eaters are vicious.
they use long claws and
Big teeth to cut into
Meat. Some dinousars are
so Vicious that they eat
there own children. Some
dinousars snatch eggs fro
nests and eat them.

Plant eaters are Gentle
dinousars. they don't hurt
other dinousars. plant
eaters have round teeth
not sharp. The tallest
dinousars of the plant
eater was (13 to 20)
feet tall. some prop
themselfs on there tail
to eat leaves from the
top of the big treetop
s.

2.

Figure 5–13 The Fnal Version of the Same Page

Editing and Publishing

Most children should be ready to finish up now. There will always be those
who need every second they can get to work on their writing and thus don't
do much revising (see the checklist in Figure 5–15) or editing (see the checklist in Figure 5–16). There are also those who finish a couple of days ahead of
schedule. Early finishers can color their illustrations, add a blurb to the back
cover, dedicate their work to someone, or write an author bio. A nice way to
celebrate these pieces is for children to create oral presentations to go with their

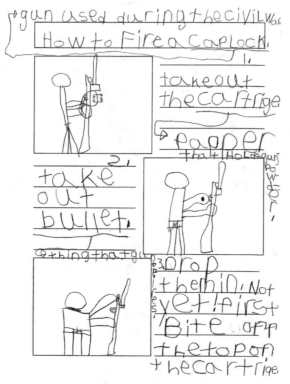

Figure 5–14 From Henry's How-To Section

written work. Children with similar topics can become a panel of experts. Perhaps parents or children from another class might come and watch presentations and ask questions.

Possible Teaching Points

● *Nonfiction writers give information in the clearest possible way, using words, pictures, and diagrams.* This point reinforces many lessons you have already taught. The idea is not that children should rush to create a lot of new material for their book. Rather, they should reflect on the material they have already created, making sure it is as clear as it can be. If they need to fine-tune a diagram or rewrite a caption, this is their opportunity to do so.

● *Commas are used to separate items in lists.* Commas are a mystery to many of us, even if we think of ourselves as writers. I'm sure I'm not the only person who has struggled with contradictory lessons about the proper uses of commas. This kind of writing often includes lists (the foods an animal likes to eat, for example), and teaching children to use commas in such a list seems to be

Revision Strategies

- Information in the pictures is also in the words.
- My piece really says what I want it to.
- I took away parts that did not belong.
- I gave support or evidence for my ideas.
- My piece is all about the same thing.
- I gave information in the clearest way I could, using words, pictures, and diagrams.

Figure 5–15 The Revision Checklist

Editing Strategies

- All word-wall words, blends, and spelling patterns are spelled correctly.
- Important words related to my topic are spelled correctly.
- I tried to use my best grammar.
- Instead of having one long sentence with a lot of *ands*, I have several sentences.
- Commas are used correctly in lists.

Figure 5–16 The Editing Checklist

the most straightforward introduction to this form of punctuation. As they edit their work, show them how to look for lists of items, actions, or descriptions (nouns, verbs, or adjectives) that might need commas. If your class doesn't seem ready for this as a whole, consider teaching the lesson to a small group.

Student Work

The teacher of the students whose work is shown here presented two nonfiction writing units, the first based on children's knowledge and experiences, the second based on research. Athena's book in Figure 5–17 is from the first unit of study and is all about making and keeping friends.

In the second nonfiction unit, a couple of months later, children were expected to write similarly structured books on topics they had researched. Because Kate had already had the experience of putting together a nonfiction book based on her personal knowledge, she now had more energy and more time to write lots of text. Figures 5–18a and 5–18b are from the part of her book of human tragedies devoted to the *Titanic*.

■ Reflection

You know what you taught; your students' reflections on this unit (see the questionnaire in Figure 5–19) will tell you what they think they learned. It is

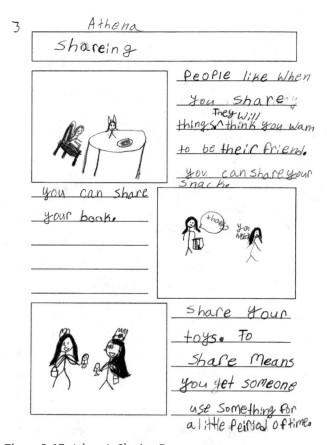

Figure 5–17 Athena's Sharing Page

In the erly 1900's 3 ships were born for a cunpany Called the white Star line. The white Star line was a Irash cunpany. One of the Ships was the Titanicl The Titanic was 11 stories high, and as long as 4 foot ball fieles. The Titanic Could fit more than 2500 People on bord. half of the Pasenjers were famlies.Titanic had a lot of food In april15 192 Titanic hitanicebrge at 1:00am

Titanic means huje and powrfle.

This way

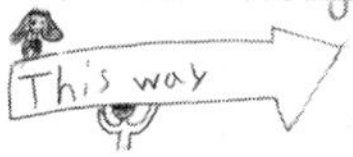

Figure 5–18a and b Kate's *Titanic* Information

at 2:00 am Titanic disappeated. Sangu into the Abise. 1500 People lost their lives. 725 People Srvived.

titanik is an Irish ship.

Figure 5–18b

Name_____ Date _____

We just researched exciting topics and made incredible nonfiction books.

*What is the most important thing people should know about writing nonfiction? _____

_____

_____

_____

_____

*What part of your book are you most proud of? Why?

_____

_____

_____

*What is hard for you about writing? _____

_____

_____

_____

_____

Figure 5–19 Research Reflection Questionnaire

always helpful to see how they interpret, and sometimes misinterpret, your teaching. Their reflections also reveal their thoughts and attitudes toward nonfiction and toward writing in general.

▪ Predictable Problems

The difficulties that seem to arrive most often in this unit relate to research and planning. This unit of study requires a lot of preparation for writing, such as note taking and reading nonfiction books as writers, studying how they are put together. Make sure you demonstrate the note taking, planning, and organizing strategies clearly. Keep an eye out for children who are not catching on so you can guide them in smaller groups.

PROBLEM	WHAT IT LOOKS LIKE	POSSIBLE SOLUTION/ CONFERENCE
Children have not chosen topics well.	• Children do not want to read much about their topics.	The problem may be that the available books on a chosen topic are too difficult or are written in too dry a style. Try to get some books that are easier and more fun to read. If this is not the problem and children just lose interest in their topics early in the study, help them find new ones that can sustain their interest longer. If they lose interest later in the study, they will not have time to choose a new topic, research it, and write about it. Try giving them a break from this piece for a day. They can help a partner or read other students' work.
	• Children have little or no prior knowledge about their topics.	You probably told children that a good topic is something they *know* and care a lot about. Despite this, there will be children who have blossoming interests in things they don't know much about. If they show a lot of enthusiasm for the new interest, give them a chance to try it out. They will have to do more research than the rest of the class, but their eagerness will give them the momentum to do this.

PROBLEM	WHAT IT LOOKS LIKE	POSSIBLE SOLUTION/ CONFERENCE
	• Children seem bored when discussing their topics.	Sometimes this lack of commitment stems from a fear of not being able to write well. It is frustrating, but we need to treat it with gentle encouragement and realistic expectations.
		Sometimes children get bored because they chose a topic they thought would be easy, rather than one that interested them. Help them take the risk of getting excited about something!
Children have not planned enough.	• Pieces are scattered. • Sections seem to be in a random order. • Diagrams or other extra features seem to be an afterthought. • Pieces contain false information.	Before they get far along in writing, make sure you have seen children's plans. If you cannot get to everyone before the students begin to write, prioritize. First see the children who have had difficulty planning in other units. Remember that, like many of the skills children acquire in second grade, planning can come slowly.
		Accept that some pieces will not flow as well as others in this unit. Schedule a time to meet with children in a small group to go over the key planning and organizing strategies.

■ Assessment

Remember to base your assessment (see Figure 5–20) not just on children's published pieces but also on their ongoing work. The pieces that were not revised and edited reveal a lot about children's internalized habits. Use the information as you plan to teach future units and to help you prepare students for the summer and the next school year.

STUDENT'S WORK SHOWS THAT I ...	NEED TO TEACH OR RETEACH THIS TO THE WHOLE CLASS	NEED TO REMIND CHILD OF THIS SKILL	NEED TO TEACH THIS TO A SMALL GROUP OR IN A CONFERENCE	NEED TO CONGRATULATE CHILD FOR HOW WELL HE OR SHE DID
Child clearly stated an opinion or idea about a text.	❏	❏	❏	❏
Child organized thoughts to support this statement.	❏	❏	❏	❏
Child kept writing focused on a single idea.	❏	❏	❏	❏
Child supported ideas with evidence from the text, using quotes appropriately.	❏	❏	❏	❏
Child used a variety of kinds of sentences.	❏	❏	❏	❏
Child chose words carefully to communicate ideas.	❏	❏	❏	❏
Child continued to develop voice as a writer.	❏	❏	❏	❏
Child spelled frequently used words correctly.	❏	❏	❏	❏
Child spelled words particular to the chosen topic correctly.	❏	❏	❏	❏
Child used end punctuation, quotation marks, and capitalization properly.	❏	❏	❏	❏
Child used commas, though perhaps not always correctly.	❏	❏	❏	❏
Child maintained consistency of voice and tense.	❏	❏	❏	❏
Child organized thoughts into effective and appropriate paragraphs.	❏	❏	❏	❏
Child participated in class conversations about literature.	❏	❏	❏	❏
Child got to work quickly.	❏	❏	❏	❏
Child managed writing tools and supplies.	❏	❏	❏	❏
Child talked with classmates about reading or writing.	❏	❏	❏	❏
Child made and used a plan to write.	❏	❏	❏	❏
Child read and reread work often.	❏	❏	❏	❏
Child referred to text as he or she wrote.	❏	❏	❏	❏
Child revised his or her work.	❏	❏	❏	❏
Child edited his or her work.	❏	❏	❏	❏
Child volunteered ideas, listened, and responded to others.	❏	❏	❏	❏
Child worked with a partner to develop and improve writing.	❏	❏	❏	❏
Child showed respect for all members of the community and their work, regardless of ability.	❏	❏	❏	❏
Child expressed disagreement in a way that promoted conversation rather than shut it down.	❏	❏	❏	❏
Child asked for and gave help with problems.	❏	❏	❏	❏

Figure 5–20 Writing About Research Assessment Chart

■ Professional Resources

Collins, Kathy. 2004. *Growing Readers*. Portland, ME: Stenhouse.

Harvey, Stephanie. 2006. *Nonfiction Matters*. Portland, ME: Stenhouse.

Stead, Tony. 2006. *Reality Checks: Teaching Reading Comprehension with Nonfiction*. Portland, ME: Stenhouse.

Closing

When I was sitting at home thinking about you sitting at home getting ready to use this book, I thought of cookbooks. I use a lot of cookbooks. The first time I make a recipe I do it as it is written. I measure out all the ingredients, making no substitutions, and I follow the directions. That's the *first* time. What happens after that is anyone's guess. I may not always feel so basil-y or lime-ish. You see, once I've made it once, I have a general sense of how it's supposed to be. I can make satisfying modifications based on my knowledge of flavors, the time of year, my mood, and the tastes of my friends. Nothing would make me happier than seeing these units taught with different flavors, based on *your* knowledge of *your* students. Bon appétit!

Appendix

Figure A–1 Introductory Narrative or Observation Paper

Figure A–2 More Challenging Narrative or Observation Paper

Figure A–3 Landscape Narrative or Observation Paper

Figure A–4 One-Box Paper, for diagrams or other large illustrations

Figure A–5 Two-Box Paper

Figure A–6 Three-Box Paper

Figure A–7 Four-Box Paper, for a List, Procedure, or Table of Contents

Figure A–8 Five-Box Paper, for a List, Procedure, or Table of Contents

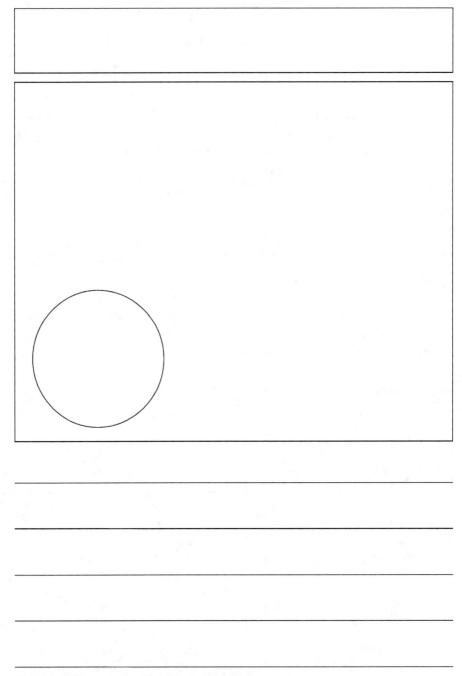

Figure A–9 Inset Paper, for a magnified part, cross section, or X-ray view

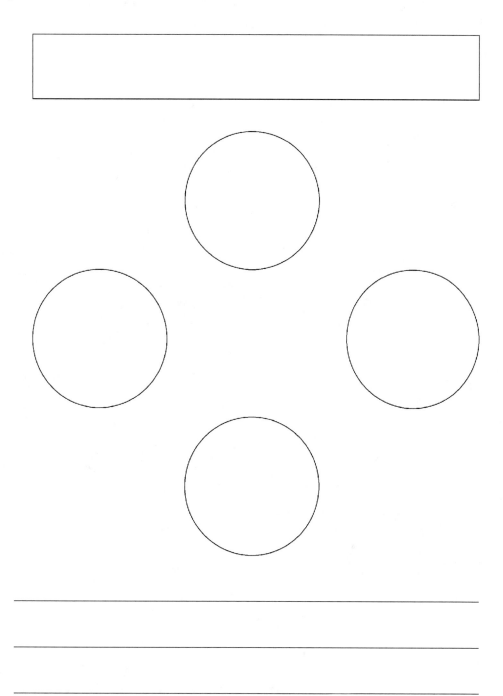

Figure A–10 Cycle Paper. Connect the circles with arrows in either direction

DATE DUE

DEC 2 2013